A Pact with Vichy

WORLD WAR II: THE GLOBAL, HUMAN, AND ETHICAL DIMENSION

G. Kurt Piehler, series editor

A Pact with Vichy

Angelo Tasca from Italian Socialism to French Collaboration

Emanuel Rota

Fordham University Press | New York 2013

Library of Congress Cataloging-in-Publication Data is available from the publisher.

Printed in the United States of America

15 14 13 5 4 3 2 1
First edition

A Nora

Contents

Acknowledgments xi

Introduction 1

1 Into the Battlefield 10

2 Learning Russian: Angelo Tasca and the Stalinization of the Communist Parties 41

3 In Limbo: Angelo Tasca and Liberal Democracy 62

4 The Road to Vichy 88

5 A Socialist in Vichy 121

Epilogue 154

Notes 171
Bibliography 203
Index 213

Acknowledgments

I have incurred great debts of gratitude in my years of work on this book. I would like to thank, first and foremost, Susanna Barrows, whose intelligence and passion guided me on Tasca's path. Martin Jay has taught me more than I ever thought I could learn. David Bidussa, Albert Russell Ascoli, John Connelly, Monika Otter, and Susannah Heschel were sources of inspiration and good friends when I needed them. Cesare Segre and Armando Petrucci taught me to love archives, and I wish I could be as thorough as they are. Valeria Tasca was kind enough to answer my questions about her father and offer me coffee while doing so. The readers for Fordham University Press have been very generous. Nikhil Rao, Nora Stoppino, Mario Stoppino, Harry Liebersohn, and Dorothee Schneider gave me fundamental suggestions to improve the manuscript and saved me from many errors; those that remain are, of course, my own. Will Cerbone and Fredric Nachbaur have been impeccable editors, and it has been a pleasure to work with them as well as with Steve Barichko, my managing editor.

Both my professional life and my research have benefited from countless conversations with David Bates, Peggy Anderson, Rebecca Manley, Alberto De Bernardi, Hee Ko, Benjamin Lazier, David Spafford, Andrew Jainchill, Marco Ruffini, Vincent Cannon, J. P. Daughton, Miriam Neirick, Veronika Fuechtner, Rob Rushing, Bob LaFrance, Vernon Minor, Barbara Will, Elisa Signori, Giulio Guderzo, Heather Minor, Elisabetta Menetti, Areli Marina, Domietta Torlasco, Maria Luisa Meneghetti, the late Ruggero Stefanini, Graziella Parati, Keala Jewell, Miguel Valladares, Paula Sprague, Leo Spitzer, Marianne Hirsch, Eugene Avrutin, Anna Montanari, and Ericka Beckman. I would also like to acknowledge the support and friendship of many others who have accompanied my life and my work during these years: Ora Gelley, Antonia Pizzigoni and Giancarlo Motta, Mark Micale, Jean-Philippe Mathy, Beppe Cavatorta, Diane Musumeci, Silvina Montrul, Anna Minardi, Nancy Castro and Gillen Wood, Marcelo Bucheli, Laura Hill, Eda Derhemi, Michael Rothberg, Michael Cole, Yasemin Yildiz, Dara Goldman, Jim Hansen, Elabbas Benmamoun, Lilya Kaganovsky, Renée Trilling, Elena

Delgado, Madeleine Viljoen, Mariselle Meléndez, Brett Kaplan, and Matti Bunzl. A number of institutions provided support for the conception, research, and production of this study: the Collegio Ghislieri of Pavia, the University of California at Berkeley, Dartmouth College, the University of Illinois, the Research Board at the University of Illinois, the Mellon Foundation, the UC Berkeley Institute of European Studies, and the European Union Center at the University of Illinois. I am grateful for the opportunity to work at a number of libraries, whose staff made it possible for me to gather the documents necessary for the completion of this book: my own home library at the University of Illinois, the Feltrinelli Foundation, the Biblioteca Nazionale Braidense in Milan, the Bibliothèque Nationale de France, the Biblioteca Nazionale Centrale in Florence, the Archives Nationales de Fontainebleau, the Fondazione Gramsci, and the Archivio Centrale dello Stato in Rome. Finally, my deep thanks to my family: my father, Romeo Rota, and his wife, Renata Cattaneo, whom I miss immensely; my mother, Agnese Legrenzi, and her husband, Eddo De Zordo; my brother, Claudio Rota; and all the friends and family in Italy, from Bergamo to Pavia to Pieve Albignola. And, of course, Leonardo and Agata. This book is for Nora.

Introduction

> Despite their certainties, despite my doubts
> I always wanted this world ended.
> Myself ended too. And it was that exactly
> which estranged us. My hopes had no point for them.
> My centralism seemed anarchy to them.
>
> Franco Fortini, "Communism" (1958)
> Translated by Angelo Quattrocchi and Lucien Rey

At the end of March 1944, Palmiro Togliatti returned to Italy from his Russian exile and announced to his comrades a radically new political strategy: the Italian Communist Party had to accept an alliance with any political group, on the left or on the right, interested in fighting against fascism for the liberation of Italy.[1] The immediate consequence of Togliatti's turn, known as the "Salerno turn," was that for the rest of World War II the Italian communists lent their support to the government led by General Pietro Badoglio, whom King Victor Emanuel III had nominated as prime minister to replace Mussolini in 1943. The fact that General Badoglio had been a key figure in the fascist regime, governor of Libya, military leader in the colonial war against Ethiopia, and supreme chief of the Italian General Staff became, in Togliatti's new strategy, temporarily irrelevant compared to the need to create a government of national unity capable of defeating the German invaders and their fascist allies. Togliatti's move procured him a place among the founding fathers of the new Italian Republic, born out of the defeat of fascism. But another man who had, with surprising and sometimes unwise consistency, proposed the same strategy, first for Italy and then for France, had ruined his own reputation by doing so. This book tells the story of that man, Angelo Tasca.

Tasca, the son of a working-class family from southern Piedmont, rose early on to become a promising star of Italian radical socialism. However, in the course of the 1920s, he became convinced that fascism was a novel and exceptional enemy, one that required a radical new strategy from the leaders of the Italian socialist and communist movements. In particular, he came to believe that only an alliance among all social and political groups interested in defeating fascism could overcome the mixture of nationalism and radicalism that fascism had concocted. For this reason, well before his decision to lend his support to the Vichy government of Marshal Philippe Pétain, a figure arguably less compromised by fascism than Badoglio, he had become suspect to his comrades, who treated him as a potential traitor. A revolutionary Marxist, equally hated by the fascists and by the members of the Communist Party, Tasca spent his life trying to convince his comrades, and anyone else who cared to listen, that unity was the appropriate response against fascism.

He paid the price for the unpopularity of his convictions and for his inability to be an effective leader within any political organization. Against his wishes, he spent most of his time in exile, first in Moscow, then in Paris, then in Vichy, and finally in Paris again. At thirty-nine, he adopted a new language and began to use French rather than Italian to write his personal diaries, his articles, and his books, and to communicate with his friends. He became a French citizen twice, the first time thanks to the support of the Popular Front government, and the second time with the help of the Vichy authorities. In the course of his life he became a left-wing socialist, a pacifist, a right-wing communist, an ex-communist, a French socialist, an antifascist, a supporter of the war against Germany, a national socialist in Vichy, and a militant anticommunist. He cultivated political and cultural relations with sectors of the French Catholic left, but he was personally an atheist. Tasca managed to live all these lives in the mere sixty-seven years of his existence.

He used many different names—Angelo Tasca, Serra, A. Rossi, André Leroux, XX—and each of these names seems to correspond to a different period of his life. He was born Angelo Tasca, but after the fascist seizure of power he became known in the ranks of the Italian Communist Party (PCI), which he had helped create, as Serra. Under that name he became briefly a potential candidate for the leadership of the PCI, with the support of the International and against the left wing of the party, led by Amedeo Bordiga, Palmiro Togliatti, and Antonio Gramsci. It was also as Serra that, in 1928, he became involved in a major conflict with Stalin, which cost him his party membership. After he moved to France, he adopted his third name, A. Rossi, and lived a semiclandestine life, without a residence permit, wanted by the Italian fascist police and attacked by his former communist comrades. He used his fourth name, André Leroux, to write articles on foreign policy in the French socialist press from before the formation of the French Popular Front to the beginning of World War II. XX, by contrast, is the signature he used for his articles during the war, first in *Le Populaire* and then, after the defeat, in *L'Effort*, a collaborationist newspaper published in Vichy.[2]

Although the creation of each pseudonym corresponded to the specific circumstances in which Tasca lived, the names quickly assumed a certain degree of independence, and he carefully exploited that. In fact, he used some of these different names simultaneously, as brand names to identify his diverse intellectual productions. As Serra, he was a professional revolutionary; as Rossi, he was the author of articles and books on the history of socialism and on fascism; as Leroux, he was a political journalist; as XX, he was a French nationalist who tried to contribute to the success of Vichy's National Revolution. This plurality of identities is the key to solving the mystery of his life.

In Italy, the historians who have written about him have concentrated mostly on Angelo Tasca and Serra, since the events of his life under those two names are indissolubly linked to the origins of the Italian Communist Party. Thanks to his activities and the journal he created after World War I, *L'Ordine Nuovo*, three of the key protagonists of the PCI, Antonio Gramsci, Palmiro Togliatti, and Umberto Terracini, took their first steps into the world of socialist politics. His expulsion from the Communist Party marked the key moment in the Stalinization of the PCI and made Palmiro Togliatti the only member of the original leadership to survive the fascist and Stalinist repression of the Italian communists. Thus it is hardly surprising that Italian historians have concentrated their attention on the relationship between Tasca and the official narrative created by the Italian Communist Party beginning in the second half of the 1920s. Was Tasca a real communist, or was he a foreign presence in the first years of the Italian Communist Party? When Gramsci and Togliatti decided to support Bordiga, who as leader of the Italian communists refused to defend Italian democratic institutions, was it because the right-wing Tasca represented a threat to the identity of the Italian communists? Was the true Italian Communist Party born only with Bordiga's marginalization and Tasca's expulsion, as asserted by the PCI's official historians? Research conducted by Paolo Spriano, Alceo Riosa, and Sergio Soave has reconsidered the role that Tasca played in the first years of the Italian communist movement, debunking the myth of Tasca's "intrusion" in the PCI and reestablishing his importance in the early phases of what became the biggest communist party in Western Europe.[3]

French historiography, by contrast, has focused mostly on XX. Thanks to the efforts of Denis Peschanski and David Bidussa, more than a thousand pages of documents from Tasca's archive on the history of Pétain's regime have been published and introduced to the historians of twentieth-century France.[4] Peschanski's analysis underlines the strange nature of Tasca's participation in the regime, which Peschanski labels an example of resistance from within Vichy.[5] Vichy represented the political expression of a component of French society, Peschanski argues, and there were people in Vichy who chose to participate in the National Revolution not in order to collaborate with Nazi Germany but despite such collaboration; Tasca was one of them.[6] From this perspective, Tasca serves as a case study of the complexity of the relations between the National Revolution, occupation, resistance, and collaboration. Peschanski uses the case of XX to reaffirm "Vichy existence" in the political and intellectual history of France, along the lines of the research pioneered by Robert Paxton, but with specific attention to the intellectual motivations of some of the National Revolution's protagonists.[7] The picture that emerges from these studies, rather than neatly dividing the history of occupied France into resistance and collaboration, provides a much more complex representation of the Vichy experiment, which gives back to the history of the period the internal debate within Pétain's pluralistic dictatorship. As Julian Jackson writes, some historical characters are "a salutary reminder of the importance of contingency in history," and Tasca is among them.[8] Thus, following Jackson's suggestion, I have tried not to read history teleologically, as if the years Tasca spent in France were only the prehistory of his time in Vichy.

My book builds upon the conclusions of both Italian and French scholars, but I have tried to approach the mystery of Tasca's multiple personalities from outside the constraints of the different national approaches, looking for the coherence of his intellectual trajectory. Soon after I began my research, I grew dissatisfied with all previous attempts, including my own, to explain Tasca's intellectual life within the framework of discrete national "cultures." Tasca obviously was neither simply "Italian" nor simply "French." More important, the problems that Tasca had to face and wanted to solve during his life were never just Italian or French. The forces that determined the course of his life were European rather than national. The events that shaped his existence were genuinely transnational phenomena, with which he unsuccessfully tried to cope throughout his life. They were the emerging ideological movements of the interwar period: communism, Stalinism, and fascism.

Tasca's exile, his attempts to hide his identity from the repressive organs of the European nation-states, and his escape from the winning forces of fascism and Stalinism appeared to me as something that Tasca shared with millions of other Europeans who lived through this age of extremes. His attempt to be a protagonist in the ideological struggles for the control of Europe after the end of World War I was simply an anticipation of the destiny of all the Europeans whose lives were changed by the ideological clash that led to World War II. Accordingly, I have highlighted Tasca's unsuccessful attempts to change the course of European politics in order to show how his personal and political life was constantly determined by events and decisions over which he had no control.

Tasca's political engagement, in fact, exposed him to the rigor of totalitarianism earlier than most Europeans. The fascist seizure of power in Italy meant for him a prison term and exile from his nation and from his family. Stalin's maneuvers to achieve absolute control over Russia and the communist movement forced Tasca out of his party. The Stalinization of the communist movement in France cost him his first job in the land where he had found refuge after leaving Moscow. The ideological aggressiveness of fascism separated him from some of his friends who, moving away from communism, embraced fascism as their new ideology. In 1939, the Molotov-Ribbentrop Pact and the temporary alliance between Russia and Germany destroyed Tasca's dreams of a broad antifascist alliance to defeat Nazism. The invasion of France compelled him to leave his house and his life in Paris for another exile. His time under Vichy—a regime that ultimately depended on the will of Nazi Germany and on the events of the war—was only the last stage of a political life in which important decisions were constantly out of Tasca's control.

Perhaps even more salient is how underdeveloped Tasca's personal life was. Historical events led him to an existence in which the only real dimension was political. There are a few documents in his archive that reveal aspects of his life other than politics. For example, Tasca was an avid reader who loved literature, history, and the humanities in general. His children and the few love stories he had in his life also left some traces in his archive. However, among the multiple personas that he invented during his long exiles, a private identity was the only one that he could not really develop, caught as he was between his revolutionary aspirations, his unstable legal status, his insecure financial situation, and his awareness of living in a time when history was happening and the future looked undetermined.

Starting in the 1930s, Tasca, who was cognizant of the larger forces that shaped his life, focused on foreign politics in order to understand the direction Europe was taking. He knew it was pointless to try to predict the success or failure of the Popular Front without taking Stalin's wishes into consideration. He also knew that fascism was an aggressive ideology that was preparing a new European war. He rightly thought that the future of France depended on decisions made in Berlin, London, and Moscow as much as on those made in Paris. Even his final lapse into Pétain's National Revolution was determined, in his mind, by his reading of the direction in which the whole of Europe was heading. Tasca believed that a new form of nationalism characterized Europe, and he wanted France and himself to be European. Thus, his last attempt to be a protagonist of European politics brought him close to the totalitarian nations that seemed to dominate the continent.

For all these reasons, in my biography of Angelo Tasca I have taken into account the history of Europe and its ideological struggle in the interwar period much more than I have focused on the diachronic dimension of a national history of ideas. Despite my personal appreciation for the attempt to create genealogies of ideas that link the sudden emergence of phenomena to long-standing national traditions, I thought that Tasca's life and his extreme ideological trajectory were better explained by focusing on the *courte durée* of the conflicts he had to face during his life. The European dimension of the events that molded his existence was in fact a new situation that Tasca and other Europeans were still poorly prepared to understand. By formation Tasca was an internationalist, and from the beginning he was more clearly exposed to transnational events than most. The circumstances of his life anticipated what all Europeans would go through during the war.

Alexander De Grand, the American scholar who has written the only published biography of Tasca, has suggested a similar transnational approach by entitling his book *In Stalin's Shadow*.[9] De Grand's study is the first to provide an account of Tasca's life in its entirety, and the issue of the international movements that conditioned Tasca's existence clearly emerges from its pages. De Grand used Tasca's immense archive to write a much-needed account of the man's intellectual development, and I have relied on his research for some of the essential details that any biographical work requires. Thanks to this advantage, I have been able to provide new material and new perspectives on aspects of Tasca's intellectual and political life that found little space in De Grand's biography.

Contrary to De Grand, whose essential focus remains on Tasca's relations with the Italian political world, I have emphasized Tasca's relations with the international world of intellectuals who were trying to reform socialism during the interwar period. To this end, I have analyzed closely the various journals to which Tasca contributed, and I have tried to recontextualize his role within the larger European debate propelled by the critics of capitalism and liberal democracy. *L'Ordine Nuovo*, *Monde*, *Esprit*, *Agir*, *L'Effort*, and all the other journals that constituted Tasca's world were important stages for the debate about the future of Europe, and Tasca was one of the protagonists of this discussion. Thus, whenever possible, I have used Tasca's intellectual contributions to these journals to guide the reader through the labyrinth of the interwar period's ideological discussions. I highlight the unorthodox alliances that were established within and across different journals and the porosity of their ideological borders, giving ample space to Tasca's ideological evolution within these debates, and I document the personal relationships that often proved more stable than the temporary ideological divisions.

In searching for a way to thread together Tasca's five pseudonyms, I have emphasized Tasca's intellectual life much more decidedly than De Grand has done in his strictly biographical approach. In so doing, I have sometimes reached conclusions that differ from De Grand's on key issues, such as the moment of Tasca's departure from Marxism and the reasons behind it, his relationship with Christianity, and the level of his involvement in Vichy. These different conclusions are based on the discovery of new documents and on a careful reinterpretation of some of the sources already used by other historians. This has also allowed me to challenge Tasca's and others' interpretations of events such as his expulsion from the Communist Party and his experience in Vichy. For example, I have documented how Palmiro Togliatti consciously used Tasca as a scapegoat for the policy adopted at the end of the 1920s by the Italian communists. In the case of Tasca's participation in Vichy, a study of *L'Effort*, lacking in previous research on his experience in Vichy, allowed me to shed new light on Tasca's support for collaboration and for a single French party. The discovery in his archive of what seems to be the only surviving document produced by his *bureau d'études* enabled me to provide an account of Tasca's activity in Vichy from 1942 to 1944, which is absent from other accounts of the life of XX. My reconstruction of Tasca's ideological development during the second half of the 1930s has also permitted me to contextualize his decision to support Pétain's regime without accepting Tasca's self-exculpatory explanation, as De Grand has partially done.

For this study, I worked for many years in Tasca's archive at the Feltrinelli Foundation in Milan and at the National Library in Paris. I have also conducted research in the French National Archives, the archives of the Italian Communist Party, and the Italian National Library in Milan (Brera). Despite the fact that five volumes of Tasca's documents have been published, making almost two thousand pages of documents available to researchers worldwide, I have preferred to work with the originals in order not to be influenced by the choices made by the editors of the published collections.

Selecting the sources I used for my research, I have paid particular attention to documents that could provide an insight on the different "force fields" that operated along Tasca's political trajectory. Work by Philippe Burrin, who used the metaphor of the force field to refer to the hegemony exercised by fascism over intellectuals and politicians who were not, or not yet, fascist, offered me an important tool to understand Tasca's ideological development.[10] However, in analyzing Tasca's case, I have also shown how the fascist force field operated in the presence of another force field, this one emanating from Stalinism, which, like fascism, both attracted and repelled intellectuals, often determining their movement from one force field to the other. In following Tasca's political development, I have emphasized how Stalin's decision to consider socialists and fascists as politically equivalent became, at least in certain ways, a self-fulfilling prophecy that pushed some intellectuals toward the force field of fascism. This has allowed me to document how the extreme polarization of the political debate in interwar Europe contributed to the failure of Tasca's attempts to ground his political projects in liberal democracy.

At the same time, however, I have sought to reject any explanation of Tasca's political trajectory that relies simply on the European political context, choosing instead to pay attention to the specific ideological elements that engendered Tasca's intellectual production. Thus, I have also used the metaphor of the force field to refer to the dynamic interactions of mobile ideological elements that coexisted in Tasca's intellectual production and which resisted his attempts to produce a synthesis.[11] In each of the following chapters (whose chronology coincides with the life of each of Tasca's five pseudonyms) I have documented the inner conflict between Tasca's attempt to remain faithful to his own humanistic version of Marxism and the political motifs he absorbed from the world of the French nonconformists.

In particular, I have shown how Tasca's desire to reconcile theory and praxis in his actions resulted in the constant frustration of both his political and intellectual endeavors. In the two crucial moments of his life, his expulsion from the communist movement and his support for Vichy, I have highlighted how Tasca's inability to transform his analysis into an effective political tool prompted him to make a difficult choice between active politics and his own understanding of the situation of Europe. In the first instance, his desire to be faithful to his own understanding of Marxism forced him out of the communist movement, frustrating his wish to play an active role in European politics. In the second instance, his desire to play a part in French politics forced him to contradict in practice most of his own analysis of European fascism. Thus the conflict between Tasca the intellectual, who tried to be consistent with his understanding of politics, and Tasca the politician, who tried to be effective in the political world, resulted in a constant oscillation between these two poles rather than in an effective synthesis.

Even in this regard, Tasca was far from being an exceptional case in the political panorama of interwar Europe. In *Les mains sales*, Jean-Paul Sartre gave a theatrical representation of the conflict between the intellectual attracted by politics and the world of communist politics.[12] In the play, Hugo, an intellectual desiring an active life, becomes a communist and is ordered to kill a communist leader, Hoederer, who refuses to follow Stalin's orders. Although Hoederer convinces Hugo that his opposition to Moscow is justified, Hugo kills him anyway, out of jealousy. At that point, the communists kill Hugo because Moscow has now adopted the politics supported by Hoederer, and Hugo is considered a traitor. In a parallel with Tasca's life, the disagreement between Moscow and Hoederer stemmed from Hoederer's refusal to break the antifascist alliance with noncommunists as ordered by Stalin. In another parallel, Hugo's inability to follow the rules of party politics ended up in an objective betrayal of the antifascist cause. As I hope this book will show, in real life Tasca played out this drama by himself, among his five identities. He thus constitutes a compelling case for the study of the complex relation between theory and politics in the age of totalitarianism.

1 Into the Battlefield

During the twentieth century, the communist movement was never afraid to manipulate its own history to serve its political goals. Josef Stalin famously instructed his secret police and his photographic experts to erase from photographs and paintings the images of revolutionary leaders who had become his enemies.[1] In Hungary, as István Rév documented, a complex system of manipulations of dead bodies and their graves was perfected to control public memory, becoming one of the legacies of the "prehistory of post-Communism."[2] In the case of Angelo Tasca, one of the key figures of the Italian radical socialist and communist movement of the early twentieth century, such an explicit and criminal manipulation did not take place. Nevertheless, historians of the Italian communist movement routinely underestimate Tasca's role in the political and cultural formation of the leadership of the Italian Communist Party.

On one hand, Tasca, who was involved in multiple conflicts with Antonio Gramsci for leadership of the Turinese socialists, is obscured by the personality and intellectual brilliancy of his more famous opponent.[3] On the other hand, the fact that Tasca's association with the Italian communists was abruptly interrupted at the end of the 1920s often makes him look like a broken thread in the history of the Italian communist movement, one that would be useless to pursue. The result is that in the long perspective on the history of the Italian communist movement, Tasca becomes a very minor presence. Since expulsion from the Communist Party of Italy (PCI) was accompanied by the drawing of a curtain of silence around the expelled, scholars who write the history of the Communist Party often relegate figures who disappeared from the party's official pictures to the ranks of minor characters.[4] Only when we abandon retrospective teleology can Tasca reemerge as a key figure among the Turinese socialists who would become early leaders of the Italian Communist Party.[5]

When a generation of promising young students with an interest in socialist politics crossed paths with Turinese young socialists, Tasca was there to greet the students and convince them to join the socialist ranks.

"The day after, coming out of school, I went to Corso Siccardi, where I met a kid who asked me: 'Who are you looking for?' and, since I did not answer, he added: 'Are you also here to become a young socialist?' It was Angelo Tasca."[6] With these words Umberto Terracini, who after the defeat of fascism became president of the Italian Constitutional Assembly, described his first encounter with socialism in the years immediately following World War I. Angelo Tasca, the person who greeted him at the entrance to the young socialists' local headquarters, was already the prodigy of the Turinese Socialist Party, whose local section of young socialists he had cofounded in 1909, while still in high school. That first casual meeting with Tasca would forever change Terracini's life, as was the case for many other young protagonists of the Turinese socialist movement.

Antonio Gramsci, who had moved to Turin from his native Sardinia, left us with a famous description of the time he spent with Tasca in his first years as a young revolutionary:

> We used to come out of the meetings of the Socialist Party as a group, surrounding the person who was our leader, and we wandered in the streets of a city already asleep. The late-night walkers stopped to stare at us because we continued our previous discussions, forgetful of ourselves and still full of passion, advancing bold proposals, exploding in sudden laughter, and taking wild rides in the realm of the imagination.[7]

Tasca, the leader Gramsci refers to, had met the Sardinian in the classrooms of the local university in 1912, when Gramsci's political identity was still unclear. Impressed by the intelligence of his new friend, Tasca immediately tried to convince Gramsci to join the socialist movement. This pressure was evident in the words Tasca wrote in a copy of *War and Peace* he gave to Gramsci at the end of the academic year: "To my comrade in study [*compagno di studi*] of today, to my comrade in battle [*compagno di battaglia*]—I hope—of tomorrow."[8] So when Gramsci made the decision to become politically active in the Italian Socialist Party (PSI), it was to Tasca that he decided to communicate his choice, readily acknowledging Tasca's political leadership.[9]

Gramsci was not Tasca's only disciple. Palmiro Togliatti, who, like Gramsci, had moved to Turin to pursue his studies at the university there, was among the group of friends who gathered around Tasca for those late-night discussions. Togliatti, whose relationship with Tasca was more formal than friendly, did not leave us with a memory of his first encounter with Tasca, but their political association lasted for sixteen years. Especially in his first years of political activity, Togliatti, who came from a conservative and monarchist family in Genoa, certainly recognized the primacy of Tasca, whose experience as a socialist had no parallel among this group of friends.[10] His political initiation, in fact, had happened years before their own.

Unlike his friends, Tasca had learned socialism at home. His father, Carlo Tasca, was a railroad worker whose socialism was marked by anarchist sympathies, as Angelo's daughter Valeria recalls. His mother, Angela Damilano, often worked as a seasonal employee in France for months at a stretch. Born on November 19, 1892, Angelo was the only son of their marriage. He inherited from his father a passion for socialism and from his mother a fascination for French culture that affected him at a very early age. At the beginning of the century, Carlo and Angela left their house in Bussoleno and moved to Turin.[11] Soon after, their marriage ended abruptly and Angela decided to leave Turin and move to Monte Carlo, where she opened a restaurant. Carlo and his son remained in the capital of Piedmont, and after finishing elementary school, Angelo enrolled in the Scuola Tecnica Giovanni Plana, where he studied for three years.[12] The Italian *scuola tecnica* was meant to prepare boys to become specialized workers and start a job at age thirteen. Upon completion of his technical studies, however, Angelo enrolled in the Liceo Classico Vincenzo Gioberti, which opened the door to a college degree. In those early years, he found in the various local organizations of the Socialist Party a way to affirm his identity as the gifted son of a worker, as well as a legitimate reason to spend afternoons and evenings in the company of other young people.

In 1909, the local sections of young socialists, as Tasca remembered years later, were "dancing clubs," where people mostly went for social activities.[13] Tasca and his teenage friends, however, cared as much about politics as they did about dancing. In the lively political climate of the years immediately before World War I, Tasca and his friends received their first political training through the activities they organized in these clubs, of which Tasca was a leader. For example, groups of young socialists who pompously called themselves "red bikers" went to villages in the countryside to try to proselytize the farmers. During these missions, which were greeted with very little enthusiasm by the villagers, Tasca learned how to speak in public and convince people of the virtues of the socialist creed. In the course of these expeditions, he developed a rhetorical style that he kept for most of his life.[14]

One of his friends, Andrea Viglongo, remembered his ability to talk to people, his natural empathy for others' problems, and his ability to speak brilliantly without being pedantic. These qualities, Viglongo claimed, stemmed from Tasca's direct knowledge of the living conditions of the lower classes.[15] Even the police reported that "Tasca, despite his ease in delivering speeches, is proper when he speaks and does not try to inflame the audience," thus offering a glimpse into Tasca's preference, even at a young age, for rational communication over more emotional approaches.[16] In their hot debates with opponents (and in particular with nationalists) on the eve of the world war, the Turinese socialists constantly needed effective speakers, and Tasca was quick in acquiring the skills required for the job. His qualities as an orator launched Tasca very early into a career in the Socialist Party and also allowed him to become, as we have seen, an effective recruiter of promising young minds for the party.

Rhetoric was not the only skill that Tasca was learning from his early commitment to socialism. At the price of neglecting school, as he confessed, Tasca became a precocious participant in the debates that animated Italian socialism in the early years of the twentieth century.[17] As he wrote in his memoirs, the socialist movement in Turin was still dominated by positivism, and in the triad "Darwin, Spencer and Marx, the last author was the least important."[18] The emphasis on evolution had, in the opinion of Turin's young socialists, the effect of pushing the socialist movement toward a reformist policy, which stressed slow and progressive change as a natural road to socialism. Tasca and the young socialists around him were determined to challenge both this approach and the older generation of socialists, whom they saw as acquiescent and politically passive. Thus, in the process of forming his political identity in relation to his older comrades, Tasca became, while still in high school, a voracious reader of publications that attacked positivism.

La Voce, the journal founded by Giuseppe Prezzolini at the end of 1908, offered the material that Tasca and his comrades needed to conduct their polemics against the old guard of Italian socialists. Tasca, and Gramsci with him, absorbed from *La Voce* a conception of the intellectual as a socially engaged figure committed to "sincerity," against the aestheticism of Gabriele Dannunzio and the political reformism of Giovanni Giolitti. They also learned from Prezzolini's publication about the political and cultural debates sponsored by the artistic avant-garde. The desire to renovate the Italian philosophical tradition through the neo-Hegelian philosophy developed by Benedetto Croce and Giovanni Gentile completed the picture of *La Voce*'s antipositivism. The role of intellectuals, Italy's "Southern Question," and the search for a new pedagogy were all themes that found their way from the pages of *La Voce* into Tasca's cultural toolbox.[19] Gaetano Salvemini, with his passionate support of Italy's southern underclasses, his coherent anticolonialism, and his battles against political corruption, was ideologically closer to Tasca and his friends than the reformist leaders of the Socialist Party were.[20]

As is to be expected from a young man in his first years in college, Tasca was more intellectually curious than ideologically coherent, but he had a good instinct that kept him away from the aggressive nationalism of some of his Italian intellectual heroes. Thus, when Salvemini broke with *La Voce* over the journal's decision to support the Italian war in Libya, Tasca and his friends immediately bought subscriptions to Salvemini's new journal, *L'Unità*, fully embracing the journal's anticolonial and antinationalist campaigns. Tasca's will to action was mitigated by a firm commitment to internationalism and by an acute sense of the Italian working class's pacifism. Viscerally socialist but unsatisfied with the coarse positivism of the Turinese cadres, Tasca was firmly convinced that socialism required the production of an autonomous working-class culture capable of challenging bourgeois culture at its highest level, and hoped the intellectual debates of the Italian avant-garde could provide new cultural weapons for such an effort.

The notion of "culture," albeit undefined in Tasca's early writings, served the purpose of stressing the human and subjective side of history over the rigid determinism of those who believed that impersonal, quasi-natural economic forces were the only engines of history. If the positivist determinism inspired by Darwinism stressed the role of nature, perhaps in the form of the economy as the "natural" side of human society, Tasca found in the notion of "culture" a theoretical tool that he could use to challenge any form of crude naturalism. Consequently, in discussions with both his comrades and his adversaries, Tasca could use the opposition between natural determinism and cultural subjectivism as a compass to orient his political judgment. Nationalism, with its quasi-racial understanding of what a community is, was repugnant to Tasca, as was the idea that the natural development of the means of production was destined to create a socialist society.

As the leader and theoretician of the Turinese young socialists, Tasca became one of the two main figures at the national congress of young socialists held in Bologna in 1912. His opponent was a Neapolitan engineering student three years older than he: Amadeo Bordiga.[21] The clash between Bordiga and Tasca dominated the congress and the following years of the left wing of the Italian socialist movement, and would never be resolved. Bordiga believed that the insistence on "culture" as a method for achieving socialism could lead only to an indefinite procrastination of the revolutionary moment. He sharply criticized the Turinese socialists led by Tasca, asking polemically: "What should be our method, theory, and culture? Should we wait for centuries in order to prepare the proletariat? No, our propaganda should be based not on theory but on sentiments, since it is the reflex of the material conditions of men in their nervous system."[22] As Bordiga articulated even more clearly in a letter published in Salvemini's *L'Unità*: "The need to study is an appropriate declaration for a congress of schoolmasters, not for a socialist congress.[23]

Tasca's reply on behalf of the "culturalists," as he, Gramsci, and the Turinese group were polemically called, affirmed exactly the opposite. "A schoolmaster," Tasca wrote, "who can create a new consciousness in his students is more revolutionary than a speaker who inflames his audience with a profusion of words against the bourgeoisie."[24] Only a clear socialist consciousness, according to Tasca, could save workers from falling into reformism when their material conditions were bettered by economic development. For the culturalists, this was the essence of the party's role: contrary to Bordiga's opinion, the party was to be the place where the critical consciousness of the workers became their collective intelligence. Tasca believed that reformism and extremism were but two faces of a similar policy, which stressed determinism over the active political engagement of workers.[25]

In his effort to present his group's positions to a national audience, Tasca provided a definition of culture that already showed signs of some of the problems that Gramsci would later try to solve. Culture, he said, was not to be confused with bookish knowledge. It was rather the process of self-reflection that allowed a worker to move from the "awareness of his miserable life" to class consciousness. Class consciousness, in fact, could be achieved only through "the habit of reflecting" and in the transformation of theory into practice. Thus, culture was the medium through which the specificity of a worker's position in the world could be transformed into the consciousness of the universal role of the proletariat.[26]

In this perspective, culture had to be understood not as the domain of a specialized group of people—intellectuals—but as a potentiality of every human being. Socialism was the realization of workers' ability to create culture, because "if the working class always had to think with somebody else's brain, [socialism] would only be the delight of a collectivist bourgeoisie in place of a republican or monarchical bourgeoisie."[27] It was the specific duty of socialist intellectuals to contribute to this process of the working class's self-discovery, providing the means that the workers needed to acquire consciousness. "We have the duty," Tasca concluded his reply to Bordiga, "to take on the responsibility of this task."[28]

At age twenty, when he was writing those words, Tasca already had strong personal reasons to consider himself not only a socialist leader but also an intellectual, and the "we" he used at the end of his article proves it. His father's decision to retire from his job, hoping to add some money to his minuscule pension through occasional employment, had turned into a disaster for Tasca's financial situation. Nevertheless, the young man managed to enroll at the university, in the department of Italian literature, counting on his father's moral support and on the occasional money that his mother could send him from France. Like Gramsci, whose economic situation was even worse than Tasca's and who, in the course of his studies, had to live in Tasca's home for a few months to save some money, Tasca was able to go through college only thanks to the help of his family. Thus Bordiga's positions, characterized by such a strong devaluation of culture, must have sounded to Tasca almost like a personal attack, since he had decided to become not a worker, like his father, but a college graduate.

The clash between Tasca and Bordiga, destined to end only with the marginalization of them both by the end of the twenties and their expulsion from the Italian Communist Party, was as much a political issue as it was a matter of personal incompatibility. Tasca was from the north, Bordiga was from the south. Tasca's father was a worker; Bordiga's father was a university professor who had Venetian aristocratic origins. Tasca studied literature, Bordiga engineering. Bordiga was charismatic, while Tasca had a passion for nearly endless discussions. Bordiga believed that politics was mostly emotions and class instinct; Tasca believed that political engagement was mostly rationality and culture. Despite all this, they both considered themselves revolutionaries who hated reformism, nationalism, colonialism, and the passive determinism of the positivist leadership of the socialist movement. They both wanted a revolution that could end capitalism and abolish the private property of the means of production. In other words, they had good reasons to be in different parties and, on the contrary, equally good reasons to be members of the same movement. What was clearly impossible as early as 1912, however, was for them to share the leadership of a political organization.

In Turin, where his leadership was unchallenged by such a charismatic opponent, Tasca's project was flourishing and his influence within his party was growing.[29] In 1913, when the first Italian elections with universal male suffrage were held, Tasca still had very little say in the electoral policy of his party. However, less than a year later, when the Socialist Party had to replace a deputy representing one of the "red" districts of Turin, Tasca and the young socialists had enough influence on the party to participate in the choice of candidate. Tasca and his comrades supported Salvemini, who was their cultural hero and a major proponent of a cultural revision of socialism. Only a technicality—Salvemini was no longer a card-carrying socialist—prevented the plan from succeeding. Nonetheless, before the problem was discovered and the idea abandoned, Tasca and his friend Ottavio Pastore had obtained Salvemini's consent to stand for election.[30] So when Salvemini was excluded, he had accumulated enough authority to propose another candidate, who was also a political hero of the young socialists: Benito Mussolini.[31]

Twenty years later, in 1934, Tasca told a French audience that in 1914 he had been too influenced by the French theorist Georges Sorel to understand how dangerous Mussolini was.[32] But he was not alone in his infatuation with the future creator of fascism. Tasca's entire group and many other young socialists in Italy recognized Mussolini as their informal leader. From the pages of *L'Avanti,* the Italian socialists' house-organ, which Mussolini edited, the theme of renewal of the Socialist Party, dear to Tasca and his comrades, was picked up in the national debate among the leadership of the party. The need to align the theoretical bases of socialism with new philosophical trends that were emerging from France, as in the case of Sorel, or from Italy, as in the cases of Gentile and Croce, united the youngsters of the party with Mussolini, who was only nine years older than Tasca. Like the young socialists from Turin, Mussolini was conducting a battle against reformism and positivism in the name of revolution and activism; also like them, he was a prodigy of Italian socialism. Thus after the failure of Salvemini's candidacy, which would have had the advantage of creating an ideal bridge between the Turinese working class and the south of the country, Mussolini was an almost natural choice for Tasca and his friends.

Since 1913, in fact, Tasca had had a personal connection with him. When Mussolini founded his new journal, *Utopia,* tellingly subtitled *Biweekly Journal of Italian Revolutionary Socialism,* he had immediately asked both Tasca and Bordiga to contribute articles. Having participated in the debate at the Bologna congress, the two were natural choices for Mussolini's new periodical, which tried to assemble many of the figures dissatisfied with the state of the Socialist Party.[33] Tasca wrote an article that revealed how closely his views matched those of Mussolini.[34] In this piece, dedicated to Giuseppe Lombardo Radice, Tasca called for a reform of pedagogy inspired by the neoidealist movement that later, under fascism, found its realization in Giovanni Gentile's reform of the Italian school.[35] Tasca's support for pedagogical activism was also in line with Mussolini's philosophy, and his insistence on the central role of schoolteachers doubtless pleased the future dictator, whose mother had been a teacher and who also had been trained as a teacher. Given these personal and ideological ties, Tasca must have felt that nominating Mussolini presented a great political opportunity.[36]

However, this second attempt to nominate someone who represented Tasca's political tendency in the Socialist Party was also unsuccessful. The local leadership of the PSI argued that since the previous representative of the district had been a worker, another worker had to take his place, and that ruled out Mussolini as a candidate. But the episode left a lasting impression on Tasca, who later in life frequently recalled the story, and who must have wondered what would have happened if the party had been able to retain Mussolini within its ranks.[37] A few months later, in fact, the beginning of World War I dramatically changed the terms of the debate among the Italian socialists. Between the beginning of the European war and the Italian decision to participate in the conflict against Germany and Austria, Tasca was at the forefront of the drama that opposed nationalists to socialists and, more important for the future of Italy, Mussolini to his former comrades.

Contrary to the majority of European socialist parties, at the beginning of the war the PSI tried to remain faithful to the Socialist International, refusing to participate in the conflict. However, the pressure of the mobilization organized by the Italian nationalists and the developments in Europe immediately created enormous theoretical problems for the Italian socialists. The war could not be ignored, and the party's call for neutrality, albeit extremely popular among Italian workers, condemned the Italian socialists to inaction. Germany and Austria appeared to the Italian socialists as symbols of reactionary politics, and the history of Italy's conflicts with Austria, which still controlled territories where the majority of the inhabitants were Italian-speakers, partially undercut the argument put forward by the supporters of neutralism that there was no difference between the two sides of the conflict. In this situation, Mussolini's decision to abandon neutrality immediately sparked a debate among all those who had been politically close to him, including the young socialists of Turin.[38]

When he heard about Mussolini's change of heart, Tasca, who had been in constant contact with him for his article in *Utopia*, immediately sent him a letter to ask him to reconsider. Mussolini's reply, which Tasca remembered as short and full of loose rhetoric, made it clear that the decision was irreversible and forced Tasca to carefully consider his options.[39] Unlike his close friends Gramsci and Togliatti, Tasca decided to remain with the majority of his party. Thus, six days after the publication of Mussolini's "Dalla neutralità assoluta alla neutralità attiva ed operante" (From absolute neutrality to active and effective neutrality), Tasca decided to write an article opposing Mussolini's decision.[40]

Tasca's article, titled "Il mito della guerra" (The myth of war), tried to pay tribute to Mussolini while rigorously contesting his political positions. "We know," Tasca wrote, "the great moral difference that separates Mussolini from the many who left socialism." With words reminiscent of a prayer, he urged Mussolini to remain in the Socialist Party: "Stay with us as our leader in this sad moment, as you were in the days of pride and expectation." Nevertheless, Tasca also insisted that Mussolini had not understood that for the Italian proletariat, war had become a "myth." After the Libyan war, Tasca said, the workers had projected onto war everything they hated in bourgeois society; it was therefore impossible to ask them to participate in it. The Italian proletariat, in Tasca's view, knew that the time had not yet come for revolution, and that workers could participate in the war only under the direction of the bourgeoisie. For these reasons, the socialists had to be prepared for the time when war revealed to the proletariat its radical opposition to capitalist society. "Despite all the love we have had for you," Tasca concluded in his article, addressing Mussolini, "we believe that the party has the duty to force you out of our newspaper."[41] Despite Tasca's evident respect for Mussolini, whom he had promoted as a candidate in Turin only a few months earlier, the issue of the war was simply too clear in Tasca's mind to leave room for any ambiguity.

A week later, it was Tasca's turn to be attacked in the pages of a socialist newspaper by a person who considered Tasca his leader: Antonio Gramsci. In "Neutralità attiva ed operante," the first article he ever published, Gramsci took up his pen to debunk Tasca's argument and defend Mussolini. The party leadership, he asserted, was abstract and ideological, whereas Mussolini was concrete and realist. Contrary to Tasca's claim, Gramsci wrote, Mussolini was not asking the workers to support a war directed by the bourgeoisie, but rather to let the bourgeoisie run its course. Thus, Gramsci concluded, if he had "rightly interpreted Mussolini's slightly confused declarations," Mussolini had asked the proletariat not to renounce its antagonism but rather to prepare itself for the revolution.[42]

Fifteen days later, however, the first issue of *Il Popolo d'Italia*, Mussolini's new newspaper, proved that Gramsci had misinterpreted Mussolini's declarations and that the former socialist leader had decided to abandon the PSI. In his memoirs, Tasca later affirmed that his association with Mussolini ended there, never to be revived.[43] His personal relationship with Gramsci, by contrast, was not affected by their dispute. Despite his firm opposition to the war, Tasca was convinced that it was a terrible mistake to expel the socialists who had declared their support for Italian intervention in the war. Since he was constantly on the verge of heresy in relation to the official positions of his party, Tasca never had any sympathy for drastic disciplinary measures against dissidents. Provided that the minority was willing to respect the decisions taken by the majority, he considered debate on the party's policy a healthy exercise. Thus, at least according to his account of the events, he was able to separate Gramsci's political motivations, expressed rather harshly in his article, from their friendship, and to maintain his admiration for his gifted friend.[44]

A few months later, when Italy intervened in the conflict, Tasca was drafted, and his collaboration with Gramsci and with the Socialist Party in general was temporarily suspended. From September 1915 to the summer of 1919, Tasca was in the military, and for the only time in his life he kept himself distant from politics. This decision kept him below the radar of the army's repressive apparatus, which, considering the socialist opposition to the war, certainly would have punished him for any direct involvement in socialist politics. It also allowed Tasca to live a fairly comfortable life—he was assigned to a regiment quartered in Turin. This privilege, which would produce comments and rumors after the war, allowed Tasca to take advantage of the time away from politics and pay attention to his personal life.[45]

A few months after he started his life in the army, Tasca and his girlfriend, Lina Martoretti, decided to get married. Martoretti, who was the sister of one of Tasca's high school friends, Renato, was nineteen at the time of their marriage, five years younger than Tasca. Her family, in Tasca's words, was "respectable" (*buona famiglia*), and her father, Carlo, was able to give financial help to the couple, who could count only on Tasca's military stipend. In a letter to his mother, Tasca said that Martoretti was "very intelligent and, above all, a very nice person," but this rather bland description should be considered in the context of Tasca's sudden announcement of his desire to marry her.[46] Their wedding was celebrated in April 1916 in Asti, Martoretti's hometown, and a year later, in March 1917, they had their first child, Carlo.

On December 19, 1917, Tasca was also able to complete his studies at the University of Turin. His undergraduate thesis on Giacomo Leopardi and the philosophy of the eighteenth century has been lost, but it must have been judged positively because Tasca graduated with honors. In a short autobiographical piece written in Vichy in 1940, Tasca described it as the study of "a generation whose excessive sensibility could be expressed only through the materialistic philosophy of *L'Encyclopédie*," but his memory easily could have been influenced by his personal situation at the time.[47] What is certainly true, however, is that the main idea of the thesis was perfectly in line with Tasca's cultural points of reference. The relation between Leopardi and the Enlightenment was in fact a privileged subject for Benedetto Croce, who inherited from Francesco De Sanctis's discussion of Leopardi's poetic production his famous distinction between "poetry" and "literature."[48] Thus, Tasca's thesis, bringing together the French Enlightenment and Italian poetry, a neo-Hegelian subject and the French Revolution, could be seen as a true mirror of Tasca's cultural interests. Until the Soviet revolution changed the perspective of Turin's working class and its leaders, this was still the cultural environment in which Tasca and his friends were operating.

L'Ordine Nuovo

When Tasca was released from active duty in the military, a job was waiting for him in the ranks of the Socialist Party, and as soon as the war was over, he prepared an article that signaled his return to political life. The essay, titled "Perché sono socialista" (Why I am a socialist), shows that during the years he spent in the military, Tasca had been reading Marx and Gramsci. For the first time, Tasca referred directly to Marx as the key figure behind his socialism, and he did so in a manner similar to that seen in a famous article Gramsci had published a year earlier, "Il nostro Marx" (Our Marx).[49]

The similarities between Tasca's description of his relationship to Marx and Gramsci's are both lexical and theoretical. Tasca started his analysis—a reply to an article by Balbino Giuliano, who had argued that Mazzini was more relevant than Marx[50]—by asserting, as Gramsci had done before him, that Marxism was not to be interpreted as a determinist proponent of the objective development of the economic structure. The core of historical materialism was to be found not in Marx's economic predictions but in his understanding of the role of the proletariat in the process of liberation of the whole of humanity. According to Tasca, a positivist interpretation, which stressed economic determinism, was incapable of seeing that behind Marx's analysis of value lay the moral problem of the exploitation of the workers.[51] The vital part of Marxism was its understanding of the process of constituting the workers as an internationalist class, conscious of its role. It was in the socialists' interest, Tasca concluded, "to excite the new moral consciousness that was forming in the proletariat."[52] Tasca was still attacking his two main ideological adversaries, nationalism and determinism, as he had done before the war, but for the first time Tasca's socialist aspirations were presented as Marxist. The problem, from a theoretical point of view, was to find a way to reconcile the humanist and moral aspirations that had animated his early years with the new philosophy he was slowly discovering.

"Perché sono socialista" shows clearly that at the beginning of 1919 Tasca's knowledge of Marx's works was already fairly substantial. His preference went not to *Das Kapital* or the other economic studies but to Marx's historical works. "The fact that economic determinism . . . should not be interpreted rigidly is proven by Marx and Engels's works that study specific historical periods: the French revolution of 1848, the Franco-Prussian war, and the Commune," Tasca wrote.[53] Against any Marxist explanation that relied simply on economic structure, Tasca quoted Marx's "Theses on Feuerbach," and in particular the third thesis, which stressed the dialectical relation between structure and superstructure and the centrality of human action.[54] Thus, like Gramsci, Tasca was trying to recover a space in socialism for human agency, a space that the reformist socialists, with their theory of the natural development of socialism from capitalism, had closed down.

Such an interpretation of Marxism derived, for both Gramsci and Tasca, from their readings of the Italian neo-Hegelian philosophers. The key authors that oriented Tasca's interpretation of Marxism were Antonio Labriola, Benedetto Croce, Rodolfo Mondolfo, and Giovanni Gentile.[55] In Tasca's words, Gentile was the author who had shown that "Hegelian dialectics was the vital part of Marx's thought," whereas Mondolfo was the philosopher who had demonstrated, against Gentile, that Marx had worked out a synthesis of naturalistic and idealistic elements.[56]

The article of Gentile's that Tasca used as a point of departure for his own understanding of Marxism was "La filosofia della prassi" (The philosophy of praxis). In this work, written in 1899, Gentile emphasized the connection between Marx and Hegelian philosophy and the centrality of dialectics for both. Gentile also stressed the relevance of the writings of the young Marx for understanding his later works, which, according to Gentile, he had unsuccessfully tried to elaborate into a system. Thus in Gentile's view, as for Gramsci and Tasca, Marx's original philosophical intuition, based on the idea that humanity realizes itself dialectically in history, had been contaminated by positivist elements, which had concealed the philosophical project under economic determinism.[57] Mondolfo, whom Tasca personally admired, had tried to refute Gentile's dismissal of Marx's materialism and his return to idealism but had accepted Gentile's analysis of the Hegelian core of Marxism.[58] Learning from both Gentile and Mondolfo, Tasca believed that he had found the theoretical tools he needed to fight his battle against the reformists as well as against revolutionaries such as Bordiga who still stressed economic determinism.[59] And although Tasca had an established reputation among the socialists at a time when a socialist revolution in Europe seemed imminent if not already ongoing, he decided that his ideas and those of his comrades needed an independent voice. So Tasca, Gramsci, Terracini, and Togliatti, on the basis of this common reading of Marxism, their desire to put culture at the center of the political battle for socialism, and their revolutionary aspirations, decided to create a journal where they could present their ideas.

They needed 6,000 lire to start their periodical.[60] Tasca requested part of that sum from Carlo Martoretti, his father-in-law. Martoretti agreed to provide half the money, though we do not know if he did so to aid the socialist cause or to help his son-in-law, who was about to become the father of his granddaughter Elena.[61] In any case, on May 1, 1919, Tasca and his friends were able to publish the first issue of *L'Ordine Nuovo,* which was presented as a weekly periodical of socialist culture. Tasca wrote the first editorial piece, entitled "Battute di preludio" (First notes), in which he presented the new publication as "something in between a newspaper and a journal," created to provide "a socialist forum for discussions, studies and research on national and international problems."[62] Gramsci was in charge of editorial policy, and his name was the only one that appeared on the masthead of the journal. The price for a copy was the modest sum of 20 cents, and the publication had eight pages. In the third issue, the journal was proud to announce that it had 179 subscribers.

From the very beginning, *L'Ordine Nuovo* tried to host some of the international authors Tasca, Gramsci, Togliatti, and Terracini found interesting, thus giving a distinct internationalist flavor to the publication. In the first issue appeared an article by Romain Rolland and one by Max Eastman. In the second issue, Henri Barbusse announced the creation of *Clarté*. In the following months, *L'Ordine Nuovo* published articles by John Reed, the Japanese labor leader Sen Katayama, and Maxim Gorky, alongside articles by leaders of the Soviet revolution of the caliber of Lenin and Bukharin. In the journal's first months, it also hosted a feuilleton, offered a history of French socialism from Louis Blanc (written by Tasca), and provided an open forum for some of its readers.

Tasca's contributions to the journal in the first year of its existence were copious. His articles covered a great number of subjects, from the aforementioned history of French socialism to political discussions on the internal life of the Socialist Party and theoretical questions about Marxism in the face of the Soviet revolution. His theoretical approach remained coherent with the approach he had developed at the end of the war, but it became slightly more refined and specific. In an article titled "Cultura e socialismo" (Culture and socialism), for instance, he affirmed the equivalence between culture and philosophy. "Culture," he wrote, "is the ability of human minds to comprehend our lives, our position in the world, and our relation with others." The capitalist economy had reduced the workers to an appendix of the machines, denying their humanity, which consists in the possibility "to choose consciously [their] own path, aware of [their] actions." The cultural asset that made the proletariat superior to the bourgeoisie, he continued, was "class consciousness." Through class consciousness, a worker could transcend his individual position in the world to become connected with "his category, his nation, and the entire world." As evident in this and similar articles, Tasca's traditional culturalism was becoming increasingly Marxist, with some of the themes that were becoming specific to the Western Marxist debate.[63]

His understanding of the socialist project, inspired by these theoretical positions, became increasingly humanist, with elements that would not have seemed out of place in the works of reactionary authors such as Thomas Carlyle. In an article entitled "La casa" (The home), for instance, he wrote: "The factory has killed the home," which continued to exist "only in the countryside, where small property has survived the law of capitalist concentration." If a city dweller had the opportunity to visit an old house outside a big city—"provided that the 'modern' grandchildren [of the home's original owner] have not had the time to sell everything"—he could see how the interior was built for the comfort of the family. Contemporary houses, on the contrary, did not show "the characteristic signs of a family, something our own to leave to our children," which pushed the workers to spend their entire lives in either the factory or the tavern. In the socialist house of the future, he predicted, the worker would have the time and energy "to notice the pretty curtains chosen by his female comrade [*compagna*], the shiny utensils hanging from the wall, the flower vase, and the distinctive cleanliness of the home."[64]

Tasca's rather traditional description of the virtues of the household, which also contained some patriarchal overtones, may have been prompted in part by his personal history. His comment that when "a woman is out most of the day the home no longer exists" and his belief that "the factory returned mothers and wives to the home" can easily be connected to his experience with his mother's long absences from home and with her decision to live where her job was. However, his desire for workers to have more private time also highlights his ability to describe the concrete circumstances and real problems of the working class, accompanied by proposals for concrete solutions that could channel families into political engagement with the Socialist Party. His effectiveness as a socialist propagandist, as Viglongo's testimony confirms, stemmed from his ability to talk to workers about their real-world problems.[65] Thus Tasca's political rhetoric did not dismiss the workers' worldview but took it seriously.

In this spirit, in a country such as Italy, where the vast majority of the popular classes were deeply Catholic, Tasca never used in his articles the language of anticlericalism. On the contrary, despite his firm atheism, he often used Christian references in order to connect with his readers, who certainly knew the Christian message better than they knew Marxism. Throughout his life, he was proud to oppose, along with the other members of *L'Ordine Nuovo*, publications such as *L'Asino* [The jackass], edited by Guido Podrecca, whose primary targets were the Catholic Church and Christianity.[66] Rather, Tasca's strategy was to show how the dominant classes had betrayed the Christian message and to present socialism as a way to fulfill aspirations expressed in Christianity. Tasca's attention to the worldview and concrete circumstances of the lower classes and his desire to engage in a permanent dialogue with the workers suggested to him and the other members of his group a respectful attitude toward religion, which they believed had to be overcome but not ridiculed.

This blend of connections to the international revolutionary movement and respect for workers' autonomy proved successful for the new publication. It benefited also from the *biennio rosso*, which began on September 13, 1919, and lasted until the beginning of October 1920, in which more than half a million workers in factories all over northern Italy took part in an unprecedented wave of strikes and seized control of industrial production. As a result, at the end of September 1919 the journal already had five hundred subscribers, and each issue sold more than three thousand copies. The revolt of the Turinese working class, events in Germany and Hungary, and the Soviet revolution were increasingly perceived by the most radical elements of the Socialist Party as a single phenomenon that could lead to the victory of socialism in Europe.

In Naples, Bordiga had created a journal of his own, called *Il Soviet*, and was organizing a faction in the PSI to boycott Italy's upcoming general elections and prepare for a Leninist revolution.[67] The Socialist Party had become a member of the Third International, and to the most radical members of the socialist movement, the revolution appeared to be mostly an issue of creating the proper organization among workers—specifically, a military organization. Learning from Leninism, as Bordiga was recommending, it was possible to take advantage of the collapse of capitalist society as long as a group of professional revolutionaries was ready for the task. The success of *L'Ordine Nuovo* among revolutionary workers could make the leaders of the journal into the Turinese Bolsheviks.

Tasca remained skeptical. He believed that the Italian proletariat had not yet sufficiently developed its culture to attract the majority of the intermediate classes to the cause of socialism. Tasca, like all those on the left of the Socialist Party, believed that the bourgeoisie was losing its ability to control Italy and that the proletariat was emerging as the class best capable of representing the nation. However, Tasca also cautioned his party about the danger inherent in the situation. If "the producers in the ranks of the bourgeoisie had consciousness of their interests, we would probably be on the verge of communism," he wrote, but "the fear of communism today still holds together the competing interests within the circle of the bourgeoisie."[68] Thus, despite the crisis and "the lack of a common program," the bourgeoisie was still capable of presenting a united front against socialism. The Italian socialists, on the other hand, were, in Tasca's judgment, poorly prepared for a successful revolution. "There are thousands of towns where we do not have a section and where we cannot organize our propaganda; there are millions of workers who do not belong to any of our organizations; there are groups that oppose any new ideas," Tasca remarked. Consequently, even if he did not say it explicitly, Tasca had little faith in the immediate success of a revolutionary uprising.

In particular, Tasca was worried about southern Italy and the petty bourgeoisie. He thought it was possible to win over considerable sectors of the middle class and of the southern farmers to the socialist cause, but, at least temporarily, they were still siding with the bourgeoisie. Therefore, the socialists needed to devote all their energies to separating those two groups from their enemies.[69] Only an intensification of the socialists' activities and an expansion of the traditional organizations of the workers' movement could lead to a successful revolution. For this reason, Tasca, who later considered the socialists' inability to win over the middle class responsible for the victory of fascism, maintained a strong attachment to organizations such as trade unions, which usually were despised by the revolutionary socialists.

Tasca, in fact, did not believe that trade unions, constantly under fire for their reformism, or even the parliamentary leadership of the PSI, accused of compromises with the institutions of bourgeois democracy, were necessarily lost to the revolutionary cause. The problem with the reformists, Tasca claimed, was that they had not sincerely tried to obtain reforms; otherwise they would have seen that "their actions would not produce the desired results." Similarly, Tasca wrote, the union leaders, "despite their desire to avoid politics," would have to face the problem of constructing a socialist state if they really wanted to better workers' material conditions. Tasca believed that with the necessary cultural preparation, the development of class consciousness could attract to the revolutionary cause sectors of the middle class as well as the reformists of the Socialist Party.

In the peculiar circumstances of Turin right after World War I, this conciliatory position toward the traditional organizations of the PSI fostered suspicions against Tasca, who, in Viglongo's account, began to be perceived, especially by Gramsci, as "a man of the mandarins." In 1920, Gramsci, "who was beginning to be the man who opposed mandarinism," attacked Tasca in *L'Ordine Nuovo*, starting a personal and political conflict between the two that, despite Tasca's enormous respect for Gramsci, was never resolved.

The conflict exploded on June 5, 1920, when Gramsci published an article in which he claimed that Tasca had betrayed *L'Ordine Nuovo*. At the end of May, Tasca had been invited to the Turin congress of the socialist trade unions, where he had presented a paper on the political value of the *consigli di fabrica*, the Italian equivalent of the Russian soviets.[70] After reading Tasca's presentation, published on the first page of *L'Ordine Nuovo* on May 29, Gramsci wrote that Tasca, "in a few hours, ruined an educational process for the working class which had taken *L'Ordine Nuovo* a year of work." Tasca's reply was so long that it needed to be printed in three consecutive numbers of the journal. In August, Gramsci published two more articles, further fostering the polemics, but Tasca's decision to accept a job as president of the Turin association of cooperatives meant that Tasca had lost the fight as far as the journal's editorial board was concerned.

In the first article of this controversy, Gramsci raised three charges against his comrade. Tasca, Gramsci argued, had decided to attend the congress without consulting the other members of *L'Ordine Nuovo*, betraying the political solidarity of the group. Tasca's presentation, Gramsci wrote, "does not in any way speak for *L'Ordine Nuovo* and does not represent an acceptable or authorized version of our theoretical position on the *consigli*." Second, Gramsci accused Tasca of being ignorant of the positions elaborated by *L'Ordine Nuovo* and, more generally, the recent literature on the subject of the *consigli*. Tasca's lack of knowledge about the subject, Gramsci asserted, was not limited to the articles published in 1919, "but reveals itself even when he talks about documents closer in time and space."[71] Finally, and most important, Gramsci charged that Tasca had not understood the novelty represented by the *consigli* and wanted to subordinate them to the trade unions. In Gramsci's conception, the *consigli* were the nucleus of the new socialist state, autonomously created by the workers, as well as the specific form of the socialist state recognized by the Third International. Tasca, Gramsci concluded, had abandoned the dictates of the International and "under the appearance of a revolutionary phraseology, [had] helped the opportunists and the reformists who have always tried to corrupt the nature of the *consigli*."[72]

In his reply, Tasca denied the legitimacy of the first accusation and the foundation of the second, but he could not deny that his understanding of the relationship between unions and *consigli* was different from Gramsci's. His belief in the relevance of all the organizations of the working class was strong, as we have seen, and it was unshaken by the appearance of the *consigli*. Unlike Gramsci, Tasca had spent his youth in workers' organizations. The very fact that it was he who was invited to speak at the congress of the Turin trade unions showed that he had a place in workers' organizations that the other members of *L'Ordine Nuovo* did not have or even want.

Even if the details of the controversy have lost their interest for us, the conflict between Gramsci and Tasca was destined to have long-lasting consequences for their relations and for Tasca's life. In his other articles on the subject, Gramsci repeated his accusation that Tasca was a "false revolutionary." This infamous epithet remained attached to Tasca, even though the journal assured its readers that there were "neither heresies nor sinners" because *L'Ordine Nuovo* was not a church.[73] To be accused of being on the right of the group was particularly damning, as a vocal segment of these revolutionaries believed that the revolution was imminent.

This sectarian mentality, which forced the communist faction of the PSI to constantly pay tribute to its most radical elements, explains why the group around Gramsci was itself on the defensive against the critiques that were coming from Amadeo Bordiga, who accused them of not sufficiently distancing themselves from Tasca. As soon as the dispute between Tasca and Gramsci ended, the entire Turin group was in turn accused of "trade unionism and [of] an overestimation of the *consigli*." During a meeting to discuss the course of action that would lead to the creation of the Italian Communist Party, Bordiga and Nicola Bombacci asked Lenin and Bukharin to censure *L'Ordine Nuovo* for its position on the *consigli* and for its support of the unity of the Socialist Party. Lenin and Bukharin refused to honor this request, but Gramsci, in reaffirming his support for the *consigli*, used his polemics against Tasca to assert that it was Tasca who had proposed a strategy contrary to that of the International. "When *L'Ordine Nuovo* was still a place for ideological exercises," he wrote, "Tasca published an editorial in favor of [maintaining] the unity of the Socialist Party." But in his polemics against Tasca, Gramsci asserted that the journal's editorial board was "against the subordination of the *consigli* to the trade unions."[74] Thus, even before the formal creation of the Communist Party, the attack against Tasca served to prove the ideological purity of the rest of the *Ordine Nuovo* group.

Even Tasca's participation in the creation of the Italian Communist Party, a few months after the end of these polemics, did not put an end to the impression that he was an interloper in this group of true revolutionaries. Though the other members of *L'Ordine* were not completely convinced that Gramsci was correct in his attacks on Tasca, they kept their dissent quiet. When the Italian Communist Party was finally created, it was the extreme left, led by Bordiga and Bombacci, that took control of the new organization.

The Failed Italian Revolution and the Birth of the Italian Communist Party

While the debate between Tasca and Gramsci was still filling the pages of *L'Ordine Nuovo*, in September 1920 metalworkers in the major industrial centers of northern Italy occupied the factories. For three months, half a million workers, armed with rudimentary weapons, took control of key parts of the Italian productive system. These three months were the culminating insurrection of the *biennio rosso*. The government, led by Giovanni Giolitti, was reluctant to take military action against the workers, while the national leaders of the trade unions were desperately seeking a political solution to the conflict. The revolutionaries, by contrast, were hoping to transform the occupation into a full-scale revolution, seizing control of the rest of the Italian economic structure.

In a meeting held on September 9 in Milan, union and Socialist Party representatives discussed the possibility of launching a revolutionary offensive, but when the unions voted on that proposal, they refused to follow the Socialist Party. Since 1907, when the PSI and the recently formed CGL (Confederazione Generale del Lavoro) had agreed to act in concert, Socialist Party had, in theory, the possibility to direct the political activities of the Unions. According to the unions' bylaws, the party had the right to take control of the CGL to pursue the workers' political goals and unify their political interests, represented by the party, with their economic interests, represented by the Unions. However, the leadership of the PSI refused to exercise that right, and when the leaders of the unions offered their resignation at a meeting at which both Tasca and Togliatti were among those present, the party's leaders refused to accept them and simply approved the idea of a compromise with the government along the lines the unions had proposed.

These events, as historian Paolo Spriano has indicated, created the conditions for a further radicalization of the communist faction of the Socialist Party. At this point, both Gramsci and Bordiga had become convinced that the Socialist Party could not be the protagonist of a revolution. Despite the differences between the two men, they increasingly wanted to part ways not only with the small reformist wing of the party, represented by Filippo Turati, but with the party itself. Giacinto Serrati, the leader of the PSI, was himself a revolutionary, but the communist faction of the Socialist Party did not trust him. As Togliatti wrote ten years later, "We fought against Turati, but we hated Serrati," since the majority of the Socialist Party appeared to them as false revolutionaries whose revolutionary rhetoric and reformist practice had confused the Italian proletariat and were responsible for the failure of the revolutionary moment.[75]

At the end of 1920, the International, misinformed on the Italian situation, also started to support the project of separating the Italian socialists from the reformists. The Russian leadership, convinced by some of the leaders of the Italian communist faction, believed that Bordiga, Terracini, Bombacci, and the other supporters of a break with the PSI could bring with them a vast majority of the Socialist Party. "They say," Grigory Zinoviev wrote, "that 75–90 percent of the party is with them. In this political situation a compromise with Serrati would do damage."[76]

However, when the moment of separation came, on January 21, 1921, the communists discovered that they were only a minority in the Italian socialist movement. In fact, at the socialist congress in Livorno, the various factions that eventually would give birth to the Communist Party received the support of only a third of the delegates, mostly young members of the Socialist Party. The Italian general elections, held five months later on May 15, 1921, further confirmed that the communists constituted only a small minority of the socialist movement. When the results of the election were announced, only 15 of the Italian communists had been elected, against 122 socialists. Bordiga's idea that the revolution in Italy simply required a truly revolutionary party turned out to have been a miscalculation.

Still, the growth of Bordiga's influence within the left of the Socialist Party led to Tasca's defeat. In Milan, as we have seen, Tasca had witnessed the inability of the majority of the Socialist Party to lead a revolution. In 1919, prior to the occupation of the factories, he and the entire *Ordine Nuovo* group had given their support not to Bordiga and his faction but to Serrati. After September 1920, when the majority of the party, led by Serrati, refused to act during the occupation of the factories, it became impossible for Tasca not to recognize that the Socialist Party needed to change substantially if the project of an Italian socialist revolution was to become a reality. However, the dramatic break with Antonio Gramsci had left him without a political group to use as a tool for his different approach to a socialist revolution. Thus Tasca, wedged between Bordiga's position and Serrati's refusal to break with the reformists, found himself without any political support. Faced with the choice between the extremism of the new Communist Party and the passivity of the Socialist Party, Tasca decided that his projects had a better chance with the communists. Despite his doubts about the line the Italian Communist Party was taking, Tasca was in fact a revolutionary and not a reformist. He believed that a revolution could be successful only if the majority of Italian workers were involved. That was why he had fought against Gramsci, who believed that the *consigli* had to act independently of the unions, and against Bordiga, who believed that the party was the only revolutionary subject. Nevertheless, he never doubted that a revolution was necessary, and he preferred to be among revolutionaries even if he disagreed with their tactics.

In 1920, during the occupation of the factories, Tasca offered clear proof of his revolutionary goals. When the occupation started, he was the general secretary of the Turin unions and had not hesitated to lead the unions and the Socialist Party of Turin in their effort to provide the workers with weapons. Like all the other members of the communist faction of the PSI, he was convinced that the occupation represented a revolutionary opportunity. For this reason, he had gone to Milan to try to convince the national directorate of the unions and of the party to do what they had done in Turin and unite the political and economic demands of the working class. Only when the leaders of the unions decided not to support the revolution did Tasca become convinced, in agreement with Togliatti, that under these circumstances the revolution did not stand a chance.[77] Revolution in Italy, he believed, was not simply an issue of organizing a group of committed revolutionaries, but required the ability to win over the majority of the workers and their organizations to the revolutionary cause.

Consistent with these insights, Tasca remained convinced even after his decision to join the Communist Party that the party's first political goal must be to continue the dialogue with the socialist workers and with the socialist trade unions. But since the identity of the Italian Communist Party was based precisely on the refusal of the faction led by Bordiga to accept any compromise with the socialist leadership, Tasca found himself in conflict with party's leaders. Thus despite Tasca's role in bringing the Turin trade unions under the banner of the PCI, he was not given a leadership role in the new party.

Tasca's positions, paradoxically, were closer to those held by the International than Bordiga's were. In 1920, the publication of Lenin's *Left-Wing Communism: An Infantile Disorder* had been the base of the political program of the Second Congress of the International, and Lenin himself had scolded Bordiga for his extremism. Lenin had written that he had too little information on "left-wing communism in Italy," but he was convinced that Bordiga's refusal to participate in the elections had been a mistake. The problem, Lenin continued, was Serrati's refusal to break with the reformist right of his party, which had given rise "to "left-wing communism . . . and to a certain extent [justified] its existence." Hence Lenin's strategy called for the expulsion of the right wing of the socialists but unequivocally identified Bordiga's strategy as a form of "infantile" extremism.[78]

So in the early 1920s, Tasca, who was in the right-wing minority of the Italian Communist Party, represented the majority of the International, which was supposed to have the unconditional obedience of the party members. This conflict between the will of the International and the will of the leadership of the Italian Communist Party created a political paradox for Tasca. In these circumstances, he was able to remain in a party that did not love him because he felt sure he fully belonged to the communist movement.[79]

The October 1922 Marcia su Roma (March on Rome) and fascist seizure of power, which Tasca later narrated in his famous *La naissance du fascisme*, further complicated his position. Since 1919, Bordiga had opposed the communists' participation in elections, convinced as he was that such a contamination of the revolutionary elements with the institutions of bourgeois democracy could only lead to confusion. Thus, even if he had had to accept Lenin's reprimand of his ideas in *Left-Wing Communism*, he was far from being convinced that the formation of Mussolini's new government under the pressure of his private army constituted a political rupture. Terracini, who fully agreed with Bordiga, even wrote immediately after the Marcia su Roma that the communists refused to call the events either a coup d'état or a revolution, expressing the hope that "the Italian proletariat could understand that the conservative classes which have used the 'white terror' and the democratic state . . . are the same thing."[80]

These positions, as absurd as they seem in the present day, help us understand the theoretical fracture that the rise of fascism created between Tasca and the majority of his party, which now included his former comrades from Turin. In turn, the break between Tasca and Bordiga helps us understand why the debate within the Italian revolutionary socialists at the beginning of the twenties paid so little attention to the fracture represented by fascism. Bordiga and his group believed that the issue was capitalism and not democracy and, coherently, they had been very critical of parliamentary democracy. In his "Theses of the Abstentionist Communist Faction of the Italian Socialist Party," Bordiga had written: "Parliamentary democracy in which citizens of every class are represented is the form assumed by the organization of the bourgeoisie into a ruling class."[81] Since Bordiga considered parliamentary democracy simply the political form of capitalist domination, he saw nothing alarming in the fascist attack on democracy. Consequently, Tasca's insistence that new developments required the unity of all the workers and even an alliance with the democratic sectors of the bourgeoisie was considered a form of political opportunism. The implication was that Tasca was seeking unity with the socialists because he was not really a communist.

Notwithstanding Gramsci and Togliatti's personal doubts, the third national congress of the Italian communists, held in Rome in the summer of 1922, fully embraced Terracini and Bordiga's approach. Despite the Third International's invitation to communist parties to establish a united front with socialist trade unions and socialist parties, the leadership of the Italian communists made only verbal concessions to the International. The Russians accused the Italians of behaving "like the old Russian Orthodox Christians, who believed that sitting at a table with the infidels was a mortal sin."[82] Trotsky told Terracini that the workers were asking "their organization, or sect, to allow them to fight for their everyday needs," not "for a glorious day after tomorrow."[83] But Bordiga and his group refused to embrace the policy of a united front.

As Spriano has shown, Togliatti and Gramsci supported Bordiga in the conflict with the International in order to prevent Tasca from emerging as the new leader of the party. Gramsci's biggest fear was that "the minority, a minority foreign to the group that had created the party in Livorno and was directed by Tasca, might take control of the party, thanks to the support of the International."[84] In fact, Tasca and Antonio Graziadei were the only important members of the PCI who openly advocated the constitution of a common front of workers and the other democratic parties against fascism.

After the victory of fascism, Tasca believed that the workers' movement would be best served not by continuing to organize the future revolution but by defending democratic institutions. He denounced the extremism of the party leadership, which on the eve of the Marcia su Roma was still speaking of "opposing the red of the communist flags to the Italian flag."

The Italian Communist Party, in his view, should have been part of a coalition that included "all the social strata interested in the fight against fascism," including Italian farmers politically represented by the Catholic Partito Popolare.[85] Despite the explicit support of the International's delegates to the congress, however, the motion proposed by Graziadei and supported by Tasca received only 13 percent of the votes.[86]

The Fourth Congress of the Communist International, by contrast, held in Moscow at the end of November 1922, fully supported Tasca's position. However, this support, which certainly gave Tasca encouragement to continue his battle in the PCI, was not sufficient to change the policy of the Italian communists immediately. Two factors prevented the International from effectively imposing its policy on the PCI. One was that the methods of the International were not yet those that Stalin would later introduce first against the Trotskyists and later against Tasca and the right of the party. The other was that the isolation of Tasca and the other members of the minority was such that they could not have effectively assumed the direction of the party. The rules of the Italian Communist Party, which prevented the creation of factions within the party itself, actually prevented Tasca from publicizing his disagreement and gathering support for his ideas. Thus, the only result that the International was able to achieve, against the will of the vast majority of the Italian communists, was the inclusion of Tasca in the leadership of the PCI.

In what appears to have been a further effort to enhance Tasca's personal prestige, the leadership of the International also elected Tasca to the Presidium, the executive group that was in charge of implementing the policy decided by the congresses. Then in April 1923, taking advantage of Tasca's knowledge of the French workers' movement, the International sent him to Paris as its representative to the French Communist Party. As a result, Tasca became one of the representatives of the International in France during the crisis of the occupation of the Ruhr, when French workers were sent to replace Germans in the occupied region, and the French communists were trying to foster solidarity between German and French workers despite their national differences. So when he returned to Italy at the end of June 1923, Tasca was no longer simply the leader of a minority group within the Italian Communist Party but a fully legitimized leader of the Communist International.[87]

Tasca's international prestige, however, did not help him within his own party, whose majority hated him personally. In 1923, when Tasca was sent for a short while to Moscow to work on reunification between Italian communists and socialists, a damaging rumor started to circulate that

Tasca had fled Italy because he lacked the courage to face the fascists. Thus Tasca had to defend his reputation while he was working under the direct orders of the International. Moreover, he immediately discovered that such rumors were believed not only by simple militants but also by some of the people who had daily contact with the leaders of the party. Hence he suspected, as he wrote in a letter he sent to the Executive Committee of the PCI on August 2, 1923, that the rumors came directly from some of the leaders of the party, or at least that they had done nothing to put an end to them.[88] The fear that Tasca could use the influence of his powerful Russian contacts to take over the party was clearly enough for some unidentified Italian communist leaders to start a defamatory campaign against him.

When we compare the rumors that surrounded Tasca with those, equally false, that surrounded Togliatti, Tasca's difficult relationship with his comrades becomes clear. Togliatti was depicted as exceptionally courageous in the face of the fascist seizure of power. The day of the Marcia su Roma, Togliatti's hagiographers maintained, he had defended the offices of a communist newspaper from fascist assault. Even if Togliatti told a different version of the story, in which he did not play any heroic part, the leadership of the party had decided to let the rumor circulate to improve the reputation of the communist leaders.[89] The different attitudes held by the Italian communists toward Tasca and Togliatti could not be clearer.

While the leaders of the Italian Communist Party were busy with these internal struggles, the fascist repression of communists, socialists, and antifascists was directly influencing the politics of the Communist Party. On February 3, Amadeo Bordiga was arrested, together with seventy-two provincial leaders of the party, forty-one secretaries of the young communists' organization, and many other members of the party leadership. On March 1, the police also arrested Giacinto Serrati. In the following months, while the fascists closed down all the communist and socialist newspapers and fascist violence increasingly targeted the entire opposition, Mussolini obtained the Italian parliament's approval of Gentile's school reform and a new electoral law.[90] In this situation, Antonio Gramsci, who had moved from Moscow to Vienna, refused to sign the manifesto of the left, which had been written in prison by Bordiga and approved by Togliatti and Terracini, formally beginning the crisis of the PCI's original leadership.[91]

Any immediate political consequences, however, were forestalled by another repressive action on the part of the Italian police. On September 21, 1923, Tasca, Togliatti, Egidio Gennari, Rita Montagnana, Teresa Noce, Caterina Piccolato, and Alfonso Leonetti were arrested in Milan, a move that left the Italian communists almost entirely leaderless. Tasca, who stayed in prison until December, was acquitted of all charges, as were all the others. When Tasca was released, shortly before Lenin's death, the majority of the PCI that previously had centered around Bordiga no longer existed. Tasca returned to Milan, where he lived underground until the summer of 1924.[92]

In April 1924, after winning a seat in the Italian parliament in the elections that saw the triumph of Mussolini, Gramsci returned to Italy, finally convinced by the International and by events to assume direct leadership of his party. His plan was not simple. According to Tasca's testimony, which was never challenged by Gramsci himself, Alfonso Leonetti, a young communist leader who had worked at *L'Ordine Nuovo,* wrote to Gramsci with the suggestion of creating a new leadership around the people of *L'Ordine Nuovo.* Gramsci's reply shows how difficult the circumstances were:

> Does our group still exist? As you can see, of the four editors of *L'Ordine Nuovo,* Tasca is a member of the minority, since he followed until the end his positions of 1920 that created the polemics between us. Togliatti cannot make a decision and is still under the influence of Bordiga's personality.... Terracini is even more extremist than Bordiga, because he has absorbed his ideas without having his intellectual abilities.... How can we revive our group?[93]

Despite these doubts, no other solution was available to Gramsci if he wished to end the conflict between the party and the International and to create an antifascist front with the socialists.

Thus in April 1924 Gramsci wrote a letter to Togliatti and Terracini, trying to convince them to form a new leadership with Tasca. "The left has created a situation which is against us," he remarked. "The minority presents itself as the majority of the International and we, who say that we are the world party, are stuck. We need to divide the minority and incorporate Tasca and [Giuseppe] Vota."[94] However, Terracini and Togliatti were not easily convinced, and Tasca, for his part, was also moving forward in his own direction. The years of division, rumors, and personal attacks had undermined the solidarity of the former friends to the point of personal resentment.

Counting on the political support of the International, Tasca, on behalf of the minority of the party, presented his own proposals in Como at the organizational conference of the PCI that was to determine the Italian theses for the Fifth Congress of the International. Thus, for the first time since 1921, the PCI was split into three organized factions: the left, led by

Bordiga; the center, led by Gramsci and Togliatti; and the right, led by Tasca. In the first months of 1924, only Tasca's faction openly criticized the policy followed by Bordiga, and this prevented Tasca from reaching an agreement with Gramsci. This situation created another paradox in the political history of the Italian communists because Gramsci, who was the general secretary of the party, was left without a majority in the party itself.[95]

Despite his intention to abandon Bordiga's policy, Gramsci, in the first months of 1924, was careful not to create an explosive conflict with the left of his party. Consequently, he did not criticize the previous positions of the PCI, which he too had helped shape, instead merely sending signals about his desire for change. In Milan, Gramsci founded a new communist newspaper and called it *L'Unità* (Unity), a clear reference to a new policy for the Italian communists as well as a direct reference to Salvemini's journal, which Tasca, Gramsci, Terracini, and Bordiga had all loved as young socialists.[96] As we have seen earlier, Gramsci also decided to present his own proposals to the party conference, probably knowing that without an agreement with Tasca or Bordiga, his ideas had no chance of winning over the majority of the party.

The history of the PCI, Gramsci claimed, was the history of three factions: Bordiga's left, the *Ordine Nuovo* group, and the group of people who had no specific affiliation at the time of the creation of the party. He and *L'Ordine Nuovo*, Gramsci continued, had always preferred to support the left, rather than the right, "because, since our polemics with Tasca in 1920, we saw the antirevolutionary [*opportunistico*] danger coming from the right."[97] The attitude of his group had not changed, Gramsci affirmed, and they still preferred the left to the right. But the situation had changed, and it was time to adopt a new strategy. If the left refused to accept the new reality, there was the danger that the conflict between the PCI and the International could result in "the rise of heterogeneous elements whose unity depends entirely on their declaration of being for the International," as had already happened with the formation of Tasca's minority faction. The right, Gramsci concluded, had already started to change its policy, eliminating some of the reasons for its conflicts with the center of the party. The left had to make a quick decision, keeping in mind that the relationship between the Italian communists and the International was the most urgent problem.[98]

Gramsci's speech was a well-crafted threat to Bordiga. He presented himself as the person who could manage the conflict with the International without excluding the left from the leadership of the party. Nevertheless, the logic of Gramsci's reasoning entailed that if the left refused to accept the new positions, a compromise with Tasca, who had declared his acceptance of the new policy of unity among antifascists, was possible. Moreover, if the left decided to boycott the new policy, the risk was that the leadership of the party could be transferred directly from the *Ordine Nuovo* group to Tasca, perverting the nature of the party that Bordiga and Gramsci's supporters had created.

Despite Gramsci's personal prestige, the vote tally clearly revealed that the PCI was still dominated by Bordiga.[99] The left received the votes of thirty-five provincial leaders and four interregional secretaries, and the right was supported by six provincial leaders and one interregional secretary; Gramsci, who was the general secretary of the party, was supported by only four provincial leaders. Thus, creating a new majority within the Communist Party was vital for Gramsci; he had to find allies before the next congress of the PCI, which had the power to overthrow him and nominate an alternative leader. Neither Tasca, whose commitment to communism had been put in question, nor Bordiga, who rejected any dialogue with the Italian socialists, was at this point willing to support Gramsci and Togliatti in their new policy.

At the following congress of the International, Bordiga restated the positions he had always held. It was wrong, he claimed, to seek an agreement with the socialists, not to mention other political parties; it was wrong to call for a "workers' government" when the goal should be a communist government. He warned the Russian communists of the danger that was coming from the right and asked for "a general correction of the International." Thus, even though the Fifth Congress of the International had tried to reorient the policy of the International to the left, Bordiga was unwilling to make concessions to the International and resolve the conflict between the Italian communists and the Russian leadership. This refusal, even before the explicit beginning of Stalin's anti-Trotskyist campaign, marked the end of his political career.[100]

Tasca, who was also a delegate to the congress, contested the left's thesis, reaffirming the need to create the broadest possible coalition to fight against fascism. He also continued to advocate abandoning the policy followed by the Italian Communist Party ever since its second congress in Rome. However, the leftist direction taken by the congress was not particularly favorable to Tasca's positions. Rather, it was the center of the party that emerged from the discussions of the Fifth Congress as the truer expression of the policy of the International. For the first time since the existence of the PCI, a resolution of the conflict between the Italian leaders and the Russian leaders seemed within reach. Consequently, Tasca lost some of his political leverage in the Italian party, as he could no longer play the card of his agreement with the majority of the International against the majority of the Italian party.[101]

During the Fifth Congress of the International, contrary to what had happened during the Fourth, Togliatti, on behalf of the leadership of the PCI, criticized Bordiga. The International's decision to change its program for the party members from a "united front" to a "workers' government" and other similar concessions to the language of the left allowed Togliatti to present the positions of the PCI as a natural evolution rather than as a reconsideration. As Gramsci had done during the organizational conference in Como, Togliatti painted Bordiga and his group as different from the center of the party and as the ones responsible for the previous direction taken by the PCI. The result was that the new executive committee of the PCI, created right after the Fifth Congress of the International, excluded all the members of Bordiga's faction but included Gustavo Mersù as a representative of Tasca's group.[102]

Tasca himself, after the conclusion of the congress, refused to become a member of the executive committee. It may be that he felt his battle was temporarily lost. Despite his commitment to the communist cause, his temperament made it difficult for him to accept someone else's leadership and a minority position for himself. Paradoxically, he must have felt that he had more possibilities when he had the support of the International against the Italian leadership than now, when the center had managed to solve the problem with the Comintern without admitting that Tasca was right. He therefore went back to Turin and for more than a year kept his political engagement to a minimum. He seized the opportunity to spend some time with his family, after years of trips between France, Moscow, and the Italian prisons. He pursued a law degree, which he doubtless intended to use more to defend himself in the case of further arrests than to practice law.[103]

On June 11, 1926, Lina Martoretti gave birth to their second daughter, Valeria. But by then Tasca had already resumed full political engagement. Gramsci had continued to pursue his new policy and had increasingly separated himself from Bordiga. By January 1926, at the time of the Lyon congress, the theses approved at the previous congress of the party had been subjected to a thorough critique.

In Lyon, an isolated Bordiga could proclaim, without provoking a strong reaction from Gramsci, that "the true precursor of 'Ordinovism's' present adherence to the tactics and general line of the International was really

Comrade Tasca and his opposition to the left at the Rome congress."[104] For a few months, the original *Ordine Nuovo* group, from Tasca to Gramsci, seemed to be working in concert again. However, Gramsci was arrested soon after coming back from the congress, and the relationship between Tasca and Togliatti, as we will see in the next chapter, would not survive the Stalinization of the communist parties.

2

Learning Russian
Angelo Tasca and the Stalinization of the Communist Parties

During the second half of the 1920s, Angelo Tasca's life was changed forever by two events he could not control: the fascist seizure of power and the Stalinization of communist parties worldwide. Fascism forced Tasca into exile, permanently separating him from Italy. The Stalinization of the Italian Communist Party deprived Tasca of his political and cultural identity, keeping him in spiritual exile for the rest of his life.

Even though the two events had an equal practical impact on the course of Tasca's life, it was his expulsion from the Communist Party that had the deepest consequences for his intellectual and ideological development. Since the age of fourteen, Tasca had known that he might well be subject to some form of political persecution by his enemies. He was a revolutionary who had always accepted the principle of class warfare. The dictatorship of the bourgeoisie, as he would have put it, had to be overthrown by all possible means, including violence. A reaction on the part of the bourgeoisie was to be predicted.[1] But to be expelled from the party he had helped create and from the political movement to which he had devoted his life was something he had not considered.

Tasca did not fail to perceive that fascism was something new. What he did not grasp was that his desire to analyze the complexity of the new phenomenon could come to be considered a form of heresy among the communists. Faithful to an understanding of Marxism as a synthesis of theory and praxis, he refused to equate fascism and capitalism, along the lines of the new Stalinist orthodoxy. Tasca's desire to reach a scientific understanding of fascism severed him from the Italian Communist Party. His desire to better understand his enemies exposed him to the maneuvers of his friends, from whom he was not expecting attacks.

Thus, even many years after the events in Moscow in 1928, Tasca told the story of his expulsion from the Italian Communist Party in a tone of surprise mixed with an acute sense of betrayal. He was surprised because he thought he represented the mainstream position of his party.[2] He felt betrayed because he was left alone to face Stalin's desire to teach the Italian

Communist Party "the Russian language."[3] However, as we shall see, Tasca's fate was determined by a power struggle that had begun before he was personally involved, and whose meaning he did not fully grasp.

The logic of the events seems to suggest that Angelo Tasca was used as a scapegoat by Palmiro Togliatti, who was engaged in his own struggle for power inside the Italian Communist Party. From the moment Tasca was sent to Moscow to represent his party, his political destiny was decided, if not in the details, then in its general course. As we shall see, Tasca's only choice was between two equally unpleasant options: a repudiation of his political past, which would have deprived him of his political identity, or faithfulness to his past, which was utterly incompatible with the new Stalinist era.

More Light

The Sixth Congress of the Communist International opened in Moscow on July 17, 1928. Delegates from all the different communist parties of the world gathered in what they considered their capital to discuss the political line of their movement. The moment was solemn. It was also critical for the life of each party, since the decisions made there were compulsory for every single militant.[4] Following Lenin's rules, all communists were encouraged to discuss the party line freely until a decision was made by the majority of the party. After the end of the debate, though, every militant was required to conform to the will of the majority, and any deviation from the party line was considered treason. The Congress of the International determined the communist orthodoxy until the next world meeting of the organization.[5]

Since the Fifth Congress, held in 1924, the communist movement had been engaged in a bitter struggle that opposed Leon Trotsky and Grigory Zinoviev to Josef Stalin and Nikolai Bukharin. Every party reenacted the conflict within the Russian leadership. During this struggle, the so-called left of the party (Trotsky and Zinoviev) had been outnumbered by their adversaries, who controlled the Russian Communist Party (headed by Stalin) and the political leadership of the International (headed by Bukharin). Thus, for four years, the rules of the communist movement had forced the members of the left to follow a party line they did not accept, practically isolating and silencing the Trotskyists.[6]

However, the struggle against the left, which in Italy had been the struggle against Bordiga, was quickly coming to an end. Stalin, who by 1927 had achieved complete control of the Russian party, was turning his attention to the International, which he needed to tame if he was to stabilize his hold on power. Stalin's project to achieve complete mastery over the communist movement, in fact, entailed a showdown with Bukharin, who led the International. In 1928, therefore, Stalin and his followers started to talk about the danger coming from the right. Everyone knew that Bukharin had come under fire, even though he was still unnamed.[7]

For the Italian Communists, the new course that Stalin intended to give to the International was important news. Like all the other communist parties, the PCI had conducted a fierce fight against its left wing. Contrary to other parties, such as the French Communist Party (PCF) where the vast majority of the members of the Socialist party joined the new party thanks to an alliance between the left and the center that only excluded the right, and against the wishes of the International, the Italian Communist Party was born out of the initiative of leftists. For this reason, bringing the Italian communists in line with Stalin and Bukharin's policy had required a dramatic reorganization of the party's leadership.[8] Palmiro Togliatti, who had been in close contact with the International since 1924, had been among the first to understand that the line coming from Moscow was different from the one decided in Rome.[9] Therefore, as we have seen, in conjunction with Antonio Gramsci he had organized the change that relegated Amadeo Bordiga to the margins of the party. This struggle against the left had been a traumatic event in the life of the Italian Communist Party and was already marking the end of the various communist parties' political independence. Togliatti, who understood the new political climate, adopted a realistic approach: unlike Gramsci, who even in jail tried to contest Stalin's methods, Togliatti tried his best not to be caught openly dissenting from the Russian dictator. [10]

Nonetheless, Togliatti's prudence was not enough to save him from falling into danger when Stalin suddenly changed political course to isolate Bukharin. Since the latter presided over the International, he was Togliatti's main point of reference in the process of coordination between the Italian Communist Party and the rest of the movement. Togliatti was still under Bukharin's influence when he took the stand to deliver his speech at the Sixth Congress of the International, and he was not fully prepared for the new situation, in which the leftist positions once strongly condemned by both Stalin and Bukharin were now being used by Stalin against Bukharin.

His ignorance of the new situation had led Togliatti to prepare a speech in which attacks against the right-wing danger, the latest fashion in the International, were carefully mixed with the traditional bashing of the left, the old orthodoxy of the movement. To this involuntary heresy, Togliatti also added his personal position, which itself diverged from Stalin's strategy. During his speech, in fact, he tried to couple his solemn condemnation of the leftist and rightist heresies with a plea for a more moderate handling of the conflicts within the communist movement. Thus, unwittingly, Togliatti himself now became suspected of heresy.[11] In a perfect example of Stalin's typical opening strategy against his real or imagined enemies, Togliatti received a signal rather than a direct threat. When the allotted time for his speech in front of the assembly was over, rather than allowing him to complete the reading of the few pages left, the presidency turned off the microphone, truncating his address—a lack of courtesy that hinted at the marginalization of the Italian leader.

Togliatti thus never had the opportunity to pronounce the only courageous words of his speech, in which, quoting Goethe's last words, he asked for "more light" in the life of the communist parties. "The proletarian avant-garde," he had written, "cannot conduct its struggle in the shadows. The leadership of the revolution cannot be formed through a struggle of fractions with no principles."[12] These words, censored by the cutting off of the microphone, were to be the last vestige of Togliatti's resistance against the Stalinization of his party, rather than the beginning of a conflict between the Italian communists and the Stalinists.[13] Learning quickly from this episode, Togliatti resisted the Russian insistence that he remain in Moscow to be part of the leadership of the Communist International. As Paolo Spriano wrote in his semiofficial history of the Italian Communist Party, Togliatti was at that point afraid to stay in Moscow.[14]

Angelo Tasca took Togliatti's place in Moscow as a member of the Seniorenkonvent, the informal leadership of the International. This decision, which changed Tasca's life forever, was made at a time when, as described by the communist Giuseppe Berti, "to bow [to Stalin's decisions] was the only way to save the natural formation of the party, preventing . . . the annihilation of its natural leadership and its substitution with one or more *leftist workers*."[15] Before narrating Tasca's role in the events, however, I need to present another episode that determined Tasca's fate without his direct participation. This episode, which temporarily conditioned the struggle between Stalin's supporters and their opponents in the German Communist Party (GCP), took place during the fall of 1928.

Tasca was in Berlin, on his way to Moscow, when Ernst Thälmann, the leader of the German party, who was very close to Stalin, was involved in a scandal. In Hamburg, the regional chairman of the party, John Wittorf, embezzled 3,000 marks from the party. Thälmann, who was a personal friend of the thief and his closest political associate, had discovered the crime but decided to cover it up to avoid personal and political damage. When the organ of the German Trotskyists published an account of the facts, an investigation conducted by Hugo Eberlein, an old and prestigious member of the party, revealed Thälmann's responsibility in the affair. The Central Committee of the German Communist Party voted unanimously to depose Thälmann. The Stalinists seemed to lose the control they had over the German party in favor of Bukharin's supporters.[16]

At that point, Stalin decided to intervene personally to rebalance the power of his supporters in the German party. He called for a meeting of the Presidium of the International and reinstated Thälmann. Such a decision, not illegal by the rules of the Communist International, was made in such a rush and under so much pressure that only the members of the Presidium who happened to be in Moscow at the time were informed of the meeting. The others, most of whom were vacationing after the Congress of the International, learned about the events only after the decision had been formalized.

This hurried decision produced some protests among the members of the Presidium who had been excluded from the meeting. The Hungarian Bela Kun and the Ukrainian Dmitrij Manuil'skij, both close to Stalin, complained about it, while the Swiss Jules Humbert-Droz, close to Bukharin, sent a letter to the International to denounce the damaging consequences of the decisions made by the Presidium.[17] Whereas Kun and Manuil'skij renounced their objections once in Moscow, Humbert-Droz maintained his, and we will see his name associated with Tasca's. Only his final repentance spared him Tasca's fate and expulsion from the communist movement.[18]

Consciously or unconsciously, in fact, Stalin had raised the level of the fight between him and his rightist opponents. His handling of the conflict within the German party proved that he was not willing to accept that members of his faction could be outvoted in any of the relevant communist parties. He also proved that he controlled the organs of the International despite Bukharin's formal leadership. Finally, he assigned a face to the right, starting the open war with Bukharin that would end with the total defeat of the latter. Stalin's famous speech against the right-wing danger in the Russian Communist Party, delivered on October 19, 1929, only five days after Tasca arrived in Moscow, set in motion the chain of events that led to the marginalization of Bukharin and to the expulsion of most of his associates.[19]

Angelo Tasca Goes to Moscow

In 1928, at the age of thirty-six, Angelo Tasca had a wife and three children. Since the end of 1926, though, he had not seen his family. As he wrote, describing the troubles of his personal life, he had had to choose, and he had chosen politics over his family. His wife, Lina, herself a socialist, had determined to stay in Italy with her children rather than follow her husband in his conspiratorial journeys through Europe.

Tasca, however, could not set foot in Italy without being arrested.[20] After the fascist regime had passed the so-called *leggi fascistissime* in 1926, which ended the last vestiges of the Italian liberal state, Tasca was arrested in Milan and brought to a prison, where he expected to spend an undetermined number of years.[21] It was only by chance that he was spared such a destiny. In one of those moments of confusion that follow a major political change, he and other communist leaders had been suddenly released and ordered to go to a police station and receive further instructions on their future. Those who actually reported to the police station, including Gramsci, were sent to the *confino* (confinement), and later were condemned to many years in prison. Tasca and some of his comrades, however, managed to disappear in the streets of Milan and escape their fate. After a few weeks, the International sent him the order to leave Italy and go to Paris, where he would create the new clandestine leadership of the Italian Communist Party together with Togliatti, who had been sent to Switzerland.[22] At the beginning of the summer of 1928, Tasca traveled from Paris to Moscow to participate in the Fourth Congress of the International.

Separated from his family, exiled, with no job other than his work as a "professional revolutionary," Tasca was happy to remain in the Soviet capital after the conclusion of the Congress when the Italian Communists nominated him as their representative. Naturally, he saw the opportunity to live in Moscow as a form of recognition of his political activity. Even many years later, writing his memoirs, Tasca recalled with pride his role as the Italian delegate at the International. The Russian leadership of the communist movement, Tasca recalled, had asked the Italian Communist Party to send to Moscow not an obscure figure but somebody who was a real leader of the PCI. Thus, according to Tasca, when Togliatti wrote a letter to the International to nominate him, he was simply following these instructions.[23]

However, Tasca did not know, or did not fully appreciate, that the Russians wanted Togliatti, not him, to stay in Moscow.[24] He also either ignored or did not know that Togliatti did not want to stay. Unlike Tasca, who never admitted or suspected that his job at the International was a dangerous one, Togliatti, as we have seen, was aware of the new situation in Moscow. Tasca, on the other hand, who had worked in the Russian capital only for brief periods after 1924, had never been personally exposed to Stalin's methods and, as he had already demonstrated many times, he was not really good at navigating the risky waters of the communist parties. Thus he probably had no idea of the level of oppression in the Soviet Union, or possibly he simply failed to understand it.

Pierre Pascal, a French communist who met Tasca in Moscow, left us a perfect picture of Tasca's naïveté in the face of the reality of the situation in the USSR, whose similarities with the fascist regime that he so deeply hated escaped him. As Pascal reported in his diary in 1927, a passionate Tasca told everyone during a visit to Moscow that the situation in Italy had become unbearable because of the repressive nature of fascism.[25] He described the new regime with a real sense of horror, saying that after 1926, all the newspapers were always lying, there was an active process of ideological indoctrination of the army, and the government had started to believe its own lies. Tasca appeared genuinely convinced that the communists were not reacting with the necessary energy to the rise of fascism because they had not yet realized the true nature of the regime. His interlocutor, on the contrary, commented in his journal that he had to resist the temptation to burst out laughing at Tasca's failure to recognize the resemblance between Russia and Italy. For Pascal, who had observed Stalin's Russia firsthand, the mixture of lies and repression that according to Tasca characterized Italy's regime was precisely what characterized the Soviet Union. Tasca, by contrast, gave no sign that he had become any more aware of the Russian reality before he went to Moscow in 1928.[26]

Moreover, Tasca was not only ignorant of the situation in Moscow but also the most likely of all the Italian communists to be in a dangerous position at the time Stalin began his attack against the right. The single most relevant aspect of Tasca's political identity within the Italian Communist Party was that he represented and had always represented the right wing of the party. Since the party's founding, Tasca had favored unity of action between workers who were members of the Socialist Party and those who had chosen to establish the new Communist Party. His position was based on practical as well as theoretical reasons.

On a theoretical level, Tasca believed that the party had to act as a collective intelligence for the working class, and not simply as a military tool for the conquest of power. The antagonism of the working class, in his opinion, had to become consciousness through a process of autonomous critical reflection if it was to become the self-conscious engine of history. The bourgeoisie had built its own culture and its own unity of intent, and so the workers had to oppose capitalism with a full social project of their own. As Tasca had been repeating since his first clashes with Bordiga, the class hatred of the proletariat for its oppressors was not enough to spark a successful revolution; political consciousness, as Lenin had affirmed, required a political party.[27] Simply being a worker was not sufficient for being a revolutionary.

On a practical level, Tasca's analysis had an important consequence. Tasca wanted the Communist Party to be active in politics, not just a military machine. It entailed the idea that the communists had to create alliances and, consequently, be ready to compromise. The leadership of the party had to conduct a tactical analysis of each concrete political situation, determining each time the political synthesis through which the party could represent the proletariat. This position, which Tasca shared with other members on the right of the communist movement, was known at the time as "situationism," because it held that the tactics of the communists could be determined only in concrete historical situations.[28] Tasca, in particular, insisted on the notion that there was a specific tempo for certain political actions, and that time was not always on the side of the communists.[29] The most relevant implication for the PCI's political tactics was that the analysis that had been conducted after the end of World War I, when the Italian communists saw a revolution as imminent, no longer applied after the victory of fascism.

Fascism and its implications for the communist movements were in fact the real center of Tasca's analysis. He insisted that it was an error to identify, at least mechanically, "fascism with the bourgeoisie, and the bourgeoisie with the social-democratic party."[30] He strongly believed in the need to mount a united front of the workers' parties, communists, and socialists against the rising threat of fascism in Italy and everywhere else in Europe. For this reason, he opposed any representation of the socialists as de facto allies of the fascists, and refused to say that the Communist Party was the only workers' party: the socialists might have been inconsistent and under the influence of the bourgeoisie, but the socialist workers were still workers.

A Marxist analysis of the situation could not, in Tasca's view, ignore the new reality represented by fascism and take comfort in the reproduction of old formulas. A policy inspired by Marxism could not disregard the fact that the workers were on the defensive and needed unity rather than abstract ideological purity. Such a position, which Tasca thought was grounded in both theoretical and practical analysis of the historical situation, was central to his political identity and clearly placed him on the right, since it implied some form of alliance between the trade unions and other organizations, on one hand, and the social democrats, on the other.

In 1926, at the time of the supposed defeat of the leftist leadership of the Trotskyist Bordiga, the centrist leaders of the PCI, including Gramsci, Togliatti, and Terracini, had accepted these ideas, but they could not accept Tasca himself. In order to secure their legitimacy in the eyes of a party that was still dominated by the left, they had to transform Tasca into an ideological bogeyman that incarnated the essence of the hated right. Thus, as Gramsci and Togliatti became the representatives of ideas that had been Tasca's, the more they wanted to stress their difference from Tasca, to avoid accusations of being the new right. The third congress of the PCI, held in Lyon at the beginning of 1926, marked the pinnacle of this strategy.

During this congress, which was supposed to create a new alliance between Togliatti and Gramsci's group and Tasca's followers, Togliatti asked Tasca not to present his ideas orally, but to prepare them for publication in the proceedings of the congress. Tasca, who was convinced that he was part of the political majority of the party, also agreed to their request not to publicize his minor disagreements, in order to maintain an image of unity among the leaders. In reality, what the publication of Tasca's objection would have revealed was how close the positions of the new leaders were to Tasca's. In a document authored by Gramsci and Togliatti and published at the end of the congress, Tasca was still labeled as the leader of a "right-wing deviation," as if his positions had been radically different from the leadership of the party.[31]

As was already customary in the PCI, the attack against Tasca was directed as much against his personal character as against his positions. He himself was labeled "impulsive," his ideas "superficial."[32] At the same time, Tasca's ideas were also considered the "political platform" of the right wing of the party.[33] For Gramsci and Togliatti, Tasca played a double political role, allowing them to position themselves at the center of the party rather than at the right of it, and permitting them to dismiss his ideas rather than consider them as the expression of a real tendency within their party.

Tasca was well aware of the trick that Togliatti and Gramsci were playing on him. In a letter sent to the Executive Committee of the PCI on March 30, 1926, he complained bitterly about the treatment that he was receiving, noting that their mockery of his positions was intended "to create artificially a right wing for the convenience of the political polemics of the party."[34] He reaffirmed his commitment to concrete analysis of specific situations and contrasted it with the tendency to refer constantly to a "superficial orthodoxy."[35] He demanded a correction of what had been reported by the party press, threatening to bring the conflict out into the open by writing his own reconstruction of the events. Yet, despite his efforts, Tasca could not manage to escape the ideological cage that had been built around him.

Togliatti, more than Gramsci, was a master at this Machiavellian art of damning Tasca as a rightist traitor while appropriating his positions. When

Togliatti went to Moscow after the third congress of the PCI to discuss the political line of his party with the Russians, he discovered that the representative of the International present at the meetings that followed the congress had identified Tasca as the leader who held the positions closest to the ones of the International.[36] Togliatti's reaction to this discovery was duplicitous. He immediately sent a letter to Gramsci and other members of the majority in which he presented his positions as very similar to the ones held by Tasca. This move surprised the recipients of the letter, who replied that they had not been aware that such a difference of opinion existed between themselves and Togliatti.[37] While he appropriated Tasca's ideas, however, he also recommended, with no further explanation, the removal of Tasca from his current position in the party.[38] While Togliatti was embracing the Bukharinist positions that would almost ruin him a year later, he was also trying to eliminate the competition coming from Tasca, who had independently arrived at positions close to the current orthodoxy of the International.

Tasca's reaction to these episodes was relatively mild. He was clearly still convinced that the hostility against him was not personal but dictated by political considerations and temporary disagreements. In reality, Giuseppe Berti, who was centrally involved in these events, was certainly right when he wrote years later that the center of the party neither liked nor trusted Tasca. Togliatti and Gramsci considered Tasca a "rightist opportunist," a "social democrat," who was in the leadership of the PCI simply because the International had imposed him on the party.[39] In other words, they saw him more as an enemy than as a fellow revolutionary, an obstacle more than an asset. Tasca, by contrast, firmly believed, even after his expulsion, that he belonged to communism. Even the most damaging stories invented about his political behavior could not shake his faith in the Communist Party and in his role in it.

It is unlikely that the temporary collaboration that Tasca and Togliatti established in 1927, at a time when all the other major leaders of the party were in prison or otherwise isolated, could have changed Togliatti's opinion of Tasca. The two had been associates for more than ten years, and Togliatti's attitude was not the result of a temporary disagreement but rather, as we have seen, the product of a consistent and enduring hostility. Togliatti, who after the end of the war became the major protagonist of the Italian communists' attempt to keep some autonomy vis-à-vis Moscow, probably had no reason to feel any sympathy for Tasca, whose authority depended on how closely his ideas matched those emanating from Moscow. Paradoxical though it may seem, Tasca could even appear to Togliatti as somebody willing to use the authority of Moscow to gain power in Italy. For more than six years, Tasca, jealously guarding his intellectual autonomy, had been isolated in his own party but supported by the Russian leadership. Thus, Tasca, who had no real interest in gaining power within the party, could be perceived as an opportunist who made use of Moscow to gain the upper hand over the leadership of a party that did not like him. The project of reunification between Italian communists and socialists—which Tasca was almost alone in favoring, and which was seen by most Italian communists as something Moscow was imposing on the PCI—could have generated the opinion that Tasca was prepared to force his will onto his party by using Russia against his comrades. The rumors of his cowardice that were spread at the time seem to suggest that, unable to criticize the International, the Italian communists were instead attacking Tasca, the man who represented the will of the International, in order to sabotage the reunification.

In contrast to Tasca, Togliatti was well aware of the difficult game played with the Russian leadership on the issue of the autonomy of the single parties, and he did not refrain from using questionable methods to avoid open conflicts with Stalin. In 1926, for instance, he refused to pass along to the International a letter that the imprisoned Gramsci had written criticizing that organization, instead privately submitting it to Bukharin.[40] This kept under wraps Gramsci's harsh criticisms of the repressive methods used by Stalin and his followers. By the same token, Togliatti was ready to manipulate a specific party in order to promote his own positions. In a letter that Togliatti wrote to Tasca, he suggested that it could be appropriate for the communist movement to artificially re-create a leftist minority in the French Communist Party in order to balance that party's rightist tendency.[41] (Ironically, Tasca would be the victim of a similar manipulation a year later.)

At the same time, though, Togliatti had always been against the systematic expulsion of dissenting party members, whether from the right or from the left, because he saw it as the end of any possible debate or criticism within the communist movement. Since he believed that the lack of discussion was detrimental to the development of a correct political line, he made a point, for as long as possible, of expressing his dissatisfaction with the expulsion of communist leaders. This had been true in his relation with the Trotskyists and would be true even in Tasca's case.[42] Nevertheless, the principle of sacrificing an individual militant for the good of the party was unquestioningly accepted not only by Togliatti but by the communist movement in general.

Considering these episodes along with the political positions held by Tasca and Togliatti, we can place the decision to send Tasca to Moscow at the end of the 1920s in its context. Tasca, the most visible leader of the right wing of the Italian Communist Party, became the Italian representative at the International when Stalin was launching an attack against the right. Togliatti was aware of this attack, as he himself had been under fire for his association with Bukharin. He therefore nominated Tasca, who knew very little of the situation in Moscow, for a position he himself did not want to occupy. Finally, Togliatti had repeatedly proven that he considered Tasca more an adversary than an ally in the PCI, and in this respect he represented the general attitude held by the majority of the leadership of the Italian Communist Party. There can be little doubt, then, that in going to Moscow, Tasca was falling into a trap.

There might be multiple reasons why Togliatti offered Tasca as a scapegoat to Stalin, though we have no proof for any of them. We can speculate that Togliatti was using Tasca, as he had done in 1926, to situate himself in the center, for if Tasca was on the right, then Togliatti could not be accused of being on the right himself. Togliatti may also have thought that somebody less identified with the right than Tasca—Longo, for example, or even Terracini—might use his position in Moscow to gain support against Togliatti and, with Stalin's consent, replace Togliatti as the leader of the Italian communists.[43] But Tasca could not possibly conduct such an operation. In any case, when Tasca went to Moscow, Togliatti's advice to him not to get involved in the controversies there was more a late scruple than a genuine concern for Tasca's fate.[44]

Stalin's Ire

In Moscow, Tasca lasted only two months. He arrived in Stalin's capital on October 14, 1928, and went straight to work in the offices of the International. Four days later he sent his first letter to the leaders of the Italian Communist Party, a letter that was centered on the so-called German question: the struggle to control the German Communist Party after the scandal surrounding its Stalinist leader, Ernst Thälmann.[45] Tasca's destiny was decided on December 19, 1928, when Stalin, talking about "the Right danger in the German Communist Party" during a meeting of the Executive Committee of the International, attacked Tasca personally.[46]

What is interesting about Tasca's activity in Moscow is not so much his effort to present his positions to the International as his struggle to be faithful to the instructions he was receiving from Togliatti and the PCI. Two days before Stalin's attack, Togliatti wrote to Tasca, "Perhaps if I had been in Moscow in your place, I would have formulated some things differently, but I approve the substance of the line you have followed up to now."[47]

Rather than favoring one of the factions that were struggling to control the German party, Tasca had simply tried to find a way to avoid the expulsion of the German right. Thus Tasca was singled out because of the line that his party had been following at least since 1926.

From the moment he arrived in Moscow, Tasca understood that the situation was intricate and that he needed to be careful, striking a balance between his ideas, the need to represent his party, and the requirements of Moscow's politics. For more than a month, he was torn between his conscience and his desire not to be crushed by the factions that were battling for power. "From my egoistic point of view," he wrote to his party on November 4 in reference to the German situation, "I wish I did not have to deal with such a big issue at the beginning of my residence in Moscow."[48] He felt himself under terrible pressure to conform to the positions of the Stalinist majority, and he probably would have complied if he had not been so convinced of the correctness of his own ideas. He was able to resist, he said, only because he was conscious that the revolution—"our revolution," as he wrote emphatically—was at stake, and the repercussions could last for a very long time.[49]

At the beginning of December 1928, Tasca realized that there his position was unsustainable. On December 4, he wrote a letter to his party in which he reaffirmed his ideas on the German question. He believed that Stalin and his majority were fueling the conflict in order to obtain the expulsion of all members of the German Communist Party who did not obey their orders, and that his effort to find a compromise was unwelcome precisely because Stalin wanted to radicalize the conflict within the German party in order to annihilate his enemies. Tasca asked the PCI to replace him with somebody who agreed, or at least did not disagree as much as he did, with the Stalinist majority. "As long as I am here," he concluded, "I am going to say what I think."[50]

The Italian Communist Party did not act, and so on December 19, 1928, Tasca was still in Moscow to listen to Stalin publicly accuse him and Humbert-Droz of being supporters of the right wing of the German Communist Party. Stalin stated that "to tolerate any longer an 'order' of things in which the Right poisons the atmosphere with Social-Democratic ideological rubbish . . . would be to go against the Comintern and to violate the elementary demands of Marxism-Leninism."[51] Stalin characterized the situation as similar to the one that had led to the expulsion of the Trotskyists from the Russian Communist Party; if Tasca and Humbert-Droz did not see that, he added, it was only because they were pretending not to see it. Stalin concluded that this meant Tasca and Humbert-Droz were prepared to support the right wing of the German communists "even at the cost of the complete disintegration of the German Communist Party."[52] Tasca's attempt to mediate between the different tendencies in the GCP earned him the accusation of being "a provincial pettifogger who tries to make out that white is black, and black white."[53] Stalin's attack culminated in the charge, directed equally against Tasca and Humbert-Droz, of having "landed in the quagmire of craven opportunism"—a phrase that, coming from Stalin, was as lethal as it was colorful.[54]

Tasca had the dubious honor of being the first target in a long series of attacks that Stalin would mount against communist leaders close to Bukharin. Arthur Ewert, Heinrich Brandler, and August Thalheimer in Germany, Humbert-Droz in Switzerland, Bohumir Smeral in Czechoslovakia, Joaquin Maurìn in Spain, Jay Lovestone in the United States, and Paul Marion in France all became victims of Stalin's purge along with Tasca, and for similar reasons. Some of the most brilliant members of the Communist movement were portrayed as bourgeois intellectuals.[55] Many of them, including Lovestone, Marion, and Tasca, later in their lives fulfilled the prophecy that had driven them out of their respective communist parties and became passionate anticommunists or, in Marion's case, even fascist.[56]

No communist party found the energy to resist Stalin's will. Even when beloved leaders, such as Lovestone, tried their best to gain the support of the majority of their parties to resist Stalinization, they ended up isolated and powerless. It was not only an ideological problem but also a financial one, since Stalin could allocate unmatchable financial resources to help his supporters. Nonetheless, the Italian Communist Party was particularly quick to distance itself from Tasca. At the same time, Togliatti, following the strategy he had adopted in the early twenties, tried to postpone Tasca's expulsion as long as he could.

Even before Stalin delivered his speech, Tasca had been able to see that his party was not trying to protect him. A young Italian communist named Gino Amadesi told the assembly of the youth movement that Tasca's position was not surprising, "given his political past" [57] Thus a young Russian communist, Chitarov, was able to report this open disavowal of Tasca to the assembly of the Presidium, where Stalin gave his speech.[58] The political leadership of the PCI had also released a public document supporting Stalin against Tasca. This document, written during a meeting in the presence of a representative of the International, was supposed to be followed by another, private document directed only to the Russian authorities and more supportive of Tasca's positions.[59] Needless to say, this second document was never delivered, and Tasca found himself completely abandoned.[60]

At the beginning of January 1929 Tasca was forced to face the reality of his isolation. Until that point he had received only the letter in which Togliatti approved of his positions. The next letter Tasca received from Togliatti, dated January 2 and containing the reply to Tasca's dramatic description of events, had a completely different tone: "Dear, we have received your letters, 24, 25, 26 [*sic*]," Togliatti wrote, "and to tell you the truth, the first thing we did was laugh."[61] Tasca's letters obviously had not moved his comrades, who went out of their way to make fun of his tragic tone.

On the day Tasca left Moscow, January 17, he and Humbert-Droz had a meeting with Bukharin to talk about the situation of the Russian party. More important than the words they exchanged was the fact that Tasca had to promise to deny that Bukharin had any part in organizing their meeting. Tasca, in his diary, characterized Stalin's political maneuvering as a combination of blackmail and pogrom.[62] Then he went back to Paris, personally and politically crushed. Togliatti, according to Berti, commented, "Finally even there [Moscow] they understood who Tasca is," and gleefully added that "sending Tasca to Moscow has proved the best way to eliminate him forever."[63]

Into Exile

The final chapter of Tasca's experience in the Italian Communist Party was written in three different moments. First came the final showdown with his party, which took place during the meeting of the Central Committee of the PCI between February 28 and March 3, 1929. Then, at the end of August, Tasca received word that he could remain in the party if he abjured his positions; he immediately refused. Less than a month later, the PCI expelled him, but he had to wait until November to receive word that the International had ratified his expulsion.

Almost at the end of this process, on October 20, he wrote a letter to his friend Fanny Jezierska telling her of the pain he felt. "I am alive, even if I suffer a little: my nerves play tricks on me. I would have needed 15 days of rest to recover. You know the nervous reaction that comes after the 'misadventure' has already taken place. But I could not get the rest I needed."[64] For the first time since leaving Italy, Tasca truly felt himself to be in exile.

Since his youth, Tasca had considered the workers' movement his real fatherland. In Paris, waiting for the final act of his expulsion, he fantasized about his imagined community with the workers of the world. "Days ago," he wrote in his journal at the end of October, "I was sitting in a very modest bistro at lunchtime. Next to me there was a worker. . . . He was reading *L'Humanité* with his face buried in the newspaper, almost to escape from the other people's attention. . . . I *felt* what connected me to that worker."[65] Despite the sense of uprootedness he experienced after his expulsion, Tasca never abandoned what he believed was a moral obligation to be true to his political convictions. Even when some of his friends urged him to do whatever he could to avoid expulsion, he refused to accept Stalin's new course.[66]

For their part, Togliatti and Stalin never tried to make it easier for Tasca to remain in the party. To the PCI's Central Committee Togliatti said that Tasca's ideas were only pointless truisms that he used to "hide the putrid dog of his opportunism."[67] "His ideas," he said under the vigilant eye of the member of the German Communist Party sent by the International to police the Italian communists, "have nothing to do with mine, his ideas deny and reinterpret the directions now given by the International."[68] Stalin himself, evidently not satisfied even by words as harsh as Togliatti's, felt compelled to intervene to remind the Italian Communists that he wanted Tasca expelled. Thus in June the new Italian representative in Moscow, Ruggero Grieco, had to inform his comrades of a resolution adopted by the Executive Committee of the International that pressured the Italians to act against Tasca. This came at a moment when, as Giuseppe Berti notes in his memoirs, the Stalinists "were organizing a moral lynching of the Italian delegation."[69] Such pressure on the Italians was clearly directed not so much against the already marginalized Tasca as against Togliatti, to ensure that he would eliminate Tasca's ideas from his party along with Tasca himself and, more important, that he would be an obedient executor of Stalin's orders.

Tasca's removal could settle the conflict between Moscow and the Italians only if the latter agreed that Tasca did not represent them ideologically. It was essential to Stalin's power that the different communist parties recognize his ideological supremacy, granting him the right to define what was orthodox and what was not.[70] For this reason, Tasca's expulsion could function as a warning to other communist leaders only if it was followed by a change in the official doctrine of the PCI. Thus the expulsion, already tragic at a personal level, had consequences that went well beyond Tasca himself.

In order to understand how Tasca's expulsion became an essential moment in the Stalinization of the PCI, it is important to consider carefully the three different yet connected charges that the communist leadership leveled against Tasca. First, they said, Tasca was mistakenly convinced that "the bourgeoisie, after the elimination of the communist movements, will eliminate the social democratic parties."[71] Second, Tasca was said to believe "in the monstrous perspective of the defeat of the communist movement and of the proletarian revolution," in contrast to the Italian communists, who thought that the present was characterized by "the radicalization of the masses, a revolutionary opportunity, and the fascistization of the social-democratic parties."[72] Finally, they claimed, Tasca wanted the Italian communists to reconsider their attitude toward "the democratic parties and so-called antifascist movements."[73] Instead of fighting against the democratic forces, Tasca proposed "to mobilize the democratic components of the petty bourgeoisie for a so-called antifascist struggle."[74] These "crimes" were inspired, the document concluded, by Tasca's fallacious analysis of two critical points, "the two fundamental theses on which the Italian communists had lately based their policy: 1. the identity of fascism and capitalism and 2. the thesis that fascism could be defeated only by a Communist revolution."[75]

The charges, which could be summarized as accusing Tasca of being an antifascist, were absolutely true. Tasca, who much earlier had been a close associate of Mussolini, had already produced a few articles for *Stato Operaio* reflecting on fascism. In these articles, Tasca emphasized the exceptional danger that the new movement represented for the entire working class.[76] This analysis of fascism, whose kernel was a reconsideration of the role of the state and ultimately of politics in Marxism, was still truly heterodox within the majority of the communist parties but was part of the political patrimony of the Italian communist leaders. By forcing the Italian communists to expel Tasca for his ideas on fascism, Stalin was compelling them to delegitimize what had constituted the specificity of their experience: the fascist seizure of power. Thus, even though the conflict that had pitted Tasca against the Stalinists in Moscow was never based on Tasca's antifascist positions, it was through his expulsion and the formulas used to justify it that most of the cultural patrimony of the PCI was discarded in the name of the new Stalinist orthodoxy.

From a traditional Marxist point of view, it was indeed difficult to reconcile the Marxist objective emphasis on economic structure with an analysis of the specificity of fascism. Moreover, it was convenient to deny that specificity. If the nature of capitalism was not changed by fascism, the communists could consider this new political movement a mere episode in the struggle against the bourgeoisie. This approach obviously had the advantage of not requiring any major change in the communists' strategy. The tactical and strategic goals remained the same: a revolution to destroy capitalism and create socialism. If capitalism was the only enemy of the communists, the distinctions between "capitalist fascists," "capitalist democrats," and "capitalist socialists" were meaningless. However, if fascism was not just another episode of class warfare but a new phenomenon that could compromise the victory of the proletariat, Marxism needed to be reconsidered. Since fascism was essentially a political phenomenon, such a revision had to be centered on a different understanding of the role of the state and of political liberties both in the capitalist world and in the construction of socialism.

In expelling Tasca on the ground of his analysis of fascism, the Italian communists accepted Stalin's strategy of an undifferentiated attack against fascism, democratic institutions, and socialist parties. Tasca, by contrast, decided to go in the opposite direction and create a Marxist analysis of fascism without the constraints of a Stalinist orthodoxy. If Marxism could not explain fascism, it was either because Marxism was not really a science or because the Marxist method had not been correctly used to analyze the historical reality. Tasca, who was still a Marxist and a communist, believed that the answer lay in the misuse of Marxist categories rather than their systematic failure.

During the last months of 1929, though, Tasca was still tempted, as he would be for most of his life, to remain politically active in a party.[77] He was one of the most brilliant minds of the PCI—even his opponents recognized that—and many groups thought that they could benefit from his help. The two that insisted the most were the Italian left-wing socialists (*massimalisti*), led by Angelica Balabanoff, and the dissident communists close to Bukharin, who were trying in Europe and the United States to create alternative communist parties. Even some Trotskyists, particularly Boris Souvarine, who was one of Tasca's personal friends, tried to convince him to work with them. Tasca refused all these offers.

The Italian socialists started to court him even before his expulsion from the Communist Party was confirmed. In *L'Avanti*, the Italian socialist organ, an article published on October 14 claimed that Tasca, who had been "the theoretician of the PCI and who was truly a great scholar," could find his way back to the "glorious house of the Italian socialists."[78] The communists close to Bukharin, for their part, invited Tasca to Germany and Switzerland to give lectures on fascism.[79] Even in the United States, *Revolutionary Age*, the new publication of the Lovestonites, reported Tasca's case as part of their own struggle against the Stalinists, citing the words of an unnamed Italian Communist who said: "We must give in on Russia and international questions in order to be able to save the Italian policy of our party."[80] The Italian Trotskyists, who had little reason to sympathize with Tasca, underscored that Tasca and Togliatti held similar positions, even refusing to publish a letter that Tasca sent them, on the ground of his past involvement in their ideological persecution.[81] Yet the French Trotskyists invited Tasca to collaborate with the journal *La Critique Sociale* and to write articles on Marxism and the present. Tasca declined all these offers because, after enduring his expulsion from his party rather than compromise his own ideas, he did not want to accept any sort of ideological compromise in another political group. Despite his tragic personal situation, he struggled to maintain his intellectual autonomy.

Among Tasca's papers there is a monthly budget that allows us to see what kind of expenses he considered fundamental for his new life in Paris: 540 lire were destined for his wife and children in Italy, 350 lire for his room and clothes, 650 lire for newspapers and books, and 120 lire for transportation, for an estimated total of 1,660 lire.[82] This sum, roughly equivalent to $1,400, was surprisingly high for a "professional revolutionary" such as Tasca.[83] So he had to find a way to meld his desire for intellectual independence with a profession that would allow him to cover his considerable expenses. Journalism seemed to him an obvious choice, and as soon as it was clear that his expulsion from the PCI was inevitable, he started to look for a position with a journal that would allow him to pursue his scholarly interests without compromising his political ideas.

The solution to Tasca's problems came from a prestigious new journal founded by Henri Barbusse and entitled *Monde*.[84] This weekly publication, which was sponsored by intellectuals as diverse as Einstein, Unamuno, and Gorky, seemed to Tasca an ideal place to publish his ideas on politics. As he wrote to Souvarine, who did not like *Monde*, he preferred Barbusse's journal to other nonconformist publications of the French left because there he could work on the issue of the unity of the workers' movement. At *Monde*, other Communist intellectuals such as the Austrian Lucien Laurat, an expert on Rosa Luxemburg, or Leon Werth, the anarchist to whom Saint-Exupéry dedicated *The Little Prince*, had created an open forum for discussion. There Tasca found what he had hoped for: a socialist newspaper where leftist intellectuals could discuss culture and politics across the traditional boundaries of party politics.

Tasca and Barbusse had known each other since the years when Tasca was publishing *L'Ordine Nuovo*, where he had enthusiastically printed the manifesto of the *Clarté* group.[85] The presence among *Monde*'s financial supporters of leftist socialists such as Georges Monnet next to the communist-leaning Barbusse granted an ideological freedom to the journal that was uncommon among equivalent publications. Beginning on November 2, 1929, Tasca wrote book reviews and a weekly commentary on the principal cultural and political journals published in Paris.

However, this job at *Monde*, which greatly helped Tasca in finding a new role for himself in France, was less important for him than his theoretical research on Marxism, democracy, and liberal institutions. His immediate plans at the beginning of 1930 involved a study of Antonio Labriola and a reading of Engels's writings on the English working class.[86] Both projects, which clearly reconnected Tasca's interests of the 1930s to his early studies in Turin, focused on clarifying the philosophical and historical roots of Marxism. Dissatisfied with the new Stalinist orthodoxy, Tasca was trying to understand how orthodox the Stalinist approach to Marxism really was.

The project to uncover the origins of Marx and Engels's thought quickly led Tasca to emphasize the Hegelian component of their intellectual production. The new element that they introduced in the history of socialism, he wrote in an unpublished study on Engels, was dialectics. According to Tasca, in Marx and Engels's early writings, it was possible to see that their central contribution to socialism had been a reevaluation of the progressive role played by capitalism. The moral component of Marx and Engels's socialism, Tasca thought, was common to most socialists. What set the founders of scientific socialism apart from their utopian predecessors was their belief in the progressive role of capitalism, because its "melting" forces can reduce all social formations to the individuals who were their original components. "The particular," Tasca wrote in Hegelian language, "has to descend to the individual before it moves back to the universal."[87] Hence, Tasca thought, it was a mistake on the part of communist parties to believe that the sublation of the individuals into the universal could be based on the forgetting of the political and civil rights that had been created by the forces of bourgeois capitalism.

According to Tasca, a reading of the early works of Marx and Engels also revealed that Marxism was a form of "humanism."[88] What Tasca meant when he used this word was that, for Marx and Engels, mankind—"or, better, humanity"—was both the actor and the telos of history.[89] Introducing dialectics as the key component of their thought, he wrote, Marx and Engels had emphasized the movement of reconciliation of "humanity in itself, in a process analogous to Hegel's idealism."[90] Thus Tasca's idea of a Marxist humanism was used to describe the dialectical process that led humanity to recognize itself as both the subject and the object of history, through a process in which capitalism played a fundamental role.

This analysis of Marx and Engels's early writings, further developed in subsequent years, helped Tasca find a position to counter the new Stalinist emphasis on the preeminence of economic structure for understanding the political situation at the beginning of the thirties. His underscoring of the role of dialectics as the philosophical base of Marxism allowed him to denounce the Stalinist reduction of the political superstructure to the economic structure as a heterodox form of positivism. His emphasis on what he called the humanism in Marxism allowed him to reassess the role of consciousness, with its ultimate reflection on the role of culture and politics, against the revolution from above that Stalin wanted to pursue in the Russian countryside.

His decision to work for *Monde,* together with his renewed interest in the history of Marxism, shows that once he was expelled from the PCI, Tasca tried to go back to the activity that had characterized his years at *L'Ordine Nuovo. Monde* provided a space for a nonconformist discussion among leftist revolutionaries that was strongly reminiscent of the original project of Tasca's journal in Turin. His research on the Hegelian foundation of Marxism temporarily brought Tasca back to the Italian Hegelian school, in particular to Labriola, Benedetto Croce, and Giovanni Gentile, who had first written about the Hegelianism of the founders of scientific socialism. In the context of the thirties in France, Tasca's intellectual production brought him to the attention of many who were looking for a socialist critique of Stalinism. As we will see in the next chapter, it was among other nonconformist thinkers that Tasca found a new home for himself, following some of them all the way to Vichy.[91] When, only four years later, the communist parties reconsidered the idea of an alliance with the socialists to fight fascism, Tasca would already be too distant from them ideologically and politically to go back to the party that he had helped to found in 1921.

3

In Limbo
Angelo Tasca and Liberal Democracy

The historical events that characterized the 1930s until the eve of World War II deeply changed Angelo Tasca. As in the previous decade, his life was determined more by the history of the great ideologies of the first half of the twentieth century than by his private decisions. The progress of the Stalinization of the communist movement, the ideological and political victories of fascism, and the reactions that these events produced in Europe directly affected Tasca's life in all its dimensions.

The unusual tempo of historical change forced Tasca to react quickly to events beyond his control. The political activism associated with fascism and Stalinism separated Tasca from some of his friends and forced him to look for a new professional career. It also transformed forever his ideological position. The simultaneity of all these transformations prevented Tasca from giving a stable structure to his thought, and his intellectual biography in this period is marked by repetitions, reconsiderations, and even sudden conversions.

As long as he maintained his job at *Monde*, Tasca was able to navigate in the familiar world of communists and communist sympathizers. But when the ideological and political development of Stalinism destroyed that environment, he had to go in search of a new political identity. This search took place at the same time as the victory of Nazism in Germany and the political success of Mussolini's regime were projecting the image of a victorious fascism onto European politics. Thus, under the pressure of the expanding ideological force field of fascism, Tasca was forced to elaborate a new personal position, trying to distinguish himself from the Stalinists, whom Tasca partially blamed for the victory of Nazism.

By the end of the period covered in this chapter, Tasca's reflections led him to embrace liberal democratic politics to an extent that became incompatible with the goals of a Marxist revolution. Thus, during the ideological march that led him to return to the Socialist Party—his first political home—he followed a trajectory that in the end made him abandon his hope in the salvific role of the proletariat. The multifarious reality of capitalism came to seem incompatible with the possibility of solving every historical contradiction through the political action of the working class alone.

This painful realization came to him right in the middle of the decade, after the equilibrium that he had achieved in the first few years of the 1930s had been shattered by the constant frustration of his political desires. In the years following 1935, France's Popular Front temporarily provided him some hope, but even then his political perspective contained an element of pessimism. He knew very well how much the life of an individual could be dramatically changed by the rise of totalitarian politics, and he was afraid that fascism and Stalinism could reach him in his French exile. He also feared that Europe was about to experience a new, devastating war, in which ideology and the will to power could create a conflict of unprecedented violence.

Looking for a New Home

During the first years of his French exile, Tasca's political life was troubled, but he also had some professional satisfaction. After his expulsion, as we have seen in the previous chapter, he found refuge among the intellectuals who gathered around the journal *Monde*, a world of radical thinkers that can be easily described as communist fellow travelers.[1] At the beginning of the thirties, under the dictates of Stalinism, the world of the fellow travelers was under fire, but the various communist parties could not easily impose the political and ideological changes Stalin required.[2] Journals such as *Monde*, which the communists had partially financed and supported in order to project an image of freedom and discussion, were asked to conform to the new orthodoxy, but at first they quite successfully resisted the new course.[3] Thus when the Stalinists launched their first attack against *Monde* (during the Second International Congress of Revolutionary Writers, held in Kharkov in late 1930), the majority of the intellectuals associated with the journal simply tried to pretend that nothing had happened.

The Stalinist attack was conducted along the same lines that had been used against Tasca a year before. The majority of the delegates at Kharkov accused Barbusse's journal of having taken "from the start an anti-Marxist position" and of failing "to base its analysis on Marxism-Leninism."[4] According to documents approved by the congress, the Revolutionary Writers' original 1927 program, which offered membership to any "writer who was against fascism, imperialist wars, and white terror," was no longer acceptable.[5] The organization had to change course to reflect the new doctrine decided by the International. *Monde*, which had been created in Moscow during the previous writers' congress, had to follow suit.[6] *Monde* was facing the same dilemma that Tasca had had to confront in 1929: either change its political line and become Stalinist, or face excommunication by the communist movement.

Barbusse was clearly inclined to follow the new party line. Even before the 1930 congress he had started to include liberal democracy among the journal's enemies.[7] *Monde,* he wrote in an editorial in October 1930, "is not only against imperialisms and any sort of fascism, but also against all the aspects of false democracy, that ultimate resort of capitalist hypocrisy."[8] This comment, which equated fascism and democracy, was the logical outcome of the refusal of the International to recognize any difference between political systems within a capitalist economy.

The consequences for the identity of *Monde,* which had been founded with the intention of creating an intellectual coalition against fascism, were potentially devastating. Had Barbusse's analysis become the editorial line of *Monde,* the distinction to be drawn between the French republic, fascist Italy, and the political projects of the German Nazis would have disappeared from the pages of the journal. Barbusse himself, who made clear in the same article that it would have been a mistake to impose a party line on the journal, seemed to be aware of the problem. For this reason, no dramatic changes were immediately introduced in *Monde*'s editorial policy, and for the next two years Stalinists and anti-Stalinists continued to share *Monde* as a common space.

During this period, from 1930 to 1932, Tasca had a brilliant career. The rise of fascism and the revision of socialism were *Monde*'s central themes and Tasca's area of specialization, so he quickly became one of the leaders of the journal. Finally free to open a discussion with intellectuals who were sympathetic to communism but not orthodox communists, Tasca felt that he had the opportunity to continue a mission that he had started with the creation of *L'Ordine Nuovo*: creating an alliance between intellectuals and workers to produce a socialist new culture. Answering the journal's call, many of the recognized heretics of European socialism, including Henri de Man, Émile Vandervelde, Jean Zyromski, Karl Renner, Henriette Roland-Holst, and Marcel Déat, agreed to participate in a virtual debate on "the ideological crisis of socialism."[9] Tasca was given the prestigious role of offering a synthesis of the debate.

The debate on the crisis of socialism gave Tasca an opportunity to express his analysis of new trends in the theory of socialism, connecting it to recent European events. Without dismissing any of the positions expressed by these different authors, Tasca tried to direct the discussion along the lines of his own reflections on democracy, revolution, and their relation to socialism. He expressed his concern about de Man's tendency to consider socialism as something akin to a religious feeling, irrational and independent of specific historical circumstances. Marxist rationalism, Tasca wrote, was no longer enough for the "mystic socialists of today."[10] De Man, Eastman, and Roland-Holst, Tasca claimed, had replaced reason with the new irrationalism championed by Bergson, James, and Freud.[11] The intellectuals around *Monde*, by contrast, still wanted to affirm the identity between reason and revolution, and to promote a social analysis based on class.

The main danger that Tasca saw in de Man's attempt to base socialism on the classless dimension of individual psychology was that it might lead to a theory of socialism that denied any role to institutions, and particularly to the organizations of the working class. De Man, Tasca claimed with his usual sharpness, was trying to replace the Stalinist formula of "socialism in one country" with the idea of "socialism in one man," ignoring the importance of trade unions, workers' organizations, and parties in the formation of class consciousness.[12] For this reason, de Man, Eastman, and Roland-Holst were not simply "beyond Marxism" (*au-delà du Marxisme*) but also beyond socialism.[13] Tasca, on the other hand, underscored the fundamental role of institutions, and in particular democratic institutions, in the construction of socialism.

Tasca also expressed his disappointment that all the participants in the debate on the crisis of socialism had ignored the most urgent problem facing the socialists, namely, "the legal and illegal offensive of fascism" against democratic institutions. The leaders of the workers' movement did not focus on "the problem of the defense of democracy," and this inability to comprehend the new realities was their real theoretical failure.[14] The communists, Tasca wrote, did not understand the fundamental role of democracy in the construction of socialism; the socialists, on the other hand, had not understood that workers could no longer rely on the bourgeoisie for the defense of democracy. The new reality of fascism, he concluded, should have convinced both communists and socialists that the defense of democratic institutions was not a conservative battle but rather the new frontier of the class struggle between the bourgeoisie and the proletariat. If the bourgeoisie was destroying its historical legacy, the proletariat was called to become the new leader of history, starting from where the bourgeoisie had exhausted its mission: liberal democracy.[15]

Tasca quite rightly complained about his comrades' lack of interest in fascism and their consequent inability to understand the new European situation. As Renzo De Felice has shown, the analysis of fascism in the first decade after Mussolini's seizure of power was marked by lack of specificity, dilettantism, and superficial analogies.[16] Not only had many liberal conservative authors completely misinterpreted the nature of the new regime, becoming implicit or explicit apologists for fascism, but also many socialists had represented fascism along the familiar lines of violent conservatism, thus understating the significance of the new phenomenon.[17] Even in the pages of *Monde*, which had made antifascism one of its central concerns, the analysis of fascism was done only by Italians; no French intellectual participated in the debate on fascism until Hitler's victory. Tasca, who was already looking for a more accurate understanding of the ideological nature of fascism, complained in the pages of *Monde* about the misuse of the word *fascism* to describe any authoritarian and reactionary regime.[18] Only an analysis of fascism in relation to its ideology, its organization, its social bases, and its methods of achieving power could offer an accurate description, provided that all these elements were considered in the specific context of the historical development of a nation. There were no ideological shortcuts.

Tasca was particularly upset by the general inability of communist leaders, both Trotskyist and Stalinist, to understand the value of democracy in the fight against fascism. In his diary, Tasca minced no words in expressing his disappointment with Trotsky, who had written: "What does the Communist Party have to defend? The Weimar Constitution? No, we will leave this to Brandler. The Central Committee has to defend the positions . . . won by the working class in Germany."[19] "But," Tasca angrily replied, "if the positions won by the working class have a connection with the Weimar constitution, do we have to defend it or not?"[20]—emphasizing the contradictions implicit in any declaration of antifascism that did not consider the question of democratic institutions.

Tasca's answer to this question was precisely what the Stalinists, at the beginning of the thirties, could not accept—so much so that they were actively trying to destroy collaboration between the different workers' parties, even when such alliances were primarily an intellectual enterprise, as in the case of *Monde*. Thus at the end of 1931, the French Communist Party tried to sabotage Barbusse's journal both ideologically and materially. Using the decisions made at Kharkov, the communists sought to force Barbusse to distance himself from the positions advocated by Tasca and others associated with the journal who did not follow the Stalinist directions. Almost a year after the Second International Congress of Revolutionary Writers, it became impossible for the members of *Monde* (as much a political group as it was a journal and its affiliates) to ignore the attack against their journal, and a public meeting was scheduled to discuss the conclusions reached at Kharkov.

During this meeting, Tasca presented his countercritique of the documents of the Second International Congress of Revolutionary Writers. Tasca attacked the resolutions approved at Kharkov with his usual toolbox of theoretical and practical considerations. The congress had ordered *Monde* "to fight not only against fascism, but also against social fascism," that is, the socialist parties; Tasca replied that, in France and everywhere else, dividing the world into two camps, one communist, the other fascist, was a mockery of reality.[21] The congress, Tasca said, was ready to imagine the world on the model of the poem by Aragon, printed in the proceedings of the congress, in which the poet invited the revolutionaries to open fire on Léon Blum and the entire leadership of the French socialist party. Such a mentality, Tasca claimed, could only favor fascism.[22]

The Communist International, Tasca went on, had abandoned the dialectical method. Instead of seeing the historical movement as the process of synthesis of the contradictions, the Stalinist method had introduced a false antinomy between the working class and the rest of the world. This operation would lead not to the identification of the working class with humanity, he told the board of *Monde*, but only to the false identification of the working class with the Red Army, as clearly stated in another poem by Aragon: "Glory to materialist dialectic and glory to its incarnation the Red Army."[23]

Barbusse, signaling again his will to conform to Stalinist orthodoxy, objected to Tasca's speech, affirming that there were indeed only two alternatives, revolution or counterrevolution. But even though Barbusse was the only member of *Monde* who openly tried to refute Tasca's arguments during the discussion, the ideological break between the founder of *Monde* and Tasca became a central moment in the life of the journal.[24] After the beginning of 1932, the polemics between the two never stopped, and their opposition became increasingly irreconcilable.

Tasca wanted to take over the political guidance of *Monde*, and even took the liberty of sending letters to Barbusse to contest his political positions.[25] All these controversies, which certainly contributed to ruining the personal relationship between Barbusse and Tasca, had little impact on the communists' strategic goal of purging *Monde*. In the face of the resistance it encountered, though, the PCF decided on different tactics. Providing Barbusse with the necessary money, in 1933 they bought a majority share of the journal through him, eliminating the members of *Monde* who, like Georges Monnet, would have opposed the journal's new political line. The decision made by the majority of the editorial board in January 1932 to nominate Tasca as the editor of the political and economic sections of the journal was only a temporary setback for the Stalinists.[26] Throughout 1932, Barbusse's publication saw a dramatic decline in the number of copies sold and an increasing deficit in its budget.[27] In July 1933, Barbusse notified Tasca, Lucien Laurat, Magdalene Paz, and all the other dissidents on the staff that in the future they would be paid only by the article, de facto transforming them into external contributors to the pages of *Monde*.[28] By August 1933, all the dissidents had resigned, with the exception of Tasca, who had no alternative job and wanted to receive as much money as possible from the new ownership. During his last four months at *Monde*, Tasca even threatened to sue the journal and asked the journalists' union to be involved in his case. In the end, he was able to receive his full salary until January 1934, along with some reparations for unfair labor practices, but he was unable to conduct a political battle within the journal.[29]

Tasca's personal life was also in turmoil. At the beginning of 1932, the relationship between Tasca and his wife, Lina Martoretti, became increasingly difficult. Immediately upon his return from Moscow Tasca had had a short affair with a young Russian émigré, but he still wanted to reconcile with the woman he had married and with whom he had had three children.[30] However, Martoretti, who was still living in Italy, did not hide her desire to end the marriage, repeatedly postponing plans to join her husband in Paris.

The letters that the two exchanged revealed Martoretti's desire to live a normal life, away from her husband's political engagement. "We could have been happy if we had lived in a freer environment, if we had not been strangled by the damn circle of politics," she wrote to him on April 3, 1930.[31] She further explained her feelings in a letter she wrote in February 1931: "I am happy to gather my belongings, also to see if I can make the decision to cross the border, if not forever, at least for some time. I will never abandon my house because you cannot imagine how good I feel when I am by myself."[32]

When Martoretti finally agreed to go to France and bring the couple's three children to meet with their father, Tasca understood that his marriage was over. Martoretti arrived in France at the beginning of the spring of 1932, but she never agreed to live in her husband's apartment at 4, Square Port-Royal, in the Thirteenth Arrondissement.[33] In February 1933, after less than a year in Paris, she decided to return to Italy without even informing Tasca. Her sudden departure threw him into a temporary state of prostration.

According to what he wrote to the Parisian police, his wife had persuaded their son, Carlo, to steal from him the money that they needed to finance their trip back to Italy. After the theft, probably to win the sympathy of the Italian police, she sought refuge in the Italian consulate in Paris. There, Tasca continued, she told the Italian authorities that she wanted to leave her husband, a famous antifascist, receiving in exchange the promise of financial support for herself and her family.[34]

When the French authorities demurred that their hands were tied, Tasca wrote a letter to the Italian general consul, complaining that his wife had come to Paris with a lover and was now taking away two of their two children, ages fourteen and sixteen.[35] His political opposition to the regime meant that he got nowhere with his petition to the Italian authorities, however, and Lina safely returned to Italy with two of their three children. Only the youngest daughter, Valeria, age seven, remained in Paris with her father.

In the middle of these personal and professional cataclysms, Tasca still managed to find the time for politics. His last two important contributions to the intellectual life of *Monde* were a comparative analysis of fascism and Nazism, presented during a seminar with the members of the journal, and a series of articles in which he tried to offer a synthetic view of the relation between Marxism and democracy. The series appeared as a small volume, *Marxisme 33*, the subsequent year and intellectually belonged to the next phase of Tasca's life; the comparative analysis of the two fascisms, as he called them, was his last attempt to discuss the nature of fascism before his more organic discussion of it in *La naissance du fascism.*

Tasca tried to highlight both the similarities and the differences between Italian Fascism and Nazism. The common elements, he believed, were the absence of a specific doctrine, nationalism, antisocialism, and social composition. Both, he added, were more movements than political parties, and were hostile to parties and the party form of organization. The circumstances of their seizure of power were, in his opinion, also similar: both had profited from the weakness of the socialists, ambiguous relations between Catholic political parties and the state, the conservatism of the Italian and German heads of state, and the weakness of the two countries' liberal governments.

As Italian fascism had done, Tasca predicted, Nazism was about to implement a form of reactionary policy, starting with the destruction of the trade unions and all the other workers' organizations. Both movements' ideological origins could be traced back to the works of Nietzsche, Sorel, the tradition of revolutionary syndicalism, and their antirationalist components, with the obvious difference of Nazism's strong emphasis on racism. The ability of the two movements to appeal to antirational, quasi-religious feelings, along with their strong liturgical elements, should have raised the question, Tasca maintained, of the potentially strong appeal of fascism even outside Italy and Germany. The main tactical goal of both movements, Tasca predicted, was to gain time to prepare for war. Only a political initiative to restructure international relations in Europe along the lines of a socialist United States of Europe could prevent the ultimate catastrophe.[36]

Much like his emphasis on the positive role of democracy, Tasca's call for political union in Europe signaled another break with Stalinism, which believed in the inevitability of war, as Barbusse had stated. However, this break happened after all Tasca's ideological connections with Barbusse and the editorial policy of the journal had been severed.

The events of 1932–33 left a permanent mark on Tasca. If his expulsion from the Italian Communist Party had been a traumatic event that he had managed to survive, the end of his experience at *Monde*, which coincided with the end of his marriage and with the Nazi seizure of power, temporarily forced him into a deeper reconsideration of his life. Long before the Nazi invasion of France, Tasca had a sense that his life was conditioned by the victorious European dictatorships. Fascism had separated him from his wife and played a part in the last, tragic days of their relationship, and its agents were constantly spying on him.[37] Stalinism had already ended his life as a communist militant and now was responsible for the destruction of his career at *Monde*. The victory of Nazism, which he rightly saw as a catastrophe that could lead to a new world war, proved to him that the strategy adopted by the Communist International could not prevent the rise of new and more aggressive fascist regimes in Europe. The convergence of these personal and political events convinced Tasca to reconsider his political affiliation.

The decision to expel Tasca and the other anti-Stalinists from *Monde* broke an important connection among the various parts of the French left, at a time when Hitler was establishing his power in Germany. Barbusse's journal, which had provided a forum in which many of the heretics of European socialism could discuss their positions in association with orthodox communists and socialists, was an important prefiguration of the politics of the Popular Front. The communists' decision to suppress that forum left Tasca and other intellectuals deeply suspicious of the sincerity of the communist leadership's antifascist sentiments.

Monde's most important contribution to the discussion within the French left, and the European left more generally, was its openness to different and even contradictory positions. Henri de Man, Marcel Déat, Gaston Bergery, and Bertrand de Jouvenel were regular contributors to the journal. Siegfried Krakauer regularly wrote analyses of the language of films, and Unamuno and Einstein contributed small pieces on philosophy and physics. Even Catholic intellectuals such as Luigi Sturzo, the founder of Italy's Partito Popolare, sent articles on the subject of Italian fascism, as did leftist intellectuals recently expelled from the Italian Communist Party, such as Ignazio Silone. Free from the constraints of political parties, these intellectuals had provided a common contribution to the debate about the European situation between the wars. Thus from its foundation until 1934, *Monde* had been able to unite, in the name of antifascism, a large coalition of forces.

During the first months of the Nazi era, when such a coalition could have played an even more important political role, *Monde*'s decision to cut off collaboration with the noncommunist intellectuals who had been acting as fellow travelers dissolved the joint effort of common ideological research in the name of resistance against aggressive fascist ideologies. Tasca, with more sadness than satisfaction, underscored in one of his diaries the absurdity of the communists' position, citing without comment *L'Humanité*'s claim that "the fact that the fascist dictatorship exists in Germany confirms the rightness of the communist tactic and strategy."[38]

Resisting Fascism

The dissolution of the coalition created by Barbusse around *Monde* unleashed a group of ideas and political projects that was to prove dangerous for the French republic. Some of the central figures who contributed to the journal—de Man, Bergery, Déat, de Jouvenel—became the protagonists of what Philippe Burrin has called "la dérive fasciste," or the fascist drift.[39]

Disillusioned with the French Communist Party, which no longer wanted them, these intellectuals started to look for an alternative to the communist strategy of the early 1930s. Some of those who were hostile to liberal democracy and had been collaborating with the communists on the basis of that hostility began to explore whether elements of fascism, which appeared to offer an alternative to liberalism and a "third way" between Western democracies and communism, could be incorporated into other political ideologies without those ideologies necessarily becoming fascist.

It was true that fascism, and in particular Italian fascism, was ideologically on the offensive at the beginning of the thirties. The regime's diplomatic and ideological victories had convinced some Italian fascists that their ideas could be exported outside Italy. Journals such as *L'Anti-Europa* and

Critica Fascista began to talk about the universal value of fascist ideology, imagining a form of fascist Europeanism. Initiatives such as the creation of the International Centre of Fascist Studies, which published documents and articles by leading fascist intellectuals and politicians, served the purpose of spreading fascist ideas in Europe. These and other initiatives were beginning to achieve some success.[40]

Fascism gained some ground among a number of intellectuals and politicians of the left in the years before the Spanish Civil War. The phenomenon was clearly not completely new either in France or in the rest of Europe; the case of Georges Valois and the Faisceau proves that an interest in fascism had existed in the 1920s. *Monde* had been very successful in that milieu, and the fact that Valois had ended up financing through his publishing house the publication of *Monde,* reentering the constellation of the left, was the best proof of that success.[41] But the situation in the thirties was clearly different.

Tasca, for his part, tried to welcome intellectuals who wanted to break with fascism. After his experience with Mussolini, he was well aware of the importance of avoiding a migration of leftist intellectuals to the fascist camp. Therefore, he supported the inclusion of ambiguous figures such as Valois in the antifascist coalition in order to prevent them from going over to the other side. He believed that if the petty bourgeoisie was left to the antisocialists, it would turn to fascism to solve its problems.[42] The winning strategy was to present socialism as the solution to social problems, not as their cause.

On the basis of this analysis, Tasca worried that the communists' decision to dissolve their alliances with other movements was creating the conditions for a new fascist offensive. In the years between 1932 and 1935, in fact, the activism of the Italian fascists signaled to him that the fight over the majority of the European population was becoming more intense, forcing the socialists onto the defensive. In particular, an increasing number of socialists were inclined to see the Italian fascists' experiment with corporatism as a positive move beyond capitalism. Tasca feared that the fascist regime's efforts might succeed in fostering illusions about the real nature of fascism. In practice, many symptoms seemed to indicate that the Italian regime was conducting a coordinated attempt to enlarge its social bases. Tasca was looking carefully at these efforts.

The news from Italy in the second half of 1933 was unsettling in that respect. In Milan, for instance, Edmondo Rossoni, an ex-socialist turned fascist, had contacted a group of moderate socialists led by Emilio Caldara, who had been the first socialist to be elected mayor of the city in 1914.[43] Rossoni, who in 1933 was working as Mussolini's undersecretary, had been the first architect of the fascist corporations, and had been in favor of new relations between labor and industrialists. During the meeting that followed, Rossoni told Caldara that he had not changed his mind about socialism, that Mussolini was still a revolutionary, and that the regime was on its way to constructing socialism.[44] Worried by this episode, the Italian antifascists told Tasca that Mussolini himself had planned this move, with the cynical purpose of winning the support of some socialists for his regime. Even though no real consequences came from this specific initiative, Tasca knew that the fascists were trying to lure some socialists to their camp.[45]

Outside Italy, the fascists were using a similar strategy, with the advantage that their offers did not need to be tested against the regime's concrete acts. Thus, some socialists manifested an interest in the economic policy of fascism, and in particular in the corporations. Hoping that a new managed economy could serve as a moment of transition from capitalism to socialism, some socialists began to study the ideas of the Italian regime, temporarily suspending judgment on Mussolini's politics.

Tasca discovered quickly that the fascist strategy was working to undermine the desire of prominent socialists to speak out openly against Mussolini's regime. For example, when Carlo Rosselli asked Tasca to intercede with Henri de Man on his behalf to publish their correspondence, he discovered that de Man wanted to obtain Mussolini's permission to go to Italy to study the corporations and for this reason did not want to draw attention to his antifascism.[46] Considering de Man's authority with many non-Marxist leftists in those years, particularly in Italy and France, his curiosity about fascism could have far-reaching consequences.[47] The fact that de Man, a cultural hero for a generation of nonorthodox socialists and antifascists including Carlo Rosselli, was opening an intellectual line of credit to Mussolini's regime, as it were, could spell trouble for the resistance against the rise of fascism in Europe.

Like de Man, many other socialists and heretics of socialism expressed a desire to study the fascist experiment with corporations. The fascist regime seized the opportunity and started to organize trips to Italy for prominent intellectuals who might become fellow travelers of the regime, following the well-established practice of the Soviets. The most famous of these trips to discover fascism would eventually lead Emmanuel Mounier, Robert Aron, Jean de Fabrègues, and Paul Marion to participate in a conference in Italy with representatives of the fascist regime in the spring of 1935 on the theme of corporations. In the summer of 1933, however, the issue of the relation between socialism and fascism was creating problems for the French socialist movement.

During the congress of the French Section of the Workers' International (SFIO) held in July 1933 in Paris, one of the delegates, Barthélemy Montagnon, told the French socialists that the crisis of socialism stemmed from the discrepancy between socialist theory and practice. Everywhere in Europe, he maintained, the economic depression had mobilized the petty bourgeoisie, creating corporatist experiments and revolutionary tendencies. In his view, the socialists had not understood the importance of this moment. Under these circumstances, either the socialists could rise to the challenge of providing an answer to the demands of the time or the fascists would do it. The creation of socialism, in fact, was no longer the monopoly of the socialist parties. There was another way, he had already declared in public, "the fascist way."[48] Under these premises, Montagnon and other members of the SFIO, led by Déat, left their party to found the experiment of neosocialism.[49]

Tasca, who knew many of the neosocialists, or Néos, was personally affected by all these events. He had collaborated with Déat at *Monde,* and he agreed with some of the Néos' critiques of the socialist parties. Like them, he believed in the need to reform the theoretical basis of socialism. He was also convinced that a race was on between socialism and fascism to respond to the demands of the moment. When he discovered that one of his closest friends, Paul Marion, had decided to follow Déat, he carefully considered the new organization, despite his disgust with fascism.[50]

Tasca and Marion had been associates since the time when they both were in Moscow as members of the right of the party.[51] Marion had been expelled from the French Communist Party at the same time and for the same reasons that had prompted the Italian communists to expel Tasca.[52] Experiencing similar difficulties in their lives, the two had become friends. At the moment of his personal crisis in 1933, Tasca even asked Marion to help him to arrange for the care of his daughter Valeria, who spent many afternoons in the company of Marion's secretary.[53] When Marion asked Tasca to join the Néos, Tasca had to explain to his friend his personal and political disagreements with the movement.

In a letter sent to Marion in the summer of 1933, Tasca left no doubt about the dangers that he saw in Déat's enterprise. He was not prepared, Tasca wrote, to replace the immobility of the French socialists with the purposeless energy of the new organization, especially because he did not believe in Hitler and Mussolini's "l'homme nouveau," created through a nationalistic mystique and sports.[54] His explicit reference to fascism in this letter clearly shows that Tasca was well aware that some of those promoting this new organization were sympathetic to the Italian regime. Rather than breaking with the socialist tradition to look for dubious "third ways," such as the one proposed by Déat, he preferred to work within the mainstream, even if he had to fight its currents.

If Déat and the Néos accepted the idea that European politics was moving in the direction of strong, authoritarian states, Tasca chose instead to stress the importance of democratic institutions for the construction of socialism. If some young Italian socialists were proposing to abandon Marx to base socialist politics on the new theories proposed by de Man, he preferred to stress the centrality of Marxism to his political projects. He responded to the Néos and to Carlo Rosselli's infatuation with de Man by publishing a series of articles, later collected in a volume, offering his antiauthoritarian, Marxist reflections.

The title that Tasca gave to this collection of articles, as we have seen, was *Marxisme 33*. The goal of the book, which he defined as a "manual of Marxism," was to restore a philological understanding of Marxism, which had been compromised by the scholasticism of its Stalinist interpreters.[55] For this reason, *Marxisme 33* was conceived as a basic textbook that could provide socialists with an anti-Stalinist version of Marxism, and Marxists with an argument against the anti-Marxism of new groups such as the Néos. Tasca believed that this approach could expose the totalitarian interpretations of Marxism as the real heresy, and enlighten workers about the antidemocratic prejudices of Stalinism. He was confident he could prove that it was possible to find in Marxism the philosophy of action required by the events of 1933. A historical account of the relation between Marxism and the democratic institutions created by the bourgeoisie could prevail against the intellectual poverty of the Stalinist interpretation. The historical method, based on rationality and clarity, had to be used to fight any attempt to abandon Marxism on the basis of bourgeois irrationalism.

In his reconstruction of the relation between Marxism and democracy, Tasca admitted that Marxism and legality seemed incompatible at the present time, since Marxism was a revolutionary ideology. He also conceded that defending the existing democracies in the name of Marxism could appear to be an absurdity. But the revolutionary project could be effective if based on the construction of an alternative legality, rather than on the simple destruction of the existing order. Marx and Engels, he claimed with his usual abundance of textual references, had never believed that socialism could be realized without going through "political democracy, republican institutions, and universal suffrage."[56]

Universal suffrage by itself, Tasca asserted, had revolutionary consequences. It was the historical duty of the proletariat to realize its revolutionary potential through a policy of alliances with the middle class and the peasants. However, Tasca believed, the bourgeoisie had been more skillful than the leaders of the proletariat in creating such alliances while simultaneously destroying democracy to keep in check the socialist potential of democratic institutions. The coalition between a fearful petty bourgeoisie menaced by the economic crisis and capitalists threatened by socialism had given birth to fascism. Therefore, the fight for socialism within the framework of democratic institutions was the only real counterstrategy for opposing fascism.

Socialism, in Tasca's conception, was to be understood as the realization of the promises of liberal democracy. Marx's critique of the "rights of man" in "The Jewish Question" suggested that democratization of the social sphere was not the antithesis of democracy, as implied by the Stalinists' attack on the institution of liberal democracy, but rather its fulfillment. It was true that without the democratization of economic relations, democratic institutions were destined to become reactionary, but they were still a precondition for social democracy. Thus, to avoid such a reactionary evolution of liberal democracy, the working class had to be the vanguard of a new process of democratization that included both the social and political spheres.[57]

Similarly, a process of democratization needed to be carried out in the sphere of international relations. Europe, Tasca believed, could be saved from war and the victory of totalitarianism only through the construction of new institutions capable of creating forms of democratic participation in the political, social, and international arenas. The alternative was another world war. But in truly democratic states, aggressive wars were impossible because the proletariat could exercise its opposition against them and defeat the aggressive tendencies of the bourgeoisie. The inability of the German social democrats to impose real democratic institutions in Germany, he believed, had allowed the German ruling class to drag Germany into a world war.[58] Only the fight for democratic institutions could spare the continent from a repetition of those events on an even larger scale.

The struggle for democracy was the arena in which the future of Europe and socialism was about to be contested. The defeat of fascism and the victory of socialism would entail the problem of the reconstruction of democracy in the states now ruled by fascist regimes. They would also entail the democratization of international relations through the project of a socialist United States of Europe.

Tasca tried to orient his political activity toward these two goals, deciding to reestablish his connections with the socialist parties (he also desperately needed to find a job). At first he looked for help to some of the people with whom he had worked at *Monde*—de Jouvenel in France, Scott Nearing in the United States, Roland-Holst in the Netherlands, and De Man in Belgium—but in the end he preferred to accept the offer from Georges Monnet and the SFIO.[59] His choice was motivated more by his refusal to follow some of his friends in what he saw as their fascist regression than by a full acceptance of the politics of the socialists. He had come to believe that the socialist parties were the only ones willing to create socialism without moving in the direction of Stalinist totalitarianism. Thus at the beginning of 1934 Tasca resumed his collaboration with the Italian Socialist Party while awaiting a new job for the French socialists as a journalist for the official newspaper of the SFIO, *Le Populaire*.

The decision to return to the party from which he had started his political career was not easy for Tasca. His critique of the socialists' shortcomings, particularly what he saw as their positivist conception of history, was still very much present in his mind. Nevertheless, since the communists were, in his view, completely subservient to the policy of Stalinist Russia and he did not believe in the radical alternatives proposed by the heretics of socialism who had abandoned Marxism, Tasca chose the socialist parties because they were parties of the working class. However, he still envisioned changing the ideological basis of the socialists, rather than accepting theirs as his own, and he marked his distance from them in many ways.

Symbolically, Tasca at first refused to join the Italian Socialist Party after he resumed his collaboration with them and the French socialists. Only in March 1935, after a year of working with them, did he agree to complete his application to become a full member of the PSI.[60] Practically, as a condition for resuming his active role in the socialist movement, he demanded to be put in charge of the theoretical journal of the Italian socialists, *Politica Socialista*, which he edited from May 1934 to August 1935. This strategy of conditional engagement, founded on his conviction that the theoretical basis of socialism needed to be changed, prompted Tasca to maintain his ideological autonomy and to cultivate political relations with groups and people who were also looking for a reform of socialism.

Therefore, even though most of the people who had participated in the *Monde* experience were taking a direction that Tasca did not like, he maintained an interest in their theoretical production, and he also cultivated relations with other sectors of the so-called French nonconformists.[61] At a point in his life when he needed to make many new choices to reorient his political and cultural activity, Tasca decided to collaborate increasingly with those sectors of nonconformism he saw as more open to a critique of the totalitarian dimension of European politics. In particular, he directed his attention to the leftist Christians gathered around Paul Desjardins at Pontigny Abbey, in the department of Yonne. Pontigny, which Tasca frequented regularly beginning in 1932, well represented the world of nonconformists, which Tasca perceived as partially akin to his own political project. Since 1929, the Church had also been the major center for diffusion of de Man's ideas in France, and through this institution Tasca was able to maintain his relationship with his Belgian friend, who, unlike the Néos, had not yet abandoned the Socialist Party.

The abbey belonged to Paul Desjardins, a writer who had sided with the Dreyfusards and who had always desired to create fraternal communities across confessional and political divisions.[62] Since 1910 Desjardins, a friend of Péguy and a progressive and fervent Catholic, had organized seminars called "Décades."[63] He invited the most promising French and international intellectuals to exchange ideas, and André Gide, Charles Du Bos, Paul Valéry, Jean-Paul Sartre, Robert and Raymond Aron, Denis de Rougemont, and Emmanuel Mounier, to mention a few, participated in these summer meetings.[64] The goal of these initiatives was to contribute to the modernization of French society through the self-reinforcement of elites endowed with technical competence: "managers with a social consciousness, bureaucrats invested in the general interest of society, socialist intellectuals and all the elites interested in promoting social transformation were the ideal candidates to participate in the Décades, where they could network and create a mutual understanding."[65] In the thirties, Tasca clearly fit the profile of those at whom Desjardins's project was aimed.

The meetings at Pontigny Abbey presented Tasca with the opportunity to discuss his positions in a more complex way than his activity as a journalist ever allowed. Desjardins greatly admired him and gave him the space to air his ideas on reforming the theory of socialism. As Desjardins wrote in a letter to Tasca, he believed that an intellectual project united Tasca, de Man, and himself.[66] This common goal, as Desjardins understood it, was to provide the socialists with a concrete set of reforms that would allow them to be ready to assume leadership of the European nations.

Tasca accepted the basic lines of Desjardins's project. Although Tasca never quite abandoned his many suspicions about de Man's theoretical efforts, his own analysis of the defeat of socialism in Germany and Italy convinced him that the socialists could be successful only if they had a plan for the resolution of Europe's economic and political crisis. As we have seen, Tasca had written in *Marxisme 33* that only the construction of an alternative legality, and not the simple destruction of the existing order, could lead to socialism. Thus when Desjardins invited him to abandon the polemical aspects of antifascism to confront the problem of the reconstruction of Europe, Tasca was receptive.[67] Under the influence of Pontigny, Tasca became convinced that de Man's idea to govern the economy along the lines of a plan democratically discussed among the different social classes could represent the solution to the problem of creating an alternative to capitalist economies.[68]

In 1934, his adoption of some of the economic solutions proposed by de Man represented the first major ideological break for the Italian. However, as he explained to his audience during one of the Décades that he led, he also maintained a distance from de Man on three essential points: the role of Marxism, the role of autonomous workers' organizations, and nationalism.

Tasca continued to consider Marx's philosophy as the continuation of the Enlightenment tradition and denounced any form of irrationalism as a fascist tendency. All revolutionary ideas, he insisted, had to remain connected to the Enlightenment. Alternative traditions that stressed "life" and irrational forces as central elements in the social and political realm were, in his opinion, unmistakably reactionary. He confessed that as a youth, when he was blinded by Gentile and Sorel, he himself had not understood this point, and it was only the emergence of Mussolini that had opened his eyes. Marx, unlike the fascists, was a legitimate son of the Enlightenment. The German philosopher had seen workers as revolutionary subjects because of their rational ability to reflect on their own material condition. Without a theory, revolutions were simple revolts with no lasting consequences. Revolutions, he proclaimed, reaffirming his critique of de Man's ideas in *Monde*, needed rational thought.[69]

On the question of the construction of a planned economy, Tasca cautioned his audience about the risks involved in abolishing independent workers' organizations, even in the name of the new interclass organizations required to discuss the economic plans. In the new climate created by the emergence of neosocialism and the fascist attempt to win support from some socialists, Tasca believed that de Man and the Néos were deluding themselves about the progressive role of fascist corporatism. Drawing on his long-standing attention to the role of intermediate bodies between the state and individual citizens, Tasca stressed that it was naive for socialists to construe fascist corporations as a form of transition from capitalism to socialism. The destruction of the workers' organizations, Tasca told his audience in Pontigny, had divided the workers, leaving them more isolated and fragmented than ever before. This atomization of the workers, which Tasca called the "original sin of fascism," could not be undone by a totalitarian regime.[70]

Equally, on the question of nationalism, Tasca wanted to stress the dangerous, unwanted consequences of de Man's ideas. Managing a national economy along the lines of a politically determined plan entailed the idea that each national government was entitled to determine what was best for its nation. De Man explicitly held that until the moment when all of Europe was governed by socialists, it fell to national governments to determine the economic plans for their nations.[71] Tasca was worried by the idea that workers, taking on themselves the political and economic responsibilities of governing their nation-states, could become the new representatives of the national communities, transforming socialism into national socialism.

The movement from internationalism to nationalism, he believed, was one of the trademarks of Mussolini's evolution and provided one of the few elements of ideological stability to be found in fascism. Tasca told his audience that when Mussolini incorporated the small Italian nationalist party into his new formation in January 1923, he accepted its ideological primacy, despite its electoral insignificance, and a similar fate could befall the socialists. The socialist parties had to do everything in their power to fight nationalism, and this meant anchoring their initiatives at the international level. For this reason, he reaffirmed, it was important to maintain the project of constructing an international community based on democratic rules. Any concession to the mysticism of nationalism had reactionary consequences.[72]

On the problem of nationalism, however, the pressure of events soon brought Tasca to accept de Man's point of view. Despite his uncompromising tone in the summer of 1934, the question of the relation between national identity and socialism was still an open problem for him. He was certainly suspicious of any contamination between nationalism and socialism, but he was also aware of the need to provide an answer to the challenge that the fascist movements were launching against the socialists on the basis of national identities. In private he tirelessly reaffirmed his hostility to national identities, but publicly he started to admit that the fascist mobilization of national sentiments was effectively undermining the class identity of the proletariat.[73] The problem, Tasca believed, was that people's identification with the nation was a sort of primordial feeling, akin to the identification with one's family, whereas class consciousness required a moment of reflexivity that could be achieved only through workers' active participation in the political process.

When at the beginning of 1935 a referendum was held in the Saar on the question of whether to reunite with Germany after fifteen years of international administration under a mandate from the League of Nations, the overwhelming vote for reunification gave Tasca a new occasion to reflect on the problem of nationalism. Despite the united engagement of the political left to defeat the Nazis, ethnic identities had been more powerful than any political arguments put forward by the antifascists. In two articles published in *Il Nuovo Avanti*, the newspaper of the Italian socialists, Tasca analyzed the reasons for the terrible defeat in the Saar referendum. His account of the Nazis' success emphasized two orders of motivation: at the political level, the ineffectiveness of an alliance between socialists and communists when there was no common and positive political project, and at the theoretical level, the failure of traditional Marxist theory to explain the persistence of nationalism. Accordingly, Tasca's solution was twofold: the ground had to be prepared in advance with a common, positive program that involved all the workers' parties, and socialist leaders had to realize that Marx's prediction that all the contradictions of capitalist societies would be absorbed into the contradiction between workers and capitalists had not come true.[74]

The second element of Tasca's analysis signaled his first major departure from Marxism. In 1847, Tasca wrote, it had still been possible to think that the nation could be sublated in the proletariat's movement toward universality; in 1935, however, only a specific political program could provide identification between the proletariat and the nation. Since capitalism had not evolved in the direction of the elimination of all the classes between the proletariat and the bourgeoisie, the proletariat needed to have a political program capable of representing the intermediate classes. Tasca phrased his new position this way: "Since the nation did not come to the proletariat, the proletariat will go to the nation."[75] Tasca's refusal to nationalize the working class had crumbled in the face of events that suggested the persistence of national and ethnic identities.[76]

In 1935, in the new political climate that the Popular Front was creating in Europe, Tasca no longer believed in a European revolution, as much as he wanted a political program that could legitimize the left as a national force in order to preserve democracy from fascism. If in 1933 Tasca was trying to tie revolution to legality, claiming that a true revolution involved the construction of an alternative legality, after 1935 legality became more important than revolution for Tasca. Under the pressure of the fascist successes, which were both political and ideological, he accepted the idea of a temporary withdrawal from revolutionary plans in order to secure the stability of the existing institutions. Since such institutions existed only at the national level, he even admitted that an antifascist policy required the temporary nationalization of the socialist movement. Concretely, this new position entailed the transformation of revolutionaries into statespeople whose legitimacy relied on their defense of democratic institutions on behalf of the working class, as well as on the ability to represent the needs of the whole nation. The practical consequences of this choice in Tasca's life became increasingly evident after 1935, and were to accompany him even through the crisis of the Third Republic.

Counseling the Prince

After the storm of the years between 1933 and 1935, Tasca's political positions remained fairly stable until 1938. Tasca was writing his book on the birth of Italian fascism, gathering sources and conducting interviews with some of the protagonists of those years. This project occupied most of his time since he wanted it to be his main contribution to the fight against fascism. Thus during those years Tasca was less prolific in documenting his own political and theoretical evolution.

The eventful years of the rise and fall of the Popular Front and the Spanish Civil War confirmed some of Tasca's predictions and reinforced his own opinions. The military threat represented by fascism offered him proof that the Italian and German regimes were leading Europe toward a new war. The political trajectory of his friend Paul Marion, who in 1936 joined the Parti Populaire Français, confirmed to him that outside the socialist parties there was a real risk of regression into fascism.[77] Finally, the decision of the French Communist Party to support Blum's government without assuming any direct responsibility in the government itself confirmed Tasca's view that the communists were not deeply committed to the defense of the French republic.[78]

Tasca tried his best to resist such events both symbolically and concretely. In the summer of 1934 his opinion of the SFIO was harsh. The leaders of the French Socialist Party, he wrote, were petit bourgeois who had replaced the nation with the party. They were "like Catholics who want to save their souls without paying too much." The political program of the SFIO, he insisted, was "a *guesdisme* established at the lowest level."[79] Nevertheless, he decided to give to the SFIO everything he could because the Socialist Party seemed to be interested in defending the French republic. The new naturalization laws approved by the leftist governments allowed him to become a French citizen, giving him a new degree of personal security and an opportunity to show his loyalty to the republic.[80] If the communists, in his opinion, were deserting France in the name of solidarity with the Soviet Union, he would become French; if some of the other nonconformists were turning fascist out of contempt for the socialists' inactivity, he would help the socialists.

Tasca could not hope to have a personal political role in the French socialist party, since its structure relied on the connection between the leaders and voters in their electoral districts.[81] Particularly in the situation of emergency experienced by the French in the second half of the thirties, it would have been impossible for him to assume a direct political responsibility. In fact, even the idea that an Italian could be involved in the decision-making process of the SFIO certainly would have offered propagandistic arguments to the socialists' enemies. In order to be most effective in his work on the pages of *Le Populaire,* Tasca needed to stay above the fray of day-to-day party business. He also adopted a nom de plume that would mask his Italian origins: André Leroux. Under this name, he regularly published foreign policy columns in the newspaper edited by Léon Blum.

Convinced that the ultimate battle against fascism was going to play out in the realm of international relations, Tasca sought to provide accurate information on the key international events of the time. The style that he adopted for these analyses was surprisingly neutral, in a clear effort to separate his personal opinions from the facts. Tasca's moderate tone and thorough analysis did not escape the leadership of the SFIO. The most important recognition of Tasca's work at *Le Populaire* came at the beginning of May 1936. Right after the socialist victory in the elections, Léon Blum told Tasca that he wanted to meet with him to hear his opinion on the formation of the Popular Front government. When Tasca told Blum that he was in favor of a government based on a coalition of all the parties of the left, from the communists to the Radical Party, the socialist leader effusively expressed his appreciation for Tasca's support of his positions.[82] For his part, Tasca had a chance to repeat to Blum his firmest political belief: despite the dangers implicit in a coalition with the communists and the Radicals, a government supported by the socialists was the only escape from a reactionary decline of French politics.[83]

Tasca was convinced that the communists' support for the Popular Front had its roots in the Soviet Union's decision to oppose German foreign policy. His analysis led him to believe that the communists could prove to be unstable allies, ready to change their positions without too many scruples. Nevertheless, he was also convinced that as long as the interests of the

Soviet Union were opposite to the interests of the fascist powers, the communists would support the government, regardless of how moderate its social policy was. Since the policy of the French communists was "weakened and distorted by their subordination to the foreign policy of the Russian state," but in line with the needs of the French and international situations, he wrote, the alliance with them could be maintained.[84] Rather than being a strategic point of view, this perspective was increasingly dictated by Tasca's new political realism.

The PCF's decision not to have ministers in the government led by Blum further reinforced Tasca's distrust. Tasca was convinced that the communists would have preferred a government led by one of the leaders of the Radical Party rather than by a socialist. The reason, Tasca believed, was that a government with a more moderate leadership would have been less threatening to the ideological position of the communists, who could have justified their support simply as a form of antifascism. Under these circumstances, it did not take too long for Tasca to translate his practical anticommunism into a more theoretical position.

Tasca was not a philosopher, but he could not accept the consequences of his discovery of historical materialism's failed predictions without trying to make sense of that failure. Not only had the predicted unification of the world under capitalism not happened, but also rising nationalism had become the most visible characteristic of the capitalist economy. Even the foreign policy of the Soviet Union, which Tasca saw as neither capitalist nor socialist, was dominated by the logic of national interest.[85] Was it possible that national feelings were destined to play a permanent part in international policy? Moreover, how was it possible, Tasca asked himself, that the identification of the proletariat with humanity had not happened?

Tasca's answer to these questions was another major step in abandoning most of his Marxist positions. Marxism, he wrote in 1936, was incomplete. Marx and Engels had abandoned their *German Ideology* project in 1846, after only three years of philosophical work. They claimed that they had finished with philosophy, Tasca wrote, but their results suddenly seemed insufficient to him. This insufficiency, Tasca suggested for the first time, was possibly the reason behind the crisis of socialism.

The main element of Tasca's new critique of Marxism was based on a reconsideration of Marx's "discovery" of the proletariat. In his *Contribution to the Critique of the Philosophy of Right*, Tasca wrote, Marx had been in search of a solution to the problem of the democratic modernization of Germany. This solution, according to Marx, had to be found in a class of bourgeois society that was, at the same time, also the totality of humanity, and so the liberation of this class had to entail the liberation of man. Faced with this problem, Tasca wrote, Marx had used the discovery of the proletariat as a philosophical shortcut that could allow him to affirm both that this class existed and that it was the product of capitalist society itself. Accordingly, Tasca reinterpreted the concept of the proletariat as Marx's philosophical escape from the rigidity of German society, which in 1846 did not show any possibility of change except through a principle so radical as to be the opposite of that society itself.

For Marx, Tasca continued, "the proletariat was one of the propositions of a philosophical syllogism" and its existence needed only to be verified in the real world.[86] Only the actual existence of the proletariat could solve the political problem of the transformation of German society in the framework of Hegelian philosophy. Therefore, Tasca wrote, if the proletariat did not exist "it needed to be invented, since its existence was indispensable to the equilibrium of the system."[87] This was also the key to understanding Marx's prediction of the disappearance of all the classes into the proletariat. Without such a disappearance, the universality necessary in Hegelian philosophy would have been unrealizable in the face of the antinomy of class conflict. Only the transformation of the proletariat into a universal principle allowed Marx to sublate (*dépasser*) the contradictions into a new synthesis.

From this reconstruction of the genesis of the Marxist discovery of the proletariat, Tasca concluded that while Marx had indeed inverted the logic of Hegelian dialectics, it was dialectics itself that needed to be critiqued.[88] Despite its insistence on the primacy of the material world, Marxism, according to Tasca, reintroduced a faith in the teleological movement of history along the lines of a philosophical project. The idea that all contradictions could finally be resolved through a universal that was also a particular seemed to Tasca to be "metaphysics." Thus dialectics, the very element that he had tried to oppose to Stalinist mechanicism, became for Tasca the real reason behind mechanicism itself.

This evolution of Tasca's attitude toward Marxism should not be particularly surprising. His accusation against Stalinism was based on the idea that Stalin was forcing the political movement of history, superimposing his own political projects on the real dialectical movement of history itself. Nevertheless, until 1935 Tasca did not doubt that the future would bring a simplification of the dynamics of capitalism to the point imagined by Stalin in 1929, with revolutionaries on one side and counterrevolutionaries on the other. When these predictions did not come true, however, Tasca felt compelled to abandon what he still had in common with Stalinism: the idea of a moment where the proletariat and the bourgeoisie would face each other in a final struggle for socialism.

His perception of the world of the second half of the 1930s no longer had room for such a simplification. Marx had believed that capitalism would unify the world, melting away all the differences, Tasca commented. Instead, the diffusion of capitalism had created multiple and competing capitalisms, and Lenin already had to update Marxism to accommodate the new reality.[89] For Tasca, the failure of Marxism to explain the persistence of multiple classes in the capitalist world entailed an even more momentous consequence: that the presumed coincidence of the proletariat with all of humanity was not a scientific discovery but rather a product of Marx's faith in the simplifying powers of Hegelian dialectics—and the root cause of the practical and theoretical crisis of socialism.

If capitalism allowed the existence of many different classes, the construction of socialism necessitated the creation of anticapitalist coalitions representative of a broad spectrum of political interests. Tasca's insistence on the need to create such coalitions against fascism thus acquired a fundamental significance. It was no longer only the need to defeat the fascist alliance between the bourgeoisie and the petty bourgeoisie that motivated Tasca, but also the idea that the workers by themselves were not a universal principle. They were merely one of the classes interested in the transformation of capitalist society. Therefore, the Popular Front, as an interclass alliance, was not only a tactical choice in a moment of crisis for the working class but also a permanent strategic requirement for the construction of socialism.

Direct proof of Tasca's theoretical and political investment in the Popular Front is provided by his treatment of the most threatening crisis that Blum's government had to face: the Spanish Civil War. Despite what might have been his personal feelings toward the Spanish republic, in his articles Tasca faithfully supported Blum's decision not to intervene. In an article published in the newspaper of the Italian socialists on November 28, 1936, for instance, Tasca became almost a spokesman for Blum's positions. After attacking Italy and Germany for their intervention in the conflict, and Great Britain for its failure to oppose the fascists' plans, he argued that France should not follow the United Kingdom down the same path. However, he did not ask for direct military intervention by France but rather merely suggested that Spanish republicans should be permitted to buy weapons on French soil.[90] Such a moderate position was particularly significant in light of the decision by many Italian antifascists, including Pietro Nenni, the leader of the Italian Socialist

Party, to go to Spain to fight fascism. The reason for Tasca's moderation, a reason that he did not reveal to his readers, was his desire to ensure the survival of the Popular Front in France.

In Tasca's private analysis, the communists' request that France send airplanes to Spain, in itself completely justified, inevitably would have broken the pact of action between the SFIO and the Radicals, leading immediately to the failure of the Popular Front government that had emerged in the elections of 1936.[91] Such a failure was a risk that Tasca did not want to run, since in his opinion the possibility of defeating fascism rested on the possibility of creating a political alternative in France and on the preservation of liberal democracies in both Great Britain and France. The fear that the Radicals might abandon the coalition if the government acted in the name of ideological solidarity made Tasca stress legality as the only solution to the Spanish conflict. For this reason, in his articles in *Le Populaire* of 1937, he carefully repeated the idea that the international community should limit itself to political pressure on the fascist powers to convince them to abandon Spain. Any militant solution, by contrast, should be discarded in the name of legality itself.[92]

Thus from 1935 to the first half of 1938, the need to support the French Popular Front enhanced Tasca's ideological transformation from a cosmopolitan revolutionary to a French citizen whose commitment was to the needs of the French government more than to international revolution. The realism he applied to foreign policy was still ideologically motivated by his loyalty to socialism, but his ideological position was increasingly pessimistic. In 1937, he said that a socialist transformation of society was possible only in countries characterized by a liberal democratic system. Only the end of the Popular Front and the events of Munich would reopen the question of Tasca's position within the Socialist Party, and even then Tasca remained committed to the idea of a large political coalition within the framework of the French republic.

4 The Road to Vichy

In 1938, while Léon Blum was still trying to salvage the Popular Front, Gallimard published *La naissance du fascisme,* Tasca's historiographical masterpiece.[1] This book sparked a debate on the danger of a fascist seizure of power in France, and its author became the recognized expert on the topic. Suddenly Tasca's opinion was valued across the political spectrum. Many intellectuals and politicians, both from the left and from the right, started to consider Tasca's opinions on fascism as relevant to France. Thanks to this success, Tasca's analyses of the international situation, which appeared daily in the newspaper of the French Socialist Party, were soon acknowledged as the semiofficial positions of Blum's party.

At this point in his career, the Italian seemed to have acquired a solid position both as a socialist theoretician and as a politician, even though this came at the cost of his personal life. His close relationships with many socialist leaders and with the constellation of radical intellectuals known as the nonconformists gave him both political and cultural influence, while he reserved for his diaries his dream of regaining control of his life from the historical drama. During the first eight months of 1939, Tasca tried to use his political and ideological influence to save the French Socialist Party from the deadlock into which factionalism had dragged it. In order to achieve this goal, he organized a meeting of the major leaders of the different socialist positions to discuss a new foundation for the French socialist party. At the same time, he tirelessly wrote articles to convince the French that Hitler must be stopped. The pact between Germany and the Soviet Union, followed by the invasion of Poland and the beginning of World War II, crashed Tasca's hopes.

Between 1938 and 1940 Tasca engaged in the slow process of maturing the ideas that later convinced him to stay in France and collaborate with the Vichy government, and it would be wrong to look for signs of a sudden conversion. Until 1940, however, Tasca was an uncompromising voice in the struggle against fascism. In his analysis, the way to oppose

Hitler was with war, not appeasement. But the French defeat forced Tasca to confront a situation that he had wanted to avoid at all costs.

A. Rossi: The Historian of Fascism

La naissance du fascisme was first published in Czechoslovakia only a few months before the arrival of German troops. Even before the book had reached bookstores, the extreme right started a campaign against its editor. The Italian government seconded the campaign (or possibly even inspired it), and the Italian ambassador in Prague addressed an official protest to the Czechoslovakian authorities. These actions prompted the Czechoslovakian Foreign Ministry to ask the book's editor not to publicize it too much, placing it in the back of bookshop windows and doing everything in his power not to stir up controversy. The editor's response to the ministry was that there was no reason to worry about publicity: more than half of the two thousand copies printed had already been sold, and the book would soon disappear from shop windows altogether. In the end, the Nazis banned the book and destroyed the few unsold copies when they occupied Prague.[2]

In France, Gallimard published the book in 1938, when Léon Blum was facing the failure of his second government and the socialists were trying to decide what to do next. The French editor who had commissioned *La naissance* had been very slow in publishing the book; it had been finished for a year before it appeared in France. Yet the timing of its publication ensured maximum resonance: the crisis of the French Socialist Party was reaching its peak, and the book seemed to offer a diagnosis of the crisis, addressing the worst fears of the French left. *La naissance* was, in fact, a book as much about socialism as about fascism.

Gallimard was the perfect choice to publish Tasca's book, and the Italian never considered any alternative. Gaston Gallimard, founder, owner, and head of the publishing house, was an admirer and personal friend of Léon Blum. He had published Blum's *Souvenir sur l'affaire* in 1935 and, two years later, *Conversations de Goethe avec Eckermann* and *L'exercice du pouvoir.*[3] In 1938, besides Tasca, Gallimard published leftist authors such as Sartre and Jorge Amado, but also rightist authors such as Drieu de La Rochelle, Georges Bernanos, and Marcel Jouhandeau (who had to find another publisher for his *Le péril juif,* but who was already a poster child for militant anti-Semitism).[4] In this context *La naissance,* published alongside Gide's *Retour de l'URSS,* Robert Aron's *La fin de l'après-guerre,* and Bertrand de Jouvenel's *Le réveil de l'Europe,* was brought out by a publisher that was not characterized by ideological intransigency and tried to favor a dialogue across ideological positions. This was exactly what Tasca wanted.

The book itself offered a perspective on fascism that was eccentric compared to the major political and intellectual schools of interpretation. Tasca's complex personal and political life gave him a perspective on the events that distanced him from existing analyses of fascism. Not bound by any specific political orthodoxy, Tasca did not have to use his book for propaganda purposes and could look back at the events he had lived as a political actor with the awareness that he was very different from the person he used to be in the twenties. Yet he could count on his firsthand knowledge of events and protagonists, from Mussolini on down, to provide insights unavailable to scholars who did not have such direct experience.

Tasca chose to publish his book under the nom de plume A. Rossi, which he had used for all his theoretical pieces since his arrival in France. He wanted his book to become a legacy of his activity. In his notebooks, he described his book as his occasion for immortality, playing with the vocabulary of Christian salvation:

> A book is a brain, a consciousness that forces readers into a dialogue, the host that repeats the miracle of incarnation. . . . I don't have any interest in "immortality" when it is meant as "celebrity." But some of the worries and aspirations that were and will always be the joy and pain of my life should not perish with my body.[5]

In order to realize such an ambitious project, he had to shield his book, and himself, from the accusation of being part of the battlefield of everyday politics. Thus Tasca used the Rossi pseudonym to distinguish his work on fascism from the articles that he was publishing in *Le Populaire* under the name of André Leroux, which provided commentaries on current foreign politics.

Another reason to adopt a more scientific outlook stemmed from Tasca's belief that "to define fascism [was] above all to write its history."[6] In this perspective, no ideological shortcut could be used without endangering the heuristic value of his work. Tasca was convinced that an imperfect understanding of fascism would have resulted in a practical advantage for fascism over its opponents. For this reason, starting on the first page of his book, Tasca wanted to state clearly that "explaining" and "reconstructing" were synonyms in historiography, and that he wanted to convince his readers through his account of the events, rather than by mobilizing preexisting ideological sympathies for his point of view.[7]

Tasca's account of the fascist victory in Italy was surprisingly coherent with what he had been saying since he was a young socialist: historical events were the result of human actions and not the outcome of objective, impersonal forces. He firmly believed that even after the failed general strike of August 1922, fascism could have been stopped if somebody—the socialists, the democrats, the Popolari, the king—had made the right decision. His goal was to provide the first full account of the fascist seizure of power, debunking both the traditional Marxist approach, which deterministically emphasized the role of capitalism in the birth of fascism, and the conservative approach, which depicted fascism as a reaction to the threat posed by communism. Recovering the centrality of politics and the concrete political behavior of the participants in the events, Tasca offered a democratic critique of fascism that put at its center the defense of the institutions of liberal democracy, denying legitimacy to any justification for the victory of fascism. If fascism won, Tasca implicitly claimed throughout his book, it was not because it was a natural evolution of capitalism or a medicine against communism, but because fascism's competitors had been unwilling or unable to defend democracy.

Faithful to the idea that the general meaning of an event could be understood only from an analysis of the particular, Tasca's book told the story of the hundreds of instances of terrorist acts, indecision, chance, fearfulness, and ideological confusion that had paved the way for Mussolini's seizure of power. Through this detailed account, Tasca was not only removing fascism from the abstraction of categories such as "capitalism" and returning it to the concreteness of its historical formation but also refuting the idea that fascism represented the resumption of orderly life in Italy. It was true that fascism had restored order, but that was only because it had been responsible for Italy's violence and chaos in the first place. Showing how violence was the main characteristic of fascist politics, Tasca pointed out how unrealistic the idea was that fascism could be used to create or maintain equilibrium in the life of a nation or on the international stage. Fascism, Tasca maintained, could be defeated but not normalized.

Only the ineptitude of the socialist camp, with its revolutionary rhetoric and its political and military weakness, explained why the fascists had managed to present themselves as a solution to the Italian problems. According to Tasca, the revolutionary language of the socialists had scared the bourgeoisie and filled the workers with hope, but the party had not managed to make the revolution a reality. Divided between a right wing that was close to both the trade unions and the socialist parliamentary group, a left wing that was close to the positions of the Third International, and an extreme left that later created the Communist Party, the Italian socialists had been paralyzed by their internal debates. Adhering blindly to their long-standing political formula, they had not noticed that the political situation was changing rapidly. Dogmatic and insincere, they had been incapable of transforming historical reality along the lines of their theory, and when the revolutionary opportunity was over, they had proved unable to transform their theory along the lines of the new historical reality.[8]

Fascism, Tasca argued, took advantage of the gap between theory and praxis that characterized its major opponents. The ideologically eclectic Mussolini was conscious of the tactical limits that principles impose on action and was open to the lessons of political action, always ready to adapt his political program to the circumstances.[9] That was how he was able to bring together different social groups, from the agrarians to the petty bourgeoisie, around generic formulas such as his interpretation of Nietzsche's "will to power."[10] By contrast, the socialists were paralyzed by their empty formulas and could not create a social alliance around the workers' movement.

The socialists' incapacity to create social alliances had resulted in their political isolation at a time when they did not have the strength to create a counterstate. Hence, Tasca wrote, their delegitimation of the dying Italian liberal state had helped the fascists destroy liberal democratic institutions. Perceived as an alien entity by the elements of the state, including the police and the army, the socialist movement had been left impotent in the face of the assault of fascist terrorism. The socialists had always refused to acknowledge that whenever the power of the state had opposed the actions of Mussolini's *squadristi*, the fascists had been quickly defeated. Hence, even when they could count on legal legitimation, as in the case of the numerous socialist city councils that were forced to resign under the menace of fascist violence, the socialists refused to ask for the protection of a state they were supposed to overthrow. The tragic outcomes had been the March on Rome, the theatrical representation of a revolution that could count on the approval of the state, and the defeat of Italian socialism, which was engaged in a verbal battle with the liberal state and the primary victim of its fall.

Tasca's concern for the role of the state in the victory of fascism was central to his book. Legality, he believed, would have killed fascism. Instead, Mussolini's movement prospered in the gray area between illegal insurrectionism and official protection.[11] Antifascists had to try to "neutralize" the state and mobilize its power because "fascism is powerless without the state and even more powerless against the state."[12] Once fascism had conquered the state machine, however, it was too late to defeat it without a massive use of military force.[13] Tasca believed that the victory against fascism could be obtained politically by making sure that the legal use of force was on the side of democracy, but this could happen only if the enemies of fascism were convinced that legality and democracy were worth defending.

In his epilogue, Tasca sought to summarize his findings on the history of the fascist movement in order to discuss its evolution after it conquered the state. Mussolini and Hitler had been capable of transferring the method and even the language of socialist mass politics into the opposite camp. However, the fascist state was the negation of politics, and the constant mobilization of the masses in the totalitarian state was a result of military training, not politics.[14] In this light, the nation itself was a victim of fascism, because the nationalization of the masses that had been initiated by democrats and continued by socialists was incompatible with the fascists' instrumental use of the masses to foster the power of the state.[15] The antifascists, therefore, ought to push forward the process of nationalization of the masses.

War and autarky were the natural outcomes of fascism. The planned economy that the fascist states had implemented functioned to support war and the needs of the fascist bureaucracy, which was the new elite of the fascist state. The fires started by fascism in its effort to destroy socialist organizations were now menacing Europe and the potential new order that, if realized, would have rendered the survival of fascism impossible. Tasca concluded his book by calling socialists to defend the practice and institutions of liberal democracy; he claimed that the coming war would be decided by the ability of ideologies to appeal for public support. "After the deluge," he wrote, "if any country survives, the sun will shine on those who have managed to preserve those foundations of humanity that fascism is trying so hard to destroy forever."[16]

In France, the public response to Tasca's book was exceptional. At the beginning of June 1938, a few months after the publication of *La naissance*, the French socialists held their thirty-fifth congress in Royan. Two months earlier, Léon Blum had resigned, thus ending the run of the Popular Front. In his speech in front of the congress, the former prime minister declared that the Socialist Party should participate in a government only on rare occasions: when there was the possibility of realizing a socialist program, or when freedom was menaced from either inside or outside France. In the latter case, he said, the socialists had a duty to try to "put their hands on parts of the governmental machine, and even more on its totality, for the simple reason of avoiding the seizure of power by other parties."[17] He added: "Many speakers recommended the reading of an admirable book indeed, the book by Rossi on the birth of fascism. The day when we see the history of German social democracy written with the same impartiality and historical precision, we will reach very similar conclusions."[18] Blum was implicitly acknowledging that he had learned the lesson about the need to use the strength of the state to protect democracy from the assaults of fascism.

Blum was not the only European socialist leader who pointed to Tasca's book as the bearer of a valuable message for his party. In Belgium, Émile Vandervelde included the book in his list of ten fundamental books for socialists, and Tasca's analysis would play a role in the internal debate of Henri de Man's party in 1939, when the party had to decide on a course of action.[19] Yet the impact of *La naissance* was even greater outside the world of the socialist parties. Back in France, the May 1, 1938, issue of *Combat* suggested the book to its readers as a manual for antifascists.[20] Marcel Déat, in three different articles—"Avertissement au socialisme," "Les classes moyennes et le fascisme," and "La leçon italienne"—pointed to the similarities between what had happened in Italy and what was happening in France, concluding that fascism was currently a risk for French society. Charles Maurras wrote an article in *L'Action Française*, and Pierre Drieu de La Rochelle, in the pages of *L'Emancipation Nationale*, used Tasca's work to affirm that in Italy socialism had proved its spiritual vacuity and the emasculatory effects of Marxism.[21]

From the socialist left to the fascist right, the French-speaking political world reacted to Tasca's book. In particular, the nonconformist left around *Esprit* and *Les Nouveaux Cahiers* were attracted by *La naissance*'s dissatisfaction with the traditional formulas of socialist politics. Tasca's analysis, a critique of the politics of socialist parties that did not break with socialism as such, was perceived as akin to the political program of the people around Emmanuel Mounier, Denis de Rougemont, and Boris Souvarine. Tasca's relationship with these ideas and people played a central part in his political life at the end of the 1930s.

Special Networks

At the beginning of 1938, Emmanuel Mounier wrote a postcard to Angelo Tasca asking him to send the epilogue of *La naissance* for publication in *Esprit*.[22] Tasca declared that he would be happy to see that portion of his book published in *Esprit*, but that Mounier needed to contact Gallimard for authorization. This proved to be more difficult than expected, and Tasca's epilogue never appeared in *Esprit*. However, these contacts produced an article on the dictatorship of the proletariat that the Italian published under the name A. Rossi at the end of 1938.

This article, although not particularly important in Tasca's production, marked the apex of a dialogue that Tasca had started around the time Mounier put out the first issue of his journal. Since 1933, in fact, Tasca and

Mounier had been intermittently in contact. When he was still working at *Monde,* Tasca had written a review of Mounier's new journal. Mounier had replied with a note in which he remarked on the differences between them, but also on the possibility of being fellow travelers in French politics. "It is for us characteristic," Mounier wrote to Tasca, "that you have understood the complete novelty of our positions and the possibilities of a collaboration on the ground of future actions."[23]

Despite this promising start, the distance between the Catholic intellectuals around *Esprit* and Tasca always proved difficult to bridge completely, mostly because of the different attitudes the two sides held toward the Catholic Church. Jacques Madaule, who wrote the review of *La naissance* for *Esprit,* acknowledged that the book was the best history ever written of Italy between 1918 and 1922 and pointed out that, despite the dangers implicit in making comparisons, the situation Tasca described for Italy during that period seemed to be similar to the situation in France at the end of the 1930s. Yet he believed that Tasca had not been completely fair in his treatment of the Partito Popolare and its leader, Luigi Sturzo.[24] He also remarked that he disagreed with Tasca's interpretation of the Vatican's policy, putting the word "policy" in quotation marks in order to underline his doubts about the legitimacy of Tasca's decision to consider the Vatican as an entity engaged in "politics."[25] Tasca's secularism was clearly an obstacle to full cooperation between him and the Catholic intellectuals at *Esprit,* but the political and intellectual climate at the end of the 1930s favored a dialogue between them in the name of antifascism.[26]

Despite the success of his book, Tasca was becoming increasingly dissatisfied with his intellectual and political life. He complained in his diary about the isolation he felt at *Le Populaire*: "All my articles are the result of a double dialogue: between me and the events, between me and my conscience. [My isolation] is a privilege, sometimes hard to bear."[27] He talked to Blum about his sense of impotence: "It has been a long time since I started feeling a malaise, which sometimes becomes anguish, before my inability to exercise a direct influence on the events."[28] His ability to foresee the course of certain events, he told Blum, had been useless because of his isolation. Moreover, he was becoming unhappy about his relations with the French Socialist Party because he thought it was impossible for him to contribute to its internal debate: only the members of recognized factions had access to the public tribunes of the SFIO, he claimed, and he was not associated with any specific faction.[29]

Tasca's desire for a more active political role in France was thwarted by his status as a recently naturalized citizen. As Tony Judt remarked in his study on the reconstruction of the Socialist Party in the 1920s, some of the socialist federations had a tradition of chauvinism to the point of localism.[30] Tasca, who could not count on personal relations with the local militants of any socialist federation, was necessarily disadvantaged in any attempt to gain influence inside the party. His isolation, which was, as he noted, the condition of his autonomy, meant that he represented only himself in the internal party debates, and the only authority he had came from his fame and work as an intellectual.

Moreover, his personal relationship with Léon Blum, built through his work at *Le Populaire*, was more an impediment than an advantage for Tasca. At a time when the conflict between Blum and Paul Faure, the secretary of the Socialist Party, was bringing the French socialists to the verge of a new split, Tasca's role as an intellectual close to Blum made Faure's faction suspicious of him.[31] As Tasca noted, the intense polarization within the SFIO left no space for an independent figure in the party. So even though Tasca would have much preferred to be the leader of his own group rather than a member of Blum's faction, any possibility that he might have an active voice in French politics was conditional, at least temporarily, on his connections to Blum and Blum's supporters.

Besides, even if Tasca had managed to overcome the problems he had as a newcomer in the SFIO, the hypernationalist French right was certainly not likely to forget that he had only recently acquired French citizenship, and they would be only too eager to use this against him. As soon as his analyses of the international scene took center stage in the French political debate, the journals of the extreme right were in fact quick to bring up his Italian birth as an argument against him. As the fascists who wrote for *Gringoire* remarked, it was useless for Tasca to hide behind pseudonyms: they knew who he was and they knew that he had been an Italian citizen until recently, so he did not have the authority to give advice to the French.[32] Tasca was very well aware that his influence depended on his ability to shelter himself behind French public figures, who could have the visibility that his birth and his past denied to him.

Facing these insurmountable problems, Tasca thought that he needed to change his life and "make a choice, make a decision between two very different roads."[33] He could either go on with the life he had conducted in the past two years, which he felt was becoming unbearable, or he could step back from his life as a militant to write the three books he desperately wanted to write. If he had been able to choose freely, he believed, he would have embraced the life of a scholar, leaving active politics and its problems behind.

How to support himself in the process, though, was not clear to him. If the government or the Socialist Party provided him with money, he would lose his independence.[34] Besides, many people depended on his financial help: his mother, his son and daughters, the Italian political refugees he was helping, and others he did not mention.[35] There was the possibility of winning the lottery—he always bought a ticket to leave some room for a stroke of luck—but if that did not happen, he still wanted to make a decision by the end of the summer of 1938.[36] If the speed of events had not prevented him from making a free choice, it is possible that Tasca would have pursued his wish to be a scholar.

Tasca's role in the Socialist Party was, as he said, more the result of his sense of responsibility, both personal and public, than an accurate representation of his political and cultural identity. Most of his ideas were connected to leftist groups that had no party affiliation in France at the end of the thirties. Some of his closest friends, such as Boris Souvarine[37] and Lucien Laurat,[38] were engaged in the usual activities of the extreme left: publishing journals critical of the existing parties and creating groups of militant intellectuals around these journals. That was what Tasca had done at *Monde* and, earlier in his life, at *L'Ordine Nuovo*. Through Pontigny Abbey, where Souvarine and Laurat's journal, *Les Nouveaux Cahiers*, organized some of its activities, Tasca was keeping his contacts and his influence in this world.

It was a relatively small world, characterized by intellectuals with inexhaustible energy and strong personal solidarity. *Les Nouveaux Cahiers* was born as a socialist version of *Esprit*, and as Daniel Villey told readers in his piece on the new journal, many of the people who wrote for *Les Nouveaux Cahiers* were also regular contributors to the pages of *Esprit*.[39] Some of these intellectuals, including Tasca, Souvarine, and Laurat, were ex-communists; some, such as Jacques Maritain, a regular contributor to *Les Nouveaux Cahiers*, were coming from the right. Many, such as Tasca, Laurat, and Denis de Rougemont, were expatriates who had adopted France as their homeland; most of them, from Gaston Bergery and his *La Flèche* to Mounier, Tasca, and de Rougemont, were supporters of a European federation. All of them were convinced that factionalism was destroying France and that their role was to overcome the divisions of party politics in order to help find the best possible solution to concrete problems through open discussion. Some of them, such as Simone Weil, another regular contributor to *Les Nouveaux Cahiers*, successfully started discussions with the opposite side, as Weil did in the letters she exchanged with Georges Bernanos. Henri de Man and his *planisme* had influenced many. Tasca, despite his affiliation with the

Socialist Party, was more aligned with these nonconformists than with the politics of the SFIO.

Even his personal life drove him in the direction of complete identification with the world that gravitated around the Pontigny abbey and its eclectic intellectuals. He fell in love with Liliane Chomette-Fernandez, a fervent Catholic who was married to Ramon Fernandez and who was studying under the direct supervision of Paul Desjardins.[40] When Chomette's marriage came apart, she began a romantic relationship with Tasca, who abandoned his plans to live outside Paris in order to stay as close as possible to her.[41] After the debacle of his first marriage, Tasca wanted to start a new life and clearly did not wish it to fall victim to political circumstances, as had happened with his first wife. Aside from the role Tasca's new love story might have played in his unhappiness with life in the Socialist Party, it is clear that Tasca was feeling the pressure of the differences between his intellectual and political lives.

Other events were also conspiring to encourage Tasca to collaborate even more with intellectuals outside the traditional world of Marxism and socialism. In Belgium, Henri de Man's ideas inspired a collaboration between Catholics and socialists.[42] Because Tasca recognized that in Italy the inability to collaborate had doomed the Catholic party and the socialists, it was an obvious step for Tasca to look at a possible collaboration between these two traditions as a "third way" between the Soviet Union and fascist Italy and Germany. At a time when a political and social revolution seemed to be more of a necessity than a political goal, it was imperative to find practical solutions to the problems involved in constructing a new state and a new economy. As Tasca had written many times, it was not enough to find concrete solutions for the problems of the day; it was also important to find timely solutions to win the race against fascism.

Tasca's desire to find alternative answers to the problems posed by fascism was shared by many other nonconformists who, equally influenced by de Man, were considering how to reform the state.[43] In fact, the same concern that Tasca had for the fascist and Stalinist challenges to liberal democratic societies was already creating the premises for conclusions that, later on, provided a fertile ground for the Vichy experiment. For instance, in the same issue of *Esprit* in which Tasca published his article on the dictatorship of the proletariat, Mounier was asking if something was valid in the formula "an antifascist fascism," created by Pierre-Aimé Touchard in the pages of the fascist journal *Voltigeur*.[44] The answer was that it was unacceptable to create a French fascist regime in order to defeat foreign fascism, as Touchard wanted. Yet, Mounier added, something should be retained of this idea if it offered the possibility of conducting a determined fight against totalitarianism, as the word *antifascist* suggested, while at the same time learning what fascism could teach them about the importance of concrete issues, such as the rapprochement of the proletariat with the middle classes, the revolutionary unity of the nation, and the reconciliation of the safety of the nation with the will to reform its system.

Paradoxically, Mounier's idea of accepting in some respects the challenge of learning from fascism was not a sign that his antifascism was weak. The real debate between intransigents (among them Tasca) and more moderate antifascists was about the significance of the new Munich agreement. Whereas *Esprit* denounced the agreement as a betrayal of antifascism, *Les Nouveaux Cahiers* took the road of a radical pacifism and in the articles written by Simone Weil urged France to appease Germany.[45] Maritain, Souvarine, Laurat, the French philosopher Alain, and many others signed a manifesto against the war, which they published in the pages of the journal.[46] Auguste Detoeuf told the readers of *Les Nouveaux Cahiers* that there were so many other injustices in the world that it was preposterous to say that a war should be started to prevent an injustice against the Czechs.[47]

Tasca, who completely supported a war against Germany, had to start an ideological fight with some of his close friends to debunk their pacifism. For this reason, he believed that an independent socialist voice was required to continue the dialogue with nonsocialist leftists. Thus at the beginning of 1939, under the editorship of Georges Monnet, Tasca and other socialists who shared this project launched a new journal, which absorbed Tasca's energies until the beginning of the war. This journal, titled *Agir*, involved some of the most prominent figures of the SFIO who were opposing the policy of appeasement. Tasca's participation in this new enterprise marked a new attempt to reform the SFIO from inside.

Another Journal: *Agir*

At the end of the summer of 1938, when Tasca wanted to retire from active political life to pursue his research, the crisis over Czechoslovakia rocked the already chaotic world of European international relations. On September 12, Hitler declared that he could no longer tolerate Czechoslovak control over the large German-speaking population in the Sudetenland. Ten days later, in a meeting at Bad Godesberg, the Nazi dictator gave Chamberlain an ultimatum: the Sudetenland had to be turned over to Germany on September 28. On September 25, the French prime minister, Edouard Daladier, went to London to discuss with his British counterpart the possibility of joint action, while the Radicals in his government coalition sought to pressure him to avoid a military confrontation with Germany. Yet Daladier was resolute in refusing Hitler's ultimatum as long as he had British support. Hitler's decision to participate in an international conference on Czechoslovakia prevented Daladier from rejecting publicly the Nazi blackmail and forced France to fall back on the British policy of appeasement. The Munich conference, held on September 29, signaled a spectacular Nazi victory and the beginning of the end of Czechoslovakia. However, when Daladier went back to France, he found a cheering crowd at the airport, saluting him as the savior of peace.

The general political climate in France was in favor of appeasement. In some newspapers, relief over the agreement was expressed as cries of joy. In *Paris Soir*, for instance, Jean Prouvost commented on the Munich agreements with these words: "Peace. Peace. Peace . . . The world breathes. We are still going to live."[48] The day after the Munich conference, Léon Blum wrote in the pages of *Le Populaire* that "there is no woman, no man in France who can refuse a just tribute of gratitude to Mr. Neville Chamberlain and to Mr. Edouard Daladier."[49] With the exception of the communists, the left of the SFIO, and a few rebels in all the other groups, the French parties found an unsuspected unity in the name of the refusal of war.[50] In the parliament, the ratification of the agreement received 535 votes; the 75 opponents were almost exclusively communists.[51]

Tasca and his friends, who were against the Munich agreements, found themselves isolated and preoccupied. On October 10, two days after the parliament granted exceptional new powers to Daladier (with the socialists abstaining from the vote), Georges Monnet went to visit Angelo Tasca. Monnet, who had been minister of agriculture in three Popular Front governments, had known Tasca since the early 1930s when, for a brief time, he had held the majority share in *Monde*.[52] As we saw, Monnet's decision to leave to Barbusse the administration of the journal had triggered the crisis of the old editorial staff of *Monde* and provoked the resignations of Laurat and Tasca. Faithful to Blum and his governmental experience, Monnet had been always committed to the unity of the socialist party, and at the congress of Royan he had tried to promote a motion encouraging synthesis among the various divisions within the French socialist party. As Bruce Graham writes, Monnet saw himself as the person in charge of restoring the party's freedom of thought in the face of the intellectual immobility generated by the division in organized tendencies.[53] Thus, Monnet, who was in constant dialogue with Tasca, shared with him the idea that the factional divisions of the SFIO were responsible for the end of a real debate within the party. Like large areas of the nonconformist left, he considered this situation potentially devastating for French democracy.

During the meeting Monnet and Tasca had in the fall of 1938, the socialist leader asked the Italian what he thought of the present situation and what he believed could be done. Tasca's answer was that for the international situation it was too early to say, as many elements depended on Stalin's decisions and on the evolution of the Spanish situation. Yet if he simply had to describe the present, he would have said that they were "submerged by ruins."[54] The outlook was slightly better for Great Britain, where the civic conscience did not allow for defeatism à la Flandin.[55] In France, however, the economic and financial crisis was bringing the country to impotence, while the French elite, simply inadequate to its historical task, lacked the necessary solutions. "The country," Tasca told Monnet, "lives under the permanent blackmail [*chantage*] of civil war and 30 or 40 billion [francs] in annual debt."[56]

The problem he saw and the solution he imagined prefigured Tasca's position in favor of Pétain's regime in the summer of 1940:

> A kind of very large *union nationale*, with very specific goals: get out of the mess, give back a scope [*ressort*] to the country, do not allow an increase in the gap between democracies and totalitarian countries. Gain a productivity [*rendement*] analogous, or bigger if possible, [to that of the totalitarian states] without sacrificing the essential of our political freedom.[57]

The feeling that France was on the verge of an irreversible crisis had convinced Tasca that new, exceptional measures were needed. He thought the situation called for a unity that encompassed the nation as a whole. The threat posed by an external enemy capable of endangering the existence of the French political space required a collective reaction by the French. If the political parties were responsible for bringing the nation to the verge of civil war, and if class warfare had left France teetering on the edge of bankruptcy, Tasca's solution was to re create the national unity necessary to preserve a common political space. Such a unity, Tasca said, could also be worth the sacrifice of some political freedom—the "unessential" part—because the alternative was to lose the battle with totalitarianism and all liberty with it.

In this perspective, the Socialist Party was an important tool, but still only a tool. "Either the socialist party takes this road decidedly," Tasca told Monnet, "or I do not see what else we can do with it."[58] At the same time, though, addressing Monnet's doubts, Tasca conceded that there was no space for a new party, especially because he believed it was possible to win the struggle in the SFIO. What they needed was support from Léon Blum and neutrality on the part of Paul Faure in order to avoid a new division within the party. If those who were for peace at any price wanted the end of Daladier's cabinet and desired political instability, the socialists' goal, Tasca said at the end of his discussion with Monnet, had to be exactly the opposite.

Monnet asked Tasca to write a motion reflecting his ideas and then went directly to talk to Blum about the matter. However, the conversation between Blum and Monnet did not produce the effects that Tasca desired. According to what Tasca wrote in his diary, Monnet called him on the phone the same night and told him that Blum agreed with their positions but was skeptical about the possibility of leading the Socialist Party in that direction. It would have been impossible, Blum supposedly told Monnet, to maintain the support of the masses with a project so radically different from that of May 1936.[59] Thus when Tasca saw Blum again at the beginning of November 1938, the plan that Tasca had elaborated with Monnet was not even part of their conversation.

Without Blum's support, Tasca put his plans on hold for a few months. In a series of meetings from the eleventh to the twenty-fifth of October 1938, the SFIO defined more precisely its position in the face of the Munich agreements. Despite their efforts, though, the division between Blum's supporters and Faure's partisans could not be completely healed. Blum and his friends believed in a military alliance with the Soviet Union against the fascist threat, whereas the Faurists were convinced that peaceful cohabitation with the totalitarian countries was possible. The disagreement on policy was also a disagreement on the causes of Europe's instability. Blum thought that the danger for peace came from the military and ideological activism of the fascist countries; Faure blamed it on the unstable and unjust order imposed at Versailles. Blum promoted a military alliance to fight fascism, whereas Faure believed that an international conference could be enough to create a new international order.

The question of a unitary socialist foreign policy became the center of a new socialist congress held at Montrouge from Christmas Eve to December 26, dates that clearly suggested the urgency of the situation. For the first time, Blum directly entered the congressional arena with his own motion. Paul Faure did the same with a resolution under his name. Both leaders were convinced that a clarification was needed and that the time for temporary compromises was over. The result, after the failure of the final attempts to draft a common position, was a victory for Blum, who held an absolute majority of the votes. Despite this clear victory, this solution did not end the feud within the Socialist Party, and the dispute continued in socialist publications. The party, divided on an issue as crucial as foreign policy on the eve of a new world conflict, was mostly occupied with an internal ideological war.

The socialists close to Paul Faure used *Pays Socialiste*, a paper they fully controlled, to promote their positions as an organized minority. Blum's supporters were not organized as a faction and did not have their own paper. *Le Populaire*, being the official organ of the party, could not serve the Blumists without further escalating the internal conflicts and depriving the party of a single voice. If the supporters of the war against Germany wanted to make their ideas more widely known, they needed their own publication to balance *Pays Socialiste*.

This situation put Tasca, who had skillfully cultivated his authority as an expert of foreign politics, in a difficult position. As a very outspoken supporter of the war against Germany, he could either risk being one of those responsible for a fracture of the Socialist Party on the eve of a major confrontation with fascism or try to preserve the unity of the party at the risk of condemning the French socialists to impotence in the face of the approaching war. Having learned from his previous experiences both in Italy and in France, Tasca tried, for once, to play by the rules imposed by party politics.

Tasca's first move was simply intended not to exacerbate the conflict. Instead of using his daily column in *Le Populaire* to advocate his position, Tasca wrote an article on the less sensitive subject of the Spanish Civil War and then ended his collaboration with the newspaper.[60] It was clear to him that using the party newspaper to give voice to the positions of the majority would have exasperated the minority.[61] Instead, a new journal founded by Monnet provided Tasca the space to publicize his plans. The new publication, titled *Agir pour la Paix, Agir pour le Socialisme*, became the voice of those who shared Monnet's commitment to the results of the Montrouge congress, while the Faurists were trying to ignore in practice what had been decided in theory. A solution to preserve the unity of the party was still needed, but Tasca was convinced that if reconciliation was at all possible, it would only be found far from the public pressure of the militants, in a place like Pontigny Abbey. Thus, Tasca tried to pursue a twofold tactic: in public, he presented his ideas uncompromisingly; in private, he looked for a compromise that could guarantee both sides that their ultimate goals were part of the Socialists' strategy.

The group that gathered around *Agir* was perfect to wage the public struggle of ideas against the pacifists in the SFIO. It included many prestigious socialists besides Monnet. Among the ten members of the editorial board were Léo Lagrange, who had been the popular vice minister for sport and leisure in the first Blum government; Pierre Viénot, who had been vice minister for foreign affairs in the first Blum government and would be one of the four deputies to be arrested in the *Massilia* affair;[62] Pierre Brossolette, a future organizer of the Resistance; Daniel Mayer, who had been a key player in the struggle against Marcel Déat and who would be responsible for the publication of the clandestine edition of *Le Populaire* in occupied France;[63] Georges Bouhey-Allex, the only socialist who voted against the Munich agreements; and Georges Izard, the cofounder of *Esprit* and a longtime political partner of Emmanuel Mounier.

Izard was a particularly significant presence. A leftist Catholic in search of an alternative between capitalism and communism, Izard had joined Gaston Bergery in 1934 in the attempt to create a new "third force" party; within that founding group, Bergery was the expert in foreign policy, Jules Roman was the economist, and he was the political philosopher. Until 1937, when he joined the SFIO, he had regularly contributed to *La Flèche*, Bergery's journal, providing a link between the Catholics at *Esprit* and the nonorthodox socialists around Bergery. His presence on the editorial board of *Agir* guaranteed the nonconformist nature of the new publication and its openness to contribution from different cultural worlds. Tasca and Izard connected the new journal to intellectuals and politicians who were not associated with the Socialist Party but who were committed to resisting fascism.

Tasca, even though he did not figure among the French socialist leaders who were part of the editorial board, played a key role in *Agir*. From February 1939 until the last issue of the journal in August of that year, Tasca regularly contributed to the pages of the biweekly publication, with articles on foreign politics and on the ideological foundations of socialism. Monnet was clearly the leader of the group, but Tasca had the role of providing a coherent ideological line for the journal and, more important at the time, that of discussing foreign policy issues from a socialist perspective.

Determining the course of French foreign policy was obviously an urgent matter, and *Agir* immediately entered the political fray with the goal of preparing France both economically and politically for the confrontation with Germany. The editorials presented the journal as the expression of the most strenuous defenders of the cultural and political heritage of the Popular Front. As a group, they had a clear leftist characterization, and their adversaries were mostly concentrated at their right. The targets of Agir's polemics were, in increasing order of importance, the right wing of the Socialist Party and its pacifism, the Radicals who were attacking the social gains achieved by the workers in the Popular Front years, and the anticommunists and the anti-Semites who were facilitating the fascist propaganda in France. The communists were also harshly criticized, but only insofar as they were not conducting a coherent antifascist struggle.[64] In other words, *Agir* presented itself as ideologically very similar to all the journals for which Tasca had worked during his life.

In the first issue, Tasca wrote a piece in remembrance of Émile Vandervelde, the Belgian socialist leader who had recently passed away, describing him as a hero of the positions held by *Agir*. The Italian mourned the former member of the Second International as a socialist who had opposed the identification between socialism and statism, an internationalist who had opposed the nationalist tendencies of de Man and others, an antifascist who had always opposed the recognition of Franco's government, and a partisan of the alliance between the Soviet Union and democracies against fascism.[65] As he would do in many other articles, which he always signed with the name André Leroux, Tasca tried to provide the group with a number of "noble fathers," from Jaurés to Marx, Proudhon to Vandervelde. Tasca, with an unusual ideological eclecticism and without the polemical edge of his previous years, seemed to be devoting his energy to the purpose of building bridges with adversaries who could be won over to his cause. Tasca was ready to offer his ideological blessing to anyone ready to join the fight against the fascists.

In the political climate of early 1939, Tasca's main task was to convince reluctant socialist militants that the imminent war was not simply another clash of imperialist nations. The Leninist analysis of World War I as an internal affair of the bourgeoisie could not be easily forgotten by the European left, and pacifism could be understood as the most radical position in the face of the oncoming conflict. In an article titled "Pacifisme bourgeois, imperialisme fasciste," Tasca, who had been a pacifist on the eve of World War I, claimed that this time the capitalists were consistently behind pacifism because of their sympathy for fascism. To fight for peace, he wrote, required a fight against fascism and against the profascist sympathies of the bourgeoisie.[66] The lesson of the previous conflict had to be unlearned if the socialist movement wanted to be faithful to its goals.

In a related article, Tasca also tried to debunk the claim that the instability of Europe derived from the unfair division of raw materials and space created by the Versailles Treaty, a central complaint raised by fascist revanchists. Tasca pointed out that the distribution of raw materials had not substantially changed from the first decades of the century, when Germany became an economic superpower. The only real economic difference between past and present derived from political reasons, not economic ones. Autarky, in fact, had been specifically designed to prepare Italy and Germany for war, revealing the intrinsically aggressive nature of fascism. The sole hope for peace involved putting military pressure on the fascist countries to force them to accept compromises and disarmament, as well as opposing fascism's imperial designs via the project of a total reorganization of Europe and the creation of a United States of Europe. While he thought a *union nationale* should govern France, pursuing this internationalist strategy would ensure that it would not transform into a nationalist *union sacrée*.[67]

Tasca's articles on foreign policy were a direct rebuttal to Faure and his friends, but they were also crafted to appeal to antifascists inside and outside the Socialist Party. In fact, the idea that the threat of war was the only way to force fascism to accept a compromise with the democratic countries had been Gaston Bergery's trademark since 1936, when Izard was still with Bergery and not yet with *Agir*. In many articles written in *La Flèche*, Bergery had claimed that if the democratic countries had been able to say no to the fascist blackmail on specific points, thus showing that they were ready to go to war, the fascists would have agreed to a discussion on the reorganization of Europe. This stop to the fascists' demands should also have been accompanied by a specific plan to reorganize the European economies on a continental basis, thus offering an honorable peace to Italy and Germany.[68] The Munich agreements had reinforced the former Radical deputy's positions, and he had been one of the few voices in France denouncing the pacts with Nazi Germany as a new step toward a European war.[69] After being temporarily separated when they had left *Monde* some years before, Tasca and Bergery were now renewing their dialogue and trying to assert their hegemony over the analysis of fascism.

Among the intransigent supporters of a military confrontation with Hitler, debate revolved around a single major obstacle: the alliance with the Communist Party and, at the international level, the Soviet Union. Bergery was against any alliance with the communists because he believed they belonged to the field of totalitarian powers rather than to the one occupied by the democratic countries.[70] On the contrary, *Agir* denounced this rabid anticommunism as an objective help to a fascist hegemony in France. Mounier's *Esprit* agreed with *Agir* and disagreed with Bergery. Bernard Serampuy (alias François Goguel) wrote in *Esprit* that on the subject of foreign policy, it was pointless "to insist on how close it [*La Flèche*'s program] is to the program of *Esprit*" because the only disagreement was on the subject of the tactical alliance with the communists, which *Esprit* supported and Bergery rejected.[71] After August 1939 and the alliance between Germany and the Soviet Union, Bergery's position emerged victorious, enhancing his personal prestige.

The point of view held by Tasca as well as by *Esprit* was predicated on the assumption, which still seemed logical after Munich, that the Soviet Union and the communist parties were willing to participate in an antifascist coalition. Only a few months later, however, the pact between the Soviet Union and Germany forced a revision of that assumption, depriving Tasca and Bergery of a major reason to dissent. By then, Bergery's notion of totalitarianism had won the battle against Tasca's idea of an antifascist alliance.

Even before this further convergence, which was destined to play a major role in Tasca's ideological evolution, *Agir* and *La Flèche* shared another idea that, in retrospect, was destined to influence Tasca: the idea that the authority of the French state had been severely diminished and needed to be restored. When he was still writing for Bergery's journal, Izard had attacked the Popular Front government for its inability to secure the power of the state. The partisans of a strong state, the Catholic intellectual said, were usually enemies of democracy, whereas the democrats never had the courage to use the state to support their convictions. Only a "democratic Richelieu" could found a true democracy, he concluded, because the authority of the state was the condition of citizens' freedom.[72] Bergery had insisted on this point, declaring that the occupation of factories during the Popular Front governments had been an illegal act that weakened the authority of the state. By breaking the law, the workers had scored a sectional victory against legality and therefore had attacked freedom.[73] Tasca, as he had clearly expressed in his book *La naissance*, was sensitive to Bergery's arguments because legality was the most effective defense against fascist violence and propaganda.

On the pages of *Agir*, Georges Monnet showed that he had been listening to Tasca. In an article on the first year of the Daladier government, the socialist leader declared that the French prime minister had put democracy in danger, breaking the spirit needed to defend it through its weak foreign policy. Yet he had to admit that public opinion recognized some merits to Daladier, above all the fact that the government had managed to stop the wave of strikes that had started with the Blum government. The French proletariat, according to Monnet, had systematically ignored all calls to stop the strikes, whether such appeals were addressed to their rationality, their sense of national interest, or even to their class interest, thereby proving the proletariat's political immaturity.[74] If Daladier was weakening democracy with his foreign policy, he had also restored legality on the internal front, albeit in a way that Monnet did not approve of.

Coming from Monnet, who had been an important minister in the Blum governments, and who was probably the politician closest to the former prime minister, this was an important admission. Even more important were the reasons behind such a critical reconsideration of the Blum experience. Certainly the socialists in the government had always been uncomfortable with the unplanned wave of strikes of the late 1930s. However, in his bitter assessment of the immaturity of the French proletariat, Monnet was making the more radical argument that the interest of the nation did not necessarily coincide with that of the proletariat, who might behave irrationally to the point of hurting both its own interest and that of the general population. Such a consideration was well in line with the Jacobin tradition but hardly related to Marxist socialism.

This connection is certainly not a surprise in the tradition of French socialism. Léon Blum had constantly presented himself as the heir of Jaurès, whose sympathies for Jacobinism, widely shared by the rest of the Socialist Party, were clearly visible in his history of the French Revolution. What is much less obvious is that in the tragic months before the beginning of World War II, the traditional Jacobin reflex that had led the French socialists to the defense of the republic was narrowing the distance between some of the leaders of the SFIO and those "heretics of the left" who were looking for an alternative to Marxist socialism. Thanks to figures such as Tasca, some of the ideas formulated in the context of the nonconformist journals were recirculated in the Socialist Party. A journal such as *Agir*, which was born at the boundary between the two worlds, provided a space where the traditional themes of the nonconformists offered new theoretical ground for the SFIO. Thus the idea of a corporative antisectionalism, capable of restoring the authority of the state without enlarging its powers of intervention, and the idea of a European union were incorporated into the language of the most important French party.

The role that nonconformist ideas could play in the Socialist Party became even clearer after the new congress held by the SFIO in Nantes at the end of May. *Agir* sided with Blum and the other leaders of the majority that had emerged at Montrouge. However, when the new congress showed a persistent and deep division between the Faurists and the Blumists, making it clear that neither a consensual separation nor a peaceful cohabitation would be possible, Tasca tried to break the deadlock.[75]

In the opening piece he wrote in *Agir* right after the congress, for the June 15 issue, Tasca made the usual indictment of the division of the Socialist Party into "clans." He pointed to the fact that when such divisions became permanent, they led to infantile extremism. As proved by what had happened in Italy, this situation only led to leftist or rightist errors, paralyzing the party in moments of crisis. Instead, the Socialist Party needed to be able to change its strategy, and even its theoretical assumptions, in the face of changing circumstances. A new initiative, he hinted, was required to shake the SFIO from its immobility.[76]

What initiative Tasca and the group of *Agir* had in mind was revealed twenty days later by *L'Ordre*, a journal where radical and socialist intellectuals, among them Julien Benda, published articles in support of a strong antifascist politics.[77] In the pages of that publication, André Stibio announced that the socialist leaders had agreed to go to Pontigny Abbey in September for a ten-day seminar to attempt to resolve the doctrinal crisis of French socialism. Paul Faure had affirmed in his speech at the congress in Nantes that the nationalization of the means of production was in need of reconsideration. Georges Izard, in the pages of *Agir*, had started a revision of the entire theoretical basis of socialism. According to the preliminary plans for the September seminar, Lucien Laurat and A. Rossi, representing their respective groups, would be in charge of the meeting; their responsibility would be to keep the discussion focused on theory. Léon Blum and Georges Monnet had already promised to attend.[78]

Tasca's dream of overcoming the internal divisions of the Socialist Party was destined to fail, however. The beginning of the war forced him to cancel the Pontigny meeting after everything had already been planned. However, the agenda for the meeting offers invaluable insight on the direction that Tasca wanted to give to the internal debate of the SFIO.

In August, references to the meeting in Pontigny, which was to be held between the eighteenth and twenty-eighth of September 1939, started to appear in the socialist newspapers and journals. Jean Lebas, who had been minister of labor in the first Blum government and minister of communications in the Chautemps government and in the second Blum government, conveyed the news of the meeting to the militants in an article in *Le Populaire*.[79] Adrien Brill, in *La Flèche*, said with some irony that the socialists were doing in 1939 what Bergery and his group had done in 1933. However, he added, it was better late than never. Besides, the organizers, Laurat and

Rossi, were men who were capable of distancing themselves from sectionalism, and this gave the initiative some chance of success.[80]

It was not surprising that Laurat and Tasca had chosen the Pontigny abbey for the meeting. As we have seen in the previous chapter, Paul Desjardins wanted to create fraternal communities that transcended confessional and political divisions.[81] Moreover, toward this end, Desjardins had devised very strict rules for his Décades, which Tasca and Laurat could apply to their initiative without taking responsibility for imposing them. The participants were invited, rather than elected as delegates by the socialist militants, and therefore they did not have to represent specific groups. The debate would not be publicized, at least while it was taking place, to ensure that participants felt no pressure from their political and electoral base. No observers were invited, and the press—socialist, independent, or otherwise—was particularly unwelcome. Consequently, the choice of Pontigny offered Tasca and Laurat the opportunity to orient the debate along the lines of their primary goals, organizing what appeared to be an informal congress of the SFIO outside the bylaws of the party.

The purpose of the Pontigny initiative was very ambitious. In writing the program for the meeting, Tasca and Laurat highlighted the need for a revision of the socialist doctrine in light of the transformation of European society after World War I. If nineteenth-century socialism was the product of Marx and Engels's analysis of the effects of the industrial revolution, they wrote, twentieth-century socialism could not survive without an effort to understand the new characteristics of capitalist Europe, shaped by World War I, the Soviet revolution, and the birth of fascism. Only an organic elaboration of new theoretical instruments of analysis, they concluded, could save socialism and the SFIO from the crisis it was living.[82]

The ten-day seminar to reform socialism was organized around a series of presentations that would provide the thread for the discussion. Tasca would have introduced the first day with a presentation on the relation between socialism and democracy in the socialist tradition and doctrine. Charles Spinasse—the inventor of the forty-hour week, who had then joined the ranks of the pacifists—was scheduled to speak on the second day, with a presentation on new economic trends. The third and the fourth days were supposed to be devoted to discussion of Laurat's presentation on the transformation of the social structure and to André Philip's lecture on the transformation of the political sphere.[83] Tasca was to present again on the theme of the working class, the masses, and the nation, followed by Monnet on the exercise and conquest of power and by Izard on the passage from capitalism to socialism. Paul Rives on planned economies, Georges Lefranc on trade unions, democracy, and socialism, and Paul Faure on the structure of the Socialist Party were going to be the last speakers of the seminar. Finally, Charles Spinasse was to have been in charge of presenting the conclusions of the discussion.[84]

As is evident from this list, all the important leaders of the SFIO had agreed to participate in the seminar, including Blum and Faure. In the spirit of the Décades, each paper was to be presented by somebody whose technical competence could be acknowledged by all the participants, regardless of possible political disagreements.[85] It is also possible to detect among the participants a common interest in the ideas of Henri de Man, who had presented at Pontigny his ideas for the reform of socialism and whose ideas on planning had influenced Tasca, Philip, Laurat, Lefranc, and Rives.[86] At the same time, Tasca and Laurat clearly kept in mind the political equilibrium of the party, assigning the opening day's comments to Tasca, a representative of the prowar socialists, and the closing day's remarks to Spinasse, who was regarded as one of the most vocal proponents of appeasement.[87]

However, even this careful balance of different opinions did not eliminate the polemics, as revealed by a letter Tasca sent to Spinasse on August 4, 1939. Spinasse had asked Pierre Viénot to intercede with Tasca to obtain an invitation for René Brunet, a former vice minister of finance in the second Popular Front government. The problem was that Brunet had worked with Georges Bonnet to reach an agreement with Germany during the crisis over Czechoslovakia, and on that occasion he had even listened to a speech by Hitler from the diplomatic box in the Kroll Opera.[88] Consequently, Georges Boris, who had been invited to Pontigny, had attacked Brunet during the Nantes congress, accusing him of being Bonnet's agent inside the Socialist Party and a Nazi sympathizer.[89] Tasca had to reply to Spinasse that he was sure Brunet was innocent of the charges but, considering the necessity of avoiding polemics, preferred to leave him out of the seminar—unless Spinasse considered Brunet's participation as a sine qua non of his participation, in which case Tasca would have accepted the ultimatum to save the meeting, whose success depended on Spinasse's presence. Spinasse apparently did not insist any further. However, the episode reveals the tone of the struggle within the SFIO, with reciprocal accusations focusing as much on the betrayal of France as on the betrayal of socialism. Even the beginning of the war, which could have ended the polemics in the name of French nationalism, only aggravated the crisis inside the SFIO.

It is difficult to know if the meeting at Pontigny could have provided the common ground the Socialist Party needed. The beginning of the war opened a new phase in the history of the SFIO before the attempt to heal the wounds incurred at Montrouge and Nantes could be completed. After war broke out, however, the meeting was cancelled, and the socialists never had the opportunity to try Tasca and Laurat's solution to their divisions. And while the planning for the unrealized conference left Tasca with the sense of another missed opportunity for the French socialists, the connections he established in the second half of 1939 with some of the right-wing socialists remained alive throughout the months of the "Phony War" and, as we will see in the next chapter, during his first months in Vichy.

Tasca Makes His Decision

The beginning of the war prevented Tasca from completing his initiative, but it gave him a new opportunity to return to *Le Populaire* as a voice respected by the whole party. When the war started, Tasca and the others who had published *Agir* decided it would be better to eliminate the conflicting tendencies within the SFIO, and so they closed their journal. When Pierre Brossolette, who had written the *Le Populaire* column on foreign policy after Tasca moved to *Agir*, was drafted, Tasca went back to his old job for the socialist newspaper. At *Le Populaire*, he signed his columns on foreign policy "XX," an anonymous signature that could not be immediately identified with him, a naturalized foreigner writing on French foreign policy during a war. His articles often appeared on the first page of the newspaper, since foreign policy had become central to the life and concerns of the French. Indeed, as Tasca had realized beginning in the mid-thirties, understanding the movements of the European states on the international stage became crucial for the life of the socialist parties.

The central issue that Tasca, Blum, and the majority of the SFIO had to confront in September 1939 was there would be no French alliance with the Soviet Union to defeat Nazi Germany. Despite the tendency of commentators to see the Russian-German pact of August 23, 1939, as the end of any such possibility, the Blumists finally lost hope only when the Red Army invaded Poland.[90] Until that moment, it was still possible for them to believe that the Molotov-Ribbentrop Pact was merely Stalin's temporary defense against the indecision of France and Great Britain. The news of the agreement between Hitler and Stalin for the partition of Poland was slow to reach France and the French socialists, but when it did, any prospect of an alliance with the communists, which the socialists had constantly pursued despite their ideological suspicions, was suddenly shattered.

It was Tasca who communicated to the socialist militants the notion that there was a secret protocol between Stalin and Hitler. On September 16, 1939, six days after pieces signed with the nom de plume XX started to appear on the first page of *Le Populaire,* Tasca told his readers that the day before, the British press had devoted many pages to Russian criticisms of the Polish policy toward national minorities. The British articles, Tasca continued, suggested that these criticisms were the ideological justification for a new partition of Poland. He was personally skeptical of these analyses, he wrote, because he could not believe that the history of Russian-Polish relations since 1921 could be transformed in the space of a few days into mere "scraps of paper." Nevertheless, he had to admit that it was impossible to predict Russian foreign policy, which depended only on Stalin's whim.[91]

Blum weighed in the next day, writing, "The anonymous friend who every day presents the [international] situation for the readers of *Le Populaire,* and whose articles have immediately gained authority and general attention, yesterday tried to cast some light on the Stalinist mystery."[92] What was known for sure was that the Russian army was on the move, and that the British press thought it was the result of a secret plan to divide Poland. The reason behind this movement of troops, Blum believed, was probably that the beginning of the war had taken Stalin by surprise, and he wanted to prepare a confrontation with Germany. However, like Tasca, Blum could not be sure that Stalin was not getting ready to add crime to crime.[93]

Tasca and Blum's incredulity, if it was not a simple maneuver to prepare the socialist militants for the tragic news, lasted only for two days. The day after Blum's article, *Le Populaire* told its readers: "The Soviets are accomplices of Hitler. The Russian troops are penetrating into Poland. The Soviet armies are fighting against the Polish armies."[94] On the same day, Blum invited French communists to declare that they were French citizens and only French citizens.[95] Tasca's article, which faced Blum's column on the first page, stated that France's situation on the western front was the same as it had been before the invasion of Poland, but for the near future a collaboration between Russia and Germany was to be expected. A war between Russia and Germany was still a very concrete possibility, Tasca added, but likely would not occur immediately.[96]

For a few days, in fact, the French socialists who had believed in the possibility of a Franco-Russian alliance had to ask themselves if France was at war with Russia. In *Le Populaire,* Blum wondered whether France's decision to declare war on Germany to defend the territorial integrity of Poland entailed the protection of Poland's eastern borders. Even if this was not the case, Blum argued, Stalin was an enemy of freedom, justice, and socialism. Blum could not believe that the French communists had not revolted at the news: "Their silence is overwhelming."[97] Tasca addressed the uncertainty of the new situation with an equal sense of desperation.

He told the readers of *Le Populaire* that the only reason France was not at war against Russia was because the Russians had declared that they were not at war. According to Russian authorities, they had simply occupied territories abandoned by the dissolved Polish government. But the reality, Tasca concluded, was that the war had been set up by the Russian-German pact.

Three days after his article on the possibility of a new partition of Poland, Tasca prepared a full analysis of the situation. In his usual column in *Le Populaire*, the Italian tried to address the concerns of those who feared an alliance of Russia and Germany against France. He warned his readers of the impossibility of analyzing a totalitarian regime with the categories used to analyze democratic countries. Totalitarian regimes had an internal logic, and only those who knew this internal logic could try to make predictions. From what he knew of Soviet Russia, however, he thought that a stable Russian-German alliance was unlikely. He believed Russia was motivated by a form of neonationalism that had nothing to do with either communism or the pan-Slavic ideology offered to justify the invasion of Poland. Only if Russia and Germany had already devised a plan for the partition of the whole of eastern Europe could the alliance last longer, and even then Russia ran the risk of sharing one border with Germany and one with Japan, both potentially hostile nations.[98]

The more news Tasca received of the new situation, however, the more pessimistic he became. As he further specified in a series of articles, nobody could count on ideological incompatibility in order to exclude the possibility of an alliance between the two totalitarian states. First, he wrote, the invasion and annexation of Poland had shown that Germany was willing to incorporate millions of people of different ethnic backgrounds into its new Reich, despite its theory of racial politics.[99] Second, he added in another article, it was true that Hitler in *Mein Kampf* had denied the possibility of an alliance with Russia, but it was also true that for Hitler ideology was less important than German war needs. Therefore it was wrong, Tasca stated, to believe that the alliance with Russia was incompatible with fascism. Hitler might consider Stalin's Russia to be much more nationalist than communist, and both regimes hated democracy enough to create an alliance against it. Thus if any conflict was to erupt between Germany and Russia, it was likely to be over hegemony in Europe, not over any ideological hostility between Stalin and Hitler.[100]

The French political horizon was deeply transformed by these events. Eight days after the news of the Soviet invasion of Poland, the French government outlawed the French Communist Party. Blum wrote that he personally thought that there were dangers in the legal banishment of a party.

However, as leader of the SFIO, he had to declare that his party was happy about the decision.[101]

Tasca's reaction to the situation was increasingly emotional. When the Soviet Union invaded Finland, Tasca's descriptions of the Finnish resistance to the invasion assumed almost lyrical tones. At the end of November he wrote in his diary: "Tonight I didn't sleep because my heart was filled with disgust and indignation. It was the result of reading the Russian note on Finland issued yesterday. The idea that the Stalinist brutes can throw themselves onto Finland causes me physical pain."[102] As in other circumstances in his life, he tried to react to discomfort with action. Tasca, Monnet, Izard, Viénot, and Daniel Mayer met at Monnet's home on January 10, 1940, to discuss the situation. Tasca, who seemed to have been in charge of the meeting, reported in one of his notebooks the conversation that took place among his closest friends at one of the most dramatic moments of his life.

Tasca was now more convinced than ever before that they needed a new theoretical synthesis to understand what was happening. He claimed that they needed to elaborate a new political program, one that did not rely on previous experience, and to create a new organization to cope with these exceptional circumstances. This new organization, he believed, was to be based on two different levels of militancy and on different levels of awareness of its goals. What he had in mind, he explained, was a form of personal solidarity that could keep them united at a time when they needed an open mind to experiment with new ideological solutions, looking beyond their fraction, their party, their class, and even their nation. The political choices that they could be forced to make might well appear heterodox, and they would need each other's ideological and practical support.[103]

This did not mean that they had to abandon the Socialist Party, however. In fact, he believed that the SFIO was still their most important tool to influence French politics. Nevertheless, they had to be aware of the fact that the communist desertion had been a catastrophe, not an opportunity. The struggle among the factions had destroyed most of the SFIO's ability to act, he said, and now their party had to face a situation where the void created by the communists' betrayal would inexorably move French society to the right. In order to be effective, they needed to be able to speak in the name of the whole party, not just a fraction of it. This required them they separate their destiny from Blum's, since Blum was "not the leader of the party"; he was "not even a leader."[104] They needed to work as a team with a spokesman, and he proposed either Monnet or Izard for the role. They needed a journal, Tasca believed, whose contributors would be the backbone of the organization. Finally, they needed contacts with members of the parliament and with local branches of the party. The goal, according to Tasca, was "to continue during the war the work that was started at Pontigny and interrupted by the war."[105]

After his sketch of the most appropriate organization for the former *Agir* group, Tasca also talked about the problem of reforming the theoretical basis of socialism. He agreed with Izard that the group should abandon Marxism. If they had the time, an analysis of Marxism would be a worthy academic enterprise, he said, but the pressure of events behooved them not to waste any time on a philosophy already a hundred years old. Replying to an objection by Mayer, he even claimed that while in theory it was important to keep the connection with the working class, since the proletariat was defined in terms of class consciousness, no working class as such existed in the USSR, Italy, Germany, the United States, or France. Tasca also cautioned the group against the emphasis that Monnet and Izard were putting on the authority of the state, a position previously held by the neosocialists.[106] If by this they meant an expansion of the powers of the state, Tasca said, it could lead directly to totalitarianism. What they needed instead was a reduction of the state's powers but an increase in its authority.

Finally, Tasca talked about the war. "From an abstract point of view," he said, "we would have preferred that the war had been waged with the democratic states on one side and the totalitarian states on the other."[107] However, it would be wrong to sacrifice France in the name of ideological purity. On the contrary, he said, they had to do everything in their power to help France survive the experience. Nobody, Tasca affirmed at the end of his speech, could accuse him of sympathy for the Italian fascist regime. However, if the safety of France depended on an alliance with Mussolini rather than on a war against him, Tasca was ready to endorse such an alliance. If France and Great Britain lost the war, he concluded, civilization would fall back "to the nightmares of the year one thousand."[108]

When we look at the ideological and political implications of Tasca's position at the beginning of 1940, it is clear that the war and the events associated with the agreements between the Soviet Union and Germany deeply affected his approach to politics. For the first time, the concept of "totalitarianism," which Tasca had never used systematically before, became central to his understanding of the European situation. In his analysis, totalitarianism was fundamentally understood as a new form of nationalism, which he saw as the origins of the policy pursued by both Stalin and Hitler. Despite the enormous differences that seemed to separate their respective ideologies, an alliance between the two despots could exist because both were above all else nationalists who used ideology only instrumentally. In

Tasca's analysis, Hitler had not hesitated to ignore his racism and incorporate Poland into the Reich in the name of the expansion of Germany, just as Stalin had not hesitated to ignore communism to conquer the remaining part of Poland. Thus Tasca came to believe that the main characteristic of the revolutions of the early twentieth century was this new form of nationalism, rather than Marxist socialism.

As a consequence, Tasca completely abandoned any faith he might still have had in the proletariat. If the proletariat did not exist as a class, as he said to Monnet and his other comrades, then a radical transformation of France and Europe depended on the actions of groups of political revolutionaries rather than those of a social group. Tasca's newly discovered passion for conspiracy proves how far he had moved from his conception of the revolution as a collective enterprise. What emerges from this document, in fact, is Tasca's idea that a specialized group of people in specific positions of power could accomplish more than an open discussion in a democratic party. The technocratic and elitist interpretation of politics that inspired Pontigny and most of the French nonconformists had finally won over Tasca. In fact, when we combine Tasca's critique of factionalism with his antistatism, and his new conception of the role of the elites with his idea of a personal connection between selected individuals, we can clearly see how Tasca, once he had lost his faith in the SFIO, began to turn completely toward the central ideas of the French nonconformists.

On a practical level, what emerges from Tasca's document is his sense of the dangers entailed by the war. Faithful to his realistic approach to politics, he thought that the only relevant goal at the time was to win the war. The risk posed by alliances that might be required to achieve this goal were, at least temporarily, less important than the risk of losing the conflict. His previous conviction that an alliance between France and Russia was desirable provided a justification for his new hypothesis of an alliance between France and Italy. Since the war seemed to be between Russia and Germany on one side and France and Great Britain on the other side, every ally was precious. If, as he wrote, the Russian-German alliance was neither an error nor a temporary deviation but rather the natural consequence of the Stalinist system, then an alliance with Italy was as legitimate as an alliance with the Soviet Union had seemed at the time of the Popular Front.[109]

In the following months, Tasca consistently tried to accomplish the goals he had set for himself and for his group at the meeting in Monnet's home. During the spring, he drafted a plan for the new journal, which was to appear monthly and was to be titled *Europe Libre: Revue Socialiste et Syndicaliste*. As had been the case with his previous plan for the Pontigny conference, the events of the war, and in particular the French defeat, prevented Tasca from carrying out his objectives. Nevertheless, we still have the detailed plan for the new publication, for which Tasca and Viénot had already found funding.[110] The document that Tasca wrote to present the new journal stressed the need to lay the groundwork for a socialist Europe free from totalitarianism and statism. A second main theme of the journal was to be the construction of a new type of state that would "free the individuals and their associations from plutocracy and autarky."[111] Finally, *Europe Libre* would support an alliance between France and Great Britain and between their respective socialist parties. According to Tasca, in fact, if the collaboration between the two democratic nations was the central condition for winning the war, the collaboration between the Labour Party and the SFIO could constitute an alternative to the statist socialism of the European socialist parties.

In foreign policy, Tasca tried his best, from his position at *Le Populaire,* to favor the alliance between France and Italy that he hoped could isolate Germany. As he had told his friends, he believed that ideological purity was inappropriate in a situation in which France had to face the German military machine, and he behaved accordingly. Obviously, he never said explicitly in *Le Populaire* that, given the situation created by the war, he considered antifascism an outdated ideology. However, in the usual impersonal style of his articles, he seized any occasion to highlight France and Italy's common interests.

His new ideas did not go unnoticed. At the beginning of April 1940, Émile Buré made it clear that other antifascists were not willing to follow Tasca on the road toward an ideologically neutral foreign policy. Writing in *L'Ordre,* Buré complained about the fact that XX (Tasca) was excessively emphasizing the common interest that France and Italy had in the Mediterranean.[112] Since on other occasions Buré had expressed complete agreement with Tasca, this explicit disagreement clearly shows that the change in Tasca's ideological position was perceived by his readers. It is interesting to note that Tasca was not moved by the critique of his ideas coming from sectors of the antifascist movement. On the contrary, in his reply in *Le Populaire,* Tasca seized the opportunity to state explicitly what he thought about the war. He wrote that France was fighting Germany not because of *Mein Kampf* but because Germany was an objective obstacle to the construction of a peaceful Europe. The relations of France with all the other nations, including Russia and Italy, depended exclusively on the actual behavior of each of them.[113] Thus, on the eve of France's defeat, Tasca was publicly declaring that antifascism and ideology were not to be used to judge the political situation of Europe.

The importance of this choice had, for a brief moment, international relevance. Even the Italian newspapers had observed the polemical exchange between *L'Ordre* and *Le Populaire*. Giorgio Sansa wrote in *La Stampa* that the French radicals were overreacting to Italian policy in the Mediterranean, whereas the French socialists were not.[114] Tasca's articles in *Le Populaire* were quoted to prove that the French socialists did not consider the conflicts between France and Italy in the Mediterranean as "fatal" to the relations between the two states. Tasca, who had hastily replied to *L'Ordre*, did not feel the need to reply to the Italian newspaper, and his silence validated the Italian reading of the contrast between the French radicals and the French socialists on foreign policy. His new instrumental attitude toward foreign policy was probably better served by the praise of the Italian journalists than by the consent of the French antifascists.

Tasca did not even feel the need to distance himself from those in the Socialist Party who were using his ideas to promote a form of nationalism. Georges Th. Girard, who had been a collaborator at *Agir*, published an article in *Le Populaire* claiming that when the nation was under attack, it was right to create a coalition of all the enemies of one's enemy, fighting the same opponent inside and outside France.[115] This article, titled "Oui, vive la nation," explicitly justified any form of political eclecticism in the name of nationalism. Girard claimed that he had learned from Tasca that workers could become the ruling class only by identifying with the interests of the general population. Since the common interest of the French was the defense of France, Girard continued, the workers could be true to themselves only by creating an alliance with all the groups who wanted to defend France. Thus the SFIO ought to fight, both internally and internationally, against those who aimed at the defeat of France, without worrying about any other ideological distinction.

Tasca's silence in the face of such a radical misunderstanding of what he had been claiming throughout his life is the best proof of his desire to forget ideology in choosing his allies for the struggle against Germany. Unable to participate personally in the war, he did everything he could to contribute to the French war effort. From the beginning of 1940 to the invasion of France, he worked at the French radio service, supervising French broadcasting directed toward Italy. Even though the programs he helped to prepare are lost, we can be sure that he tried his best, as he was doing on *Le Populaire*, to prevent an alliance between Germany and Italy in the war against France. As we will see in the next chapter, when Italy finally joined the Germans, he prepared a final broadcast to denounce the cowardice of Mussolini's government, which was his last act of militant antifascism. Even before the French defeat, most of the elements that would become central in his choice for Vichy were already in place in his mind. However, as long as the war lasted, Tasca's political eclecticism was still firmly on the side of practical antifascism, albeit no longer on the side of ideological antifascism. With the defeat, however, Tasca's choice assumed more sinister characteristics.

5 A Socialist in Vichy

On September 3, 1944, Angelo Tasca spent the day in his apartment in Vichy, writing in his diary. At night, three young men knocked on his door.[1] One of them, who identified himself as Captain Chartons (or Chartrons), said that Tasca was under arrest and that they had come to take him to prison. Tasca noticed that they were armed with submachine guns and displayed a foulard with the colors of the French flag. When Tasca asked to see the warrant for his arrest, the captain replied rather harshly that he did not need to provide any explanation. After this brief exchange, the soldiers took Tasca on a thirty-five-mile trip to the military prison in Clermont-Ferrand, where he spent the rest of the night in a cell. Neither the three men nor the prison authorities bothered to tell him the reason he had been arrested.[2]

Despite the distress of being in jail, Tasca felt quite relieved by the developments of that night. As soon as the Germans left Vichy, groups of partisans had started to look for him. Quite naturally, Tasca was scared. On September 2, just one day before his arrest, a vehicle armed with a machine gun and displaying the insignia of the Francs Tireurs et Partisans Français (FTP) had stopped at the Hôtel de la Paix and at the Hôtel des Princes, and the partisans had asked for Tasca/Rossi.[3] Unable to find him at the hotels, the men had gone to his office, where they had spoken with Tasca's secretary, Madame Rollin, pressing her for Tasca's home address without identifying themselves. However, the symbols of the French Communist Party on their vehicle left little doubt as to their identity. By sheer chance Tasca's temporary absence had spared him arrest by the communists, whose goal, Tasca believed, was not to arrest him but rather to kill him.[4]

By 1944, Tasca had already survived many encounters with the police. Eighteen years earlier, as an Italian communist leader, he had twice been detained by the fascist police. Only by a miracle had he managed to escape the fate of Gramsci and the other communist leaders captured on that occasion. After his expulsion from the Communist Party, he had almost been arrested a third time, while crossing the border between Switzerland and France. On that occasion, he had simply forgotten the false name on his passport, thus awakening the interest of a policeman who was addressing him by that name. Much more recently, at the end of October 1943, it had been the French police who had started to look for Leroux/Rossi in his apartment in Paris. His friends told the police that the Italian journalist who went by those names had moved back to Italy many years earlier.[5] His stay in the military prison in Clermont-Ferrand was only the latest episode in a life lived on the brink of illegality.

Trained as a professional revolutionary, Tasca knew enough to start organizing his defense as soon as he arrived in prison, even before he knew exactly what the charges against him were. On September 6, after two days of reflection, he asked for permission to write a letter to Colonel Prince, the regional intendant of the police. In this letter, and in many others that followed, Tasca affirmed that he had been an undercover agent of the Resistance since 1941.[6] It was therefore essential that he be released as soon as possible, in order not to compromise his military and political work. To prove his role, he explained, he only needed to contact the French and Belgian authorities who were aware of his work. His arrest, he claimed, had been an innocent but potentially dangerous mistake.

Apparently Colonel Prince was not moved by Tasca's claim, and the Italian had to wait another week before he could talk to anybody in charge of his case.[7] Only on September 11, during an interrogation that lasted all day, Tasca learned why the three men had taken him into custody. To his surprise, he was not in prison for what he had done in Vichy during the past four years. Instead, he had been arrested because he was accused of preparing a fascist conspiracy against the French government in Algiers. Under his direction, according to the charges, virtually all the forces hostile to the new order that the Allies were creating in Europe—the Synarchie, the Trotskyites, the Forces Françaises de l'Interieur (FFI), the Spanish embassy, the Cagoule, and General Leclerc—were plotting to overthrow the government. Tasca was public enemy number one of the new republic, it seemed.

The charges could not withstand any serious scrutiny. The person who had denounced Tasca, a Russian who was working at the Centre d'Écoutes, clearly had been overzealous in his accusations.[8] For unknown reasons, he wanted to portray Tasca as the most dangerous person in Vichy and had accused him of everything that came to his mind. The result looked more like a Stalinist version of the fascist "Judeo-plutocratic-Masonic conspiracy" than a credible accusation. Even in the confusion of the time, this construction must have looked ridiculous. Nevertheless, it took the prosecutor one month before he decided to free Tasca from the military prison, on the evening of October 12.[9]

During the time he spent in jail, Tasca refashioned his public persona to distance himself from the Vichy regime. He now started to present himself as an agent of the Resistance, puzzling all his friends, who were convinced that he had been faithful to Vichy. He also claimed that he had been an agent since 1941, and thus among the first to join the ranks of the Resistance on French territory. In his letters to the authorities, Tasca was distancing himself not only from the last days of Pétain's regime but also from Vichy as such.

In his private correspondence, Tasca drew a more prudent self-portrait. Aware that his friends knew him too well to accept wholesale his new persona, he offered a more ambiguous account of his relation with Vichy. In a letter to André Julien, one of his closest friends and the temporary guardian of his daughter Valeria, Tasca wrote: "Since 1941, and mostly from November 1942, I have a hundred times risked execution in the service of the Resistance."[10] The first date he mentioned, 1941, was the same date he was presenting to the authorities. The second, November 1942, was a date that he never mentioned in his public letters and one that would soon disappear from Tasca's account of his Vichy years.

The difference between these two dates is central to understanding the relationship between some Vichy supporters and the Resistance. It is obvious that if Tasca joined the Resistance in 1941, he had mentally abandoned the regime after the meeting between Pétain and Hitler in Montoire that marked the beginning of collaboration between Vichy and Germany. In that case, Tasca would have decided to distance himself from the regime because he had been against the collaboration between France and Germany. But if Tasca's activity for the Resistance began after November 1942, he had abandoned Pétain's regime only when the Germans ended the last vestiges of French independence by occupying the whole of France. Tasca's case can provide an interesting answer to the question of when the various Vichy leaders changed camps.

But it will not be a univocal answer. Tasca managed to make the first date, 1941, credible to the French authorities. Thanks to the testimony of Paul Cavyn, the leader of the Belgian underground in southern France, who testified that Tasca had passed him information on the regime and had informed him of the possible arrest of Belgian agents, he even received a gold medal from the Belgian king.[11] With the help of this medal, he was able to present himself not only as someone who had changed his mind on Pétain's regime but also as a hero. Tasca used this new status to testify in the trials of some of his friends accused for what they had done in Vichy, people as diverse as Paul Marion and Georges Monnet.[12] However, looking at the documents, it is easy to see that a gray area existed in Tasca's attitude toward the regime, which makes it difficult to pinpoint something that we can call the beginning of his Resistance period.

When we consider the reasons people decided to resist the Nazi occupiers, we see a plurality of motivations and behaviors. Some people fought against the German invaders, some fought against fascism, and others fought in the name of democracy. The political goals of the different groups were not necessarily the same. The French communists who fought so bravely after the invasion of the Soviet Union certainly would have preferred communism to liberal democracy as their ultimate goal. Yet there were also those who would have been willing to turn against the communists in the Resistance rather than allow them to realize their goal. If we focus our attention on Vichy, we can see the same differences and conflicts about the ultimate goals of the regime that we can see in the Resistance. For this reason, Tasca's case can be understood only through the history of his time in Vichy.

Tasca's lifelong goal was to contribute to a successful revolution. Beginning at the end of 1940, he started to lose faith in the ability of the regime to lead the kind of revolution that he had in mind, though he still saw no alternative to the regime itself. A revolution, in Tasca's mind, could not be imported into France by the victorious armies of the Allies. Moreover, he never fully understood the choice of those who left France after the armistice. In his mind, politics had not ended with France's defeat, and he felt that the socialists needed to continue to exercise an influence on the French government. Thus he saw the decision to leave France as a form of evading the political responsibilities imposed by the country's defeat.

This misplaced sense of responsibility prevented him from allying himself with the exiled French government led by de Gaulle, and especially with the French communists, whom he considered responsible for the defeat. However, it certainly did not prevent him from desiring the ultimate victory over Germany, even though for the moment this seemed out of the question. Therefore, there was no contradiction in Tasca's mind between participating in Pétain's National Revolution and making his small contribution to the German defeat. It seemed unjust to him that the people who had left France considered those who had stayed traitors and that the Resistance mechanically equated participation in the regime with support for Germany, and so after his arrest he did not hesitate to exploit the contradictions implicit in the narrative of the Resistance.

As we will see, Tasca's alternative analysis of the situation in France after the German invasion was extremely complicated, sometimes even baroque. The constant motif in his actions was a form of French nationalism, which he thought should unite right and left, national question and social question, in order to end the social and political conflicts in France. As had happened many other times in his life, he was almost alone in his project, supported by occasional allies but never simply imitative of other people's ideas. It was to these personal projects that Tasca remained attached throughout his experience in Vichy, and he never fully recovered from them, even after the war.

The Construction of a New Regime

When the French defeat emerged in all its tragedy, at the end of May 1940, Angelo Tasca was still working in Paris, where, thanks to his political connections and to his work at the French national radio service, he had access to information coming from the front. Unlike many Parisians who had already left the city and found refuge from the Germans in provincial France, he was still in the French capital on June 8, when he received the order to move to Tours with all the personnel of the radio service. On June 10, Tasca heard the news of Mussolini's declaration of war against France, which offered a new confirmation of the French defeat. With the French government already dispersed in the French provinces and the Parisian centers of power abandoned by their legitimate occupiers, Tasca took it upon himself to broadcast a message in reply to the Italian declaration of war, which in that moment of disarray became the only immediate official French reply to Mussolini's war speech.

In his broadcast, Tasca denounced the Italian decision to participate in the war when "the German army was only a hundred kilometers from Paris."[13] If Germany won the war, Tasca predicted, the destiny of Italy could only be servitude to Germany, which would be the real winner, while Mussolini's regime would be only "a jackal attracted by the smell of a corpse."[14] Therefore, on behalf of the French, he invited the Italians to fight against Hitler and his accomplices, who were already "preparing the grave" for the Italians. "The cause of a new Italy, free and great, [was] defended by all those who were resisting Hitler and his accomplices" because "those who want peace and justice among equals want Hitler's defeat on all fronts."[15]

This message was, for a long time, Tasca's last opportunity to state publicly what he thought of the present situation of France and Europe. Even though he still spoke about a German victory as if it had not yet happened, he knew that the war was over for the French state. Therefore, he placed his hopes for the defeat of Germany and fascism on a revolt by the people of Europe against the winning fascist governments. At the time, however, he knew that such a revolt was extremely unlikely in the short term, and so a different solution had to be found for the immediate future. Obviously, what the French could do, beyond the moral revolt he referred to in his radio broadcast, was unclear to him, as it was for the vast majority of French citizens. Thus, when he moved from Tours to Bordeaux right after June 10, he still did not know what his or France's destiny would be.

It was in Bordeaux that he learned that Pétain had requested an armistice from Germany. There Tasca, against the advice of some of his friends, also made the decision to remain in France. Pierre Viénot, a friend with whom he had worked at *Agir*, obtained for him documents that would allow him to board the *Massilia* and go to Casablanca with the French deputies who refused to accept the armistice.[16] His name was also added to the list of passengers of a British boat that was to transport French dignitaries to London.[17] Despite these opportunities, Tasca refused to leave, he later claimed, because he rejected the idea of "giving in to panic, evading his duty to share the destiny of millions of people who were also in that situation because of the responsibility of a movement [the SFIO] in which he had been a militant."[18] Even if we do not believe Tasca's testimony regarding his motivations, other socialists who were Tasca's close friends were making a similar choice.

Georges Monnet, in particular, who had been the leader of Tasca's anti-Munich fraction in the SFIO, after opposing the armistice as a socialist minister in Reynaud's government, accepted Pétain's legitimacy and voted for the inclusion of socialist ministers in Pétain's new government. The goal was to avoid the risk that Pétain's supporters might destroy the republican institutions after the military defeat.[19] Even Blum did not oppose the decision to support Pétain conditionally, and on July 9, 1940, when he had to cast his vote on whether to assign constitutional powers to the old marshal, he abstained, despite his personal opposition.[20] By that time, however, Tasca, who had moved from Bordeaux to Vichy, had already gone further in his support for the new French government than his friends in the leadership of the SFIO.

According to the testimony of François Chasseigne, confirmed by Bergery, when the moment came to vote on Pétain's constitutional powers,

"Tasca played a decisive role in rallying a number of socialist deputies who had great regard for him to the marshal's cause. First, he urged them one by one to vote. Then, indefatigably, when some had doubts, he convinced them all over again."[21] At a moment of immense confusion, Tasca used his cultural capital and his personal prestige to pressure sectors of the French left to support the new government, seeming to be one of the few socialists who was sure about what needed to be done.

This activity certainly did a lot to introduce Tasca to the new regime and provide him with powerful connections at a time when his future in France was insecure. Even if he had many friends who were destined to play roles of primary importance in the new order that emerged after the collapse of the Third Republic, including Gaston Bergery and Charles Spinasse, Tasca was still a member of the left of the socialist party and a former vocal supporter of the Popular Front. His political identity could easily look suspicious to the new Vichy elites.[22] He was a political emigrant, a naturalized citizen, and an Italian socialist at a time when sympathy for Italy was scarce among the French; these reasons easily could have been sufficient to marginalize him completely in Vichy. His full support for the creation of the regime itself, however, won Tasca the chance to have an active role in Vichy politics beginning in the summer of 1940.

Tasca's assistance in the creation of the new regime should not be underestimated. Among the people who "had great regard for him," there were members of the left of the Socialist Party who were among the sternest opponents of the armistice and of the abolition of the constitution of the Third Republic. Georges Monnet was certainly one of them, and Tasca, who had been his friend since the time of *Monde*, must have played an important role in convincing him to abstain in the vote that assigned constitutional powers to Pétain. Thus if Pétain was approved by almost all of the socialist deputies, and if Blum found himself isolated among the French socialists, abandoned even by those such as Monnet who had been his closest allies in the party, it was because of Tasca's actions in July 1940. Tasca, in fact, invested all his energies in the attempt to give legitimacy to the new regime.[23]

In the thirty days between his departure from Paris and the French parliament's vote to assign constitutional powers to Pétain, Tasca had seized on the logic that had inspired the socialists' initial decision to have representatives in Pétain's government, and taken it to an extreme. Jef Rens, who talked to him several times during the summer of 1940, said that Tasca wanted to play the role of the "socialist consciousness" of the new regime, with the intent to counter the pressure on the new regime that was coming from the right and the extreme right. Tasca's self-appointed role stemmed from his analysis of the French political system, which he thought could be endangered if the French socialists decided not to participate in the political life of the new regime.

Since the outlawing of the PCF in 1939, Tasca had expressed his concern for the future of the French republic, fearing that the entire French political spectrum could be pulled to the right by the disappearance of the communists from parliamentary politics. Tasca believed that political systems rested on a dynamic equilibrium, and so the sudden disappearance of a political party could create the conditions for an imbalance on the political spectrum. As he explained in a document written for other Vichy socialists in August 1940, in the French political situation created by the German invasion, the problem of balancing the political forces on the ground applied both to the presence of socialists in Vichy, to balance the antirepublican right, and to the entire Vichy regime, to balance the Nazi presence in France.

Accordingly, at the beginning of August 1940, Tasca and other socialists who supported Pétain began to organize their presence in the regime. Tasca's role in the creation of this group was unquestionably fundamental. Tasca had chosen the other central figures of the group, Rives and Spinasse, as keynote speakers for the socialist meeting that he had planned for Pontigny in September 1939, with the aim of bringing together the left and the right of the socialist party in order to renew the theoretical basis of socialism. Of the group that gathered in August 1940, however, Tasca was the only exponent of the former left of the party, so his role was paramount in giving the appearance that the entire spectrum of political positions in the SFIO participated in the group. Without Tasca, only the fraction of the SFIO that had welcomed the Munich agreement and opposed the war against Germany would have been represented.

During these meetings, the Vichy socialists decided to create a newspaper to give voice to their positions, and so at the beginning of August 1940, *L'Effort*, the journal of the group, joined the ranks of authorized publications.[24] In August 1940 Tasca wrote a document outlining his ideological contribution to this new publication. It is of particular relevance for understanding Tasca's evolution during the traumatic first months after the French defeat. Although the political logic that Tasca tried to follow in the summer of 1940 was not new for him, he went through an important ideological transformation as the regime took shape. This document offers the key to understanding Tasca's reactions to the new context.

His analysis started from his own evaluation of French public opinion after the defeat. The breakdown of the Third Republic, Tasca argued, had curtailed the ability of the French to act politically. The dissolution of the political sphere in France had forced the French to regress to a state in which an elementary form of national consciousness dominated public opinion. The hopes that the French put in the military actions of Great Britain, despite "the tragic episode of Mers-el-Kébir," was proof that the French were still not ready to organize resistance against the Germans by themselves and wished for a miracle to restore their national independence.[25] The combination of nationalistic feelings and the desire for an "English miracle" was the origin, Tasca believed, of French hostility toward the Vichy government: it both reminded the French of their defeat and imposed on them the political responsibility to act without waiting for the Germans to be vanquished.[26]

Tasca hoped that the Vichy government would succeed in being recognized by the French as their legitimate government, thus restoring a French political sphere. "If the French are still looking too much outside France [for the rebirth of their national community]," he wrote, "it is because a great hope for salvation [*salut*] from inside France has not yet reached them." If the people did not recognize the Vichy government as their representative, this entailed the risk that another political power would emerge to fill the void, according to a political law that Tasca called "l'appel du vide." The consequence, in Tasca's opinion, could be the division of the French into two different groups, to the advantage of the German invaders. What France needed was "a single center of power, around which the resurgent national feelings could be shaped." Tasca believed this power could exist only if it had the support of the entire country.

His desire to see a single center of power in France encompassed both the French state's relationships with the German occupiers and the internal life of the new state. Tasca believed that the key to the successful re-creation of a French political sphere around Vichy was to overcome the political divisions of the last days of the Third Republic. "The left and the right [had] mutually paralyzed each other," he said, so much so that any political decision had become impossible within the Republican government. The creation of a new national unity was therefore necessary to achieve the conditions for a French reaction against the Germans. The Pétain experiment had to succeed because Vichy was the only opportunity to create "a unitary movement capable of surpassing the old divisions between left and right, monarchists and republicans, conservatives and revolutionaries." Without such a unity, the war would be lost a second time.[27]

Tasca believed that the German occupiers were actively trying to prevent unity among the French political parties. They also wanted to prevent the identification of the French people with the Vichy government. The Germans, Tasca wrote, did not rely on any specific French party or politician to realize their goals, but tried "to confuse all of them and oppose one to the other in a policy aimed at creating a situation of deep division in France."[28] The experience of the National Party of Labor in Bohemia-Moravia, according to Tasca, had taught the Germans the danger implicit in the creation of national parties. These parties could become the focal point of a policy of resistance against the occupiers, and the Germans wanted to avoid the organized expression of French nationalistic feelings in the form of a party. The French state, contrary to the desires of the occupiers, had to become the expression of the national consciousness of the French, even at the expense of not being immediately popular with the French themselves. "The present situation does not offer easy popularity to any government," Tasca wrote, but national leaders had to "turn toward the country with a missionary spirit" in an attempt to awaken France.

The tool that the leaders could use to achieve their mission was the "fusion of the social and the national," as Tasca thought Hitler, Mussolini, and even Stalin had done.[29] In Tasca's opinion, the French government did not need to follow the specific direction taken by the Germans, the Italians, and the Russians, but needed to find its own national road to a successful revolution, under the difficult circumstances of the German occupation. Thus, the goal of re-creating a national political sphere had to be coupled with a social transformation that could lead France into an economic system different from capitalism. Only the solution of the social question in conjunction with the national question could create the unity of left and right that Tasca advocated, because European socialism had already died with the death of capitalism. "No matter how the war ends," Tasca wrote, "capitalism, socialism, and democracy as they existed in the last century and a half are dead."[30] France could save itself only by finding its own solution to the new situation and by creating a "new order" for itself.[31]

Tasca believed that his analysis ought to have specific practical consequences. In order to realize the unity of the different French political traditions, he thought that a single French party should be created.[32] This party was to be "hierarchical but plural," capable of reaching "every village" and being the imaginary place where the National Revolution could continue to grow even if part of the country was "separated under unfortunate circumstances from the central authority."[33] In Tasca's opinion, only such a party could create a connection between French society and Vichy, bridging the gap between public opinion and Pétain's regime. The single party was to work as the intermediary between the state and the citizens, allowing citizens to communicate their needs to the ruling elite and giving the government a way to explain unpopular decisions to the general populace. The requirements of life under the occupation, Tasca remarked many times in the document, could be fulfilled only if a real unity could be forged between all the representatives of the people and the entire French population, and such a unity required communication.

Tasca was aware of the psychological and practical problems that the government had to solve if it was to become legitimate in the eyes of the French. The most important and most unpopular policy that Vichy had to explain was collaboration. The anti-German feelings of the French citizens could paralyze the government in its attempts to seek an agreement with the Germans on the future of France, but "collaboration with the Germans," Tasca wrote, "is a necessity."[34] Tasca thought that the majority of the French people were hostile to collaboration but not ready to transform their hostility into active resistance. On the contrary, the needs of everyday life would force French citizens into individual collaboration with the German administration while maintaining passive forms of resentment against the occupiers. If Vichy wanted to perform the functions of a French state, it needed to provide the services that the citizens required and overcome the mental reservations that the French had about the practicalities of governing under military occupation.[35]

This project, Tasca claimed, called for the support of the occupiers, who held all the levels of power and easily could have denied Vichy the authority it needed to work as an independent agent. Therefore, the Vichy regime needed collaboration in order to achieve three fundamental goals: to work out an independent policy, to present itself as a legitimate representative of the French people, and to organize the rebirth of France. France had "to be taken in hand" and led toward a policy that "allowed the French to abandon their blinding and passive hatred for the Germans and start a great enterprise where they could collaborate with the Germans without fear of losing themselves and their independence."[36]

Tasca was perfectly aware of the ideological and political implications of what he wrote in his article for *L'Effort*. At the ideological level, Tasca's idea that a successful National Revolution had to combine the social and the national echoed the words he had used to describe what he saw as one of the main ideological characteristics of fascism. In his articles on Nazi ideology for *Monde*, Tasca had explicitly argued that the union of social and national elements in the framework of a revolutionary ideology was the essence of fascism. In particular, in his article titled "Nationalisme ou socialisme," he had written that the most reactionary element in Hitler's "socialism" was its fusion with nationalism.[37] So when in 1940, after the German invasion, he invited his friends around *L'Effort* to use a combination of those two elements to prepare a French National Revolution, he was consciously inviting them to incorporate into their political program one of fascism's central ideological elements.

Moreover, if we look back at Tasca's critique of the thought that emerged from some of the nonconformists of the thirties, we have an even clearer sense of his ideological transformation after the French defeat. For instance, commenting in 1936 on Jules Romains's plan to reform the Third Republic, which became known as the "Plan du 9 Juillet," Tasca labeled the project as a typical example of those "third ways" between fascism and socialism that tried to combine elements from both ideologies. In Tasca's analysis, the fascist elements of the plan were (1) the idea of a reform of the state conducted by an authoritarian government; (2) the suspension of the constitution in order to assign constitutional powers to a government, exempting the government itself from the legal limits imposed by a constitution; (3) its anti-Marxism; (4) the proposal to reform the economy along the principles of Proudhon's socialism and corporatism; (5) the prohibition of strikes; and (6) the preeminence of the executive branch over all the other powers of the state. Comparing Tasca's own analysis of Romains's plan with the political architecture of Vichy and with Tasca's support for the transfer of constitutional powers to Pétain, we can fairly conclude that in the final days of the Third Republic Tasca had joined the ranks of the French nonconformists who had been trying to combine socialism and fascism.

The way had been prepared for Tasca's ideological turn by some of the political ideas of his nonconformist friends. In his days at *Monde*, as we have seen, Tasca had been surrounded by people such as Marcel Déat and Paul Marion, who had preceded Tasca in his ideological trajectory. The idea that France needed to incorporate some of the political features of the victorious European totalitarian states had been discussed at length among the nonconformists. Mounier's article on the formula of a "fascist antifascism" is a case in point.[38] The defeat of France had finally convinced Tasca that Europe was in the middle of a revolution radically different from the one he had imagined in his youth. This fascist revolution had assumed divergent national characters in Italy, Germany, and the Soviet Union, but it had also common features, starting from the union of social and nationalistic elements. Faithful to his long commitment to deriving his political actions from his analysis of the reality of Europe, Tasca tried to learn from a political situation in which democracy, his "humanistic" version of socialism, and traditional capitalism seemed to have been defeated by an alliance between Germany, Italy, and the Soviet Union.

After a loss that looked like a rematch of World War I, Tasca became what we can call a "rational supporter" of Vichy. *Vernunftrepublikaner*, "rational republicans," was the name given to the intellectuals who supported the Weimar Republic as a rational choice rather than a sentimental one. Moving away from conservatism, they had started to favor liberal democracy because they believed that liberal democracy was the way of modernity.[39] Not unlike them, Tasca accepted the way of the future, which seemed to go in the direction of the totalitarian states, and he supported Pétain because he believed that liberal democracy had lost its battle in Europe. Still, Tasca was willing to use all the means at his disposal to ensure that the National Revolution served France rather than Germany. Indeed, as is clear in his writings for *L'Effort* in the summer of 1940, Tasca believed that the most important political goal of the National Revolution was the liberation of France from German occupation. However, the liberation of France seemed to him to depend on the ability of the French to borrow the ideological strength of the fascist powers.

Like the Weimar *Vernunftrepublikaner*, who wanted to adopt the institutions of liberal democracy without accepting its spirit, Tasca wanted to infuse a French pluralistic spirit into authoritarian institutions. Totalitarian societies, he wrote, had achieved a level of social unity so great that they had easily defeated the pluralistic societies of the West, and so it was vital for totalitarianism's adversaries to achieve a similar level of unity. To accomplish this, French society had to avoid what Tasca was calling the "French curse"—the inability to pursue "social progress without falling under the influence of foreign nations, yesterday Bolshevik Russia, today Nazi Germany."[40] Thus, contrary to the Parisian collaborationists, who wanted to establish an ideological solidarity between Germany and France, Tasca wished to learn the secret of fascist success to use it against the fascists themselves.[41] This project closely resembled the "antifascist fascism" advocated by Mounier.

Tasca had witnessed the collapse of the Third Republic; he had seen the Germans enter France without any sign of spontaneous popular resistance. He took this collapse as an indication that the regime did not have the popular support that everybody thought it had. He blamed the communists for the disorientation of the popular classes and the French elites in general for the weakness of the state. He believed that the winners were not just militarily but also politically stronger than the losers. He thought that the occupation would last a long time and therefore required a modus vivendi between the occupiers and the French. With all these elements in mind, he was convinced that the only chance for a reunification of France, perhaps many years in the future, was for the unoccupied part of France to preserve a national memory and autonomous institutions. Tasca's lack of faith in Great Britain's ability to win the war by itself, at a time when the war between Germany, the USSR, and the United States had not yet started, was the final factor that led him to support Vichy. His teleological conception of history, in which defeat was a sign of at least temporary weakness, is the key to understanding his choice.

We should also add that what we could call a misplaced sense of moral responsibility was part of Tasca's justification for collaboration with the winning forces of fascism, which he despised. Besides his belief that such collaboration was necessary, his choice had, in his own mind, a paradoxical moral foundation. In the context of those months, Tasca was convinced that he was not betraying his values, but rather making the ultimate political sacrifice for his adopted land.

Since the end of 1938, Tasca had begun to think that the looming war was demonic in nature. "What is really unbearable for me," he noted in his diary, "is the spectacle of this world, where Good and Evil exchange their positions, and equally contribute to the common ruin. Brute force enlists itself in the service of justice, and conscience abandons its path to take refuge in violence."[42] Tasca went so far as to call this paradoxical effect of the events the war's "diabolical side." In that situation, he wrote, "conscience, which does not know how to find its own resources and use them, becomes an obstacle to the use of force."[43] Even before the defeat of France, Tasca was reflecting on a paradoxical situation in which the normal criteria used to decide between right and wrong appeared not only useless but even an obstacle to the pursuit of justice.

His way out of the "diabolical situation" was to dream of a messianic role: "If my individual sacrifice could open the path for a better humanity, I would not hesitate and I would accept the possibility of redemption with a very deep feeling of relief," Tasca wrote in one of the few passages of his journal in which he abandoned the impersonal language of politics.[44] He added: "I wish that my sacrifice could be anonymous, and I do not care if the memory of my act would be lost or even cursed."[45] This moral paradox, to damn himself to try to better the condition of humanity, was probably the result of a flawed reading of the historical events, but for Tasca, and not just for him, it was subjectively true. Our understanding of his collaboration should consider this point of view.

Under the "diabolical" circumstances of the war, Tasca's decision was certainly reinforced by the opposite but mirroring decision of the French communists. With the pact between Germany and the Soviets of the summer of 1939, as we have seen, Tasca had begun to believe that the French communist leaders had abandoned France and the French workers in the name of solidarity with Stalin. As he would try to prove with the three books he began writing during the occupation, he believed that the French communist leaders had accepted the compromise with the Nazis in order to save the Soviet Union from the war. His duty, he thought, was the opposite: to take responsibility for the defeated French people. If the French communists had chosen to privilege the alliance between the USSR and Germany over their ties with their fellow countrymen and their antifascism, Tasca made the opposite choice: to privilege his ties to France over his personal commitment to militant antifascism. Thus, following the logic evident in his dream of playing the role of humanity's savior, Tasca saw himself as living out the moral and political consequences of the communists' desertion; he felt he had a personal duty to act with the same ruthlessness as his opponents, whether fascist or Stalinist. He believed that it was his moral obligation to ensure the safety of the French people, who had been invaded by the Nazis and betrayed by the Stalinist leaders of the PCF, even if his actions looked immoral and his reputation would be tainted.

During those first days of the regime, Tasca shared with all his closest friends his analysis of the situation. Therefore, after the war, all the people with whom he had been in contact during the summer of 1940 were reluctant to believe that Tasca had been a supporter of the Resistance since the spring of 1941.[46] Both Tasca's analysis of the political situation of France and his moral reflections on war seemed irrelevant from the point of view of those friends when confronted with the actual policy that he derived from those thoughts. This policy, which advocated collaboration with the Germans and the construction of a single party under the regime, meshed with the projects of people such as Paul Marion, who had wanted a semifascist transformation of France long before the war. In the months immediately after the occupation, it also meshed with the political goals of the person who was running the French government: Pierre Laval.[47] Thus, when Tasca denied after the war that he had worked with the circles around the politician most closely associated with the policy of collaboration, he was not telling the truth.

Tasca's conviction that uniting around the government was the only way to prepare the future salvation of France—a belief shared by the other leaders of *L'Effort*—left no room for opposition to the government itself.

Thus, when the first issue of *L'Effort* appeared on August 4, 1940, the political project advocated by the newspaper was not only compatible with Laval's policy but so perfectly in line with it that Laval himself, according to Tasca, financed the new publication. In just a week, even the ambitious subtitle of the newspaper, *Organ Socialiste pour la Reconstruction Nationale*, disappeared, to be replaced by the more orthodox *Pour la Reconstruction Nationale*, probably to avoid even the appearance of a political venture different from the general direction of the so-called National Revolution. Accordingly, during the months in which Tasca wrote in its pages, *L'Effort* never criticized any aspect of the policy pursued by Laval, including collaboration with the Germans.

When the newspaper appeared, Tasca was enthusiastic. He immediately sent copies of the new publication to the Juliens, who were taking care of his daughter Valeria, and who had remained in Paris. He received an embarrassed reply, but, as he had done with Viénot and Rens, he refused to listen to the critiques of the regime that came from his socialist friends who opposed the armistice. His decision to sign his articles in *L'Effort* with XX, the same signature that he had used in the pages of *Le Populaire*, proves that he believed that *L'Effort* could claim to be the successor of SIFO's official newspaper, whose publication had been suspended and whose editor was now working on *L'Effort*.[48]

In *L'Effort*, as he had done in *Le Populaire*, Tasca wrote a daily column that analyzed the events of international policy, using a style that emphasized more the news itself than his own commentary. The only direct comments that Tasca made in his articles explicitly supported Vichy and its policy. For instance, in an article discussing the French-Japanese agreement that assigned to Japan a de facto protectorate in Vietnam, Tasca wrote, "It is enough to think a little about the international situation created by the defeat to understand that the French government has tried to save whatever it could in a situation that has become difficult if not dramatic."[49] Only rarely did Tasca's ideas emerge more directly, and even then only because they were in perfect consonance with the regime's official perspective on the war. In an article on the German war against Great Britain, for example, Tasca wrote that the British resistance could prolong the war, "but we do not believe that it can effectively change the European situation." For this reason, Tasca concluded, France had "to choose its destiny, and be successful in its effort of European collaboration without subordinating this policy to the battle of England."[50] Most of the time, however, Tasca preferred to convey his ideas through his seemingly neutral account of the events, rather than explicitly stating his position.

Even more than during the last days of the Third Republic, his status as a naturalized immigrant must have prevented Tasca from directly stating his point of view on the war and foreign policy. This limitation did not stop him from seeking to communicate his political ideas to the readers of *L'Effort*, but he had to do so by carefully selecting the news on which he commented rather than by speaking frankly. A typical example of his strategy can be seen in an article he wrote on October 10, 1940, on the political situation in Norway. In his description of the events in the Scandinavian country, Tasca emphasized how the Germans had decided to outlaw all the Norwegian parties—with the exception of Quisling's—precisely at the moment when they had decided to unite into a single party. By forbidding the creation of such a single party, Tasca concluded, the Germans had been able to impose a new order on Norway. What Tasca had in mind in writing this article was clearly the French situation, in which he supported the creation of a single party to force the German occupiers to discuss their political choices for France with French representatives. The Norwegian case, Tasca implicitly suggested, proved that the Germans did not want such single parties to be created, for fear that they could be successful in mobilizing the population against the occupiers. Therefore, Tasca implied, if the Germans did not want to see a single party, the French who wished to oppose the Germans should support its establishment.[51]

Tasca left any less cryptic statements of the policy favored by the newspaper to Spinasse and Rives, who were the public face of *L'Effort*. However, his own personal history, from *L'Ordine Nuovo* to *Monde*, proves that he had never been willing to work for a publication whose political line he did not fully support. During his months of work at *L'Effort*, Tasca was in constant contact both with Spinasse, with whom he felt politically more in tune, and with Rives, who was running the newspaper from Bellerives-sur-Allier, the small village right outside Vichy of which Rives was the mayor.[52]

Since the first days of *L'Effort*, in fact, both Rives and Spinasse made explicit references to Tasca's contributions. In his first signed articles in *L'Effort*, Paul Rives paid a real tribute to Tasca, writing that the ideas behind the newspaper were coming from the thwarted meeting that Tasca had organized for SIFO. "A few days before the war," Rives wrote, "an assembly was to have taken place in Pontigny to develop ideas for the revision of socialism. The war did not stop those ideas."[53] Spinasse, for his part, showed an even stronger consonance with Tasca's analysis in many of his editorial pieces, often repeating the ideas expressed by Tasca in the essay that he had written in the summer of 1940. In an article titled "Au service de la France," Spinasse even seemed to embrace the same logic that had moved

Tasca in his choice for Vichy, writing: "We could wait in the security of our profession for a miracle, an English miracle or a Russian miracle or an American miracle; but we do not believe in miracles. We prefer danger to inaction and misalliances [*mésalliances*] to solitude." There is no evidence in Tasca's diary or in his communications with his friends that his opinions differed from those expressed daily in the pages of *L'Effort*.

Moreover, when we look at the names of the people who contributed to *L'Effort*, we can see that the newspaper welcomed articles by many of the intellectuals who had participated in the debate organized by Tasca in *Monde* on the theoretical crisis of socialism. During the first months of the new journal's existence, de Man published an article in support of the idea of collaboration with the Germans.[54] Marcel Déat, for his part, wrote several pieces to support the creation of a single party that would function as an intermediate body between civil society and the state.[55] And Bergery published articles advocating reform of the French state without waiting for the conclusion of the war between Germany and Great Britain.[56] Thus Tasca, who no longer had any objections to the idea of coupling socialism and nationalism, found himself in the company of those heretics of socialism whom he had abandoned at the beginning of the thirties in the name of internationalism.

Tasca's acceptance of Vichy nationalism put him in the position of sharing the moral and political responsibility of the regime for what was certainly the most horrific feature of its nationalist ideology: anti-Semitism. At the beginning of October 1940, in fact, anti-Semitic references started to appear in the pages of *L'Effort*. On October 9, Spinasse, who had been finance minister under the Popular Front, published an article in support of an economic reorganization of Europe to allow the different national economies to work as a system. On the second page appeared an article with no signature reporting that Walther Funk, the German minister of economy, and Raffaello Riccardi, the Italian minister of exchange and currencies, had planned a meeting to talk about the economic reorganization of Europe along the lines of the countries' national interests, in a Europe freed from "Judaic capitalism."[57] Nine days later, on October 18, 1940, *L'Effort* published an article to comment on the new *statut des juifs*, which appeared on the same day in the *Journal Officiel*. In this piece, the anonymous author affirmed that Jews and foreigners were to be blamed for the defeat. The new regime, the article continued, had no interest in vengeance, but the Jews, who were said to be incapable of social life, had to be put in a position where they could not cause further damage.[58] The day after, when the text of the *statut des juifs* was published on the first page of *L'Effort*, Tasca published an article on the Balkans and neither then nor later commented, in his articles or elsewhere, on the anti-Semitism of the regime.

The lack of references to anti-Semitism in Tasca's diaries or publications suggests that he probably considered the new policy of the regime one of those "misalliances" that Spinasse had described as the price to pay for the future of France. Nevertheless, if we consider Tasca's reaction to the other limitations imposed by Vichy on those French citizens who did not conform to its nativist and racist standards, we can certainly conclude that he did not think such policies were unacceptable. The laws promulgated by the regime to limit the freedom of foreigners on French territory, in fact, directly affected Tasca, who fell into the category of those immigrants whose naturalizations were suspended pending review by the Vichy authorities. Tasca's reaction to this new situation, which left him in a legally dangerous condition, was simply to reapply for citizenship. Thus, even in the face of a legal procedure that reminded him that French nationalism could exclude even its own supporters when they happened to be born outside France, he reacted by reaffirming his alliance with the his new country.

This legal problem ended up changing Tasca's life. On October 24, 1940, Hitler and Pétain met in Montoire and initiated the policy of collaboration that Tasca and *L'Effort* had always advocated. The newspaper welcomed the meeting, and both Rives and Spinasse reaffirmed *L'Effort*'s commitment to collaboration. Tasca also continued to publish his regular articles on foreign policy without giving any sign of disapproval of the events. His articles on the American elections of 1940 occupied almost the entire first page of the newspaper. Then, after his article on the election of Franklin Delano Roosevelt to his third term as president on November 8, 1940, Tasca's signature disappeared from the pages of *L'Effort*.

After the war, Tasca claimed that he had left *L'Effort* because he disapproved of the policy started in Montoire. However, this choice would have been in open contradiction with what he had supported since August 1940. Moreover, in documents written in 1941, Tasca continued to talk about the need for collaboration with the Germans. And even after the war, he continued to quote the article that he had written in the summer of 1940 (albeit not the part on the necessity of collaboration) in order to explain his political program in Vichy.[59] Since in his postwar testimony Tasca had a specific interest in lying about his role in Vichy, it seems more likely that Tasca's decision to temporarily suspend his work at *L'Effort* was inspired by the need to keep a low profile while his naturalization was being reviewed.

An important piece of evidence supports this interpretation of the events: as soon as he regained his citizenship, in April 1941, Tasca again started to publish articles in *L'Effort*. Tasca later claimed that he had resumed his job for the newspaper only as a cover-up for his activity for the Belgian Resistance, with which he made contact in February 1941. However, none of the people who testified on Tasca's behalf after the war ever mentioned that. Moreover, we can add that Tasca himself had likely proposed the person who substituted for him in his regular column on *L'Effort*, Georges Th. Girard. Girard, who had worked at *Agir* despite his sympathies for the right of the SFIO, had a real admiration for Tasca and had followed him from *Agir* to *L'Effort*.[60] So the problems posed by Tasca's naturalization review, which delayed a process that he had expected to be completed by December 1940, seem to be the only logical explanation for Tasca's decision to suspend his collaboration with the newspaper that he had helped to create.

The problem with Tasca's application started by chance. Thanks to the help of Charles Vallin, who was a member of the committee in charge of reviewing naturalizations granted in the thirties, and with the support of his powerful friend Henri Moysset, who was general secretary of the vice presidency, Tasca had received a quick and smooth review. However, at the very last minute, the whole process seemed to stop and the Vichy police summoned Tasca to be interrogated by a prosecutor.

Under the threat of deportation and even arrest, Tasca learned from Moysset that his application had run into trouble because of some checks sent to him in the spring of 1940. As he would later learn from the police, Tasca had received 50,000 francs from Pierre Viénot at his address in Paris. The money was supposed to pay for the expenses of a new journal, *Europe Libre*, which Tasca had planned to publish with Viénot and the other members of the *Agir* group.[61] When the money arrived, however, he had already moved to the south, and the letter with the checks, unable to reach its destination, had become suspect in the political climate of Vichy.

What the police found in the envelope was a small treasure for the paranoid mentality of the authoritarian regime. The checks, coming from the bank account of Viénot, a former junior minister of the Popular Front government, had been signed by Viénot's wife, whose maiden name was Mayrisch, and were made out to a naturalized French citizen who was working for the French radio service. This curious constellation attracted the attention of Jean-Louis Tixier-Vignancour, a lawyer and the future guru of the French extreme right, who wanted to use the checks against Viénot. Since Viénot was one of the four parliamentarians arrested for the *Massilia* affair, any zealous attempt to damage him might be rewarded with a political career.[62] Thus, Tixier-Vignancour managed to convince himself and the police that the checks were proof of corruption. Viénot, according to Tixier-Vignancour's overactive imagination, had received money from a Czechoslovakian named Mayrisch to corrupt a functionary who was working at the French radio service. The purpose of the corruption was to support a bellicose French attitude against Germany. The corrupted functionary was, of course, Tasca.

This unbelievable story of international intrigue was enough for the police and a judge to invite Tasca to a police station for questioning. Nevertheless, either because Tasca managed to convince the police of the absurdity of the story or because no one wanted to incur the displeasure of Tasca's powerful sponsor, Henri Moysset, the charges were soon dropped. The affidavit that Moysset had given him, stating that Tasca "has given, is now giving, and will be required to give services equal to his intelligence and his ardent French sentiments," left no doubt that the investigation was concluded.[63] At the end of this small adventure, on April 17, 1941, Tasca was reawarded citizenship.[64]

During those months of forced political inactivity for Tasca, the political situation of Vichy changed dramatically. On December 13, Laval had been removed from the vice presidency and then arrested. With the temporary disappearance of the key politician of the first months of the regime, Tasca believed that it was time for him to begin reconsidering his experience in Vichy. Both his project of a single French party and that of uniting the French under Pétain appeared to him to be moving in a different direction than he had imagined. Even his plan for collaboration between France and Germany in order to allow the Vichy regime to develop real power over the territory under its control seemed to have come to a sudden halt with the reaction against Laval's policy. Thus Tasca began to believe that he needed to find a new role for himself within the regime. His ties to Moysset offered him a new opportunity to exercise influence on Vichy's politics when, after the resolution of the problem with his citizenship, Admiral Darlan came to dominate the political stage of Pétain's state.[65]

Multiple Personalities

Tasca had direct knowledge of the power struggle within the pluralistic dictatorship of the regime, and he did not like it. In his journal he provided an unsympathetic account of the events that had destroyed his dreams for the regime. On all three major issues that he considered essential for the success of the National Revolution—the creation of a single party, collaboration, and the conjunction of social and national issues—he believed that the regime had failed.

The rivalries among Pétain's entourage, Laval, Bergery, Déat, and the parties of the right (in particular L'Action Française and Doriot's Parti Populaire) had effectively put an end to the project of creating a single party around the Rassemblement National Populaire. At the beginning of 1941, he already described the Rassemblement as nothing more than "a committee for propaganda" in the hands of Paul Marion.[66] Even more hostile was Tasca's opinion of the Légion Française des Anciens Combattants, the Rassemblement's major competitor for the role of single party. He described it as a tool in the hands of the extreme right and as an organization completely unfit for the purpose that he attributed to the National Revolution. In his view, the Légion's foreign-policy goal was revenge against Germany and its internal-policy goal was revenge against the French left.[67] Without this single party, he believed, the government lacked a tool that would create a connection with the people and which he thought was indispensable for a successful revolution. "The abandonment of the project of a single party," Tasca wrote, "has made impossible the creation of an atmosphere favorable to reconciliation, which could have rallied around the regime the half of the country" that had voted for the Popular Front.[68]

He disliked both Laval's internal policy and the way in which he had managed the issue of collaboration, but he disliked even more the coalition that had managed to dismiss him. Laval's arrest, he wrote, had been the "greatest joy for the newspapers of the extreme right."[69] In Tasca's opinion, Laval had been, and in early 1941 still was, opposed by all the people who wanted to "lead France toward a monarchy or a deeply reactionary system."[70] "Laval did not deserve such an honor," Tasca wrote, "but the dynamics of the different positions made him the major obstacle for the ideas of L'Action Française and its allies, supporters of an 'ultra' restoration."[71] Because Laval's power had been generated by a vote of the French parliament and was still dependent on that form of legitimacy, Tasca thought that "to attack Laval was to attack the French deputies, and an attack against the French deputies was an attack against Laval."[72] A coalition of forces led by the extreme right and hostile to collaboration had defeated Laval in the name of a political project that was even more dangerous than Laval's subordination to the Germans: a reactionary design that aimed at restoring an absolute monarchy in France and eliminating all the vestiges of the republican tradition. Tasca wrote that the regime had been polarized around either the extreme right or around Laval, pushing toward him, "which is to say toward the Germans, people little inclined to collaboration, especially in the spirit and the practice of the old prime minister [*président du conseil*]."[73]

France, according to Tasca, had not yet resolved the problem of the union between the social and the national, which he saw as essential for the success of the regime. René Belin's participation in the government as a socialist representative had failed to meet Tasca's expectations. When Belin had been offered a ministry, Tasca wrote, "I vigorously pushed him to accept for the same reasons that had convinced me to support the vote for the reform of the constitution proposed to the National Assembly."[74] But Belin, according to Tasca, had quickly crossed the line that separated *planisme* from bureaucraticism.[75] He had been incapable of imposing a transformation on the French economy, prevented from doing so by the hostility of the right, whose power was overwhelming in Vichy. The result had been the failure of Belin's project for a *charte du travail* and of his entire social policy.[76] Tasca's long standing critique of *planisme* and corporations allowed him to see very clearly that Belin's *charte du travail* did nothing to democratize the economy. It simply added the bureaucratic regulation of capitalism. Whereas Tasca's goal was to subject the state to the democratic control of producers, Belin's plan allowed incompetent bureaucrats to interfere with the life of the producers.

Robert Paxton has noted that "if service as a shield was the primary justification for the existence of a sovereign French government under German occupation, its failure had already become painfully clear by the end of 1940."[77] Tasca's perception of the failure of his ambitious projects for the regime seems to confirm Paxton's analysis. However, Tasca still saw no better alternative to the regime itself. He remained convinced that the future of France depended on the ability of the French to discover the reasons behind the failure of the Third Republic and to find a solution for this failure by themselves. Even if Germany had been defeated in the war by a coalition of powers, the problem of France would have remained, Tasca believed. France had to find its own path if it did not want to be the passive recipient of foreign models, whether English, German, or Russian.

Tasca was particularly afraid of the possibility that the Soviet Union might enter the war against Germany. This event, he feared, could erase the memory of the Russian-German alliance, making the fight against communism extremely difficult. In the event of a war between Germany and Russia, he wrote in May 1941, French public opinion could split between those who wanted a British victory in order to defeat the Germans and those who wanted a revolution. "Churchill will provide the first as gift to the French," he wrote, "and Stalin the second."[78] The only alternative to the National

Revolution, Tasca believed, was the victory of either Nazism or communism, which he saw as little different. Thus the "first tool to fight against communism," he affirmed, "is to make the National Revolution the passion of France."[79] As he had begun to believe since the defeat, the alternative to the National Revolution was not internationalism but the imposition of foreign models on France.

As Tasca worked to prevent this from happening, he increasingly disengaged himself from his neosocialist friends in order to engage with the circles of antitotalitarian Catholics present in Vichy. These groups were both anticommunist and anti-Nazi and had the advantage of playing a much greater role than the small groups of socialist traitors who supported the regime. In particular, Tasca established a very close relationship with Henri Moysset, whose political star was on the rise and who reached the peak of his influence when Darlan became vice president in February 1941.[80]

To characterize this change of alliances as a major shift in Tasca's political vision would be misleading, however. As described in the previous chapter, after 1938 Tasca oscillated between the nonconformist Christians and those socialist groups that were more open to nonconformist ideas. His personal friendships with Laurat, Souvarine, and de Rougemont, his assiduous participation in the Décades at Pontigny, and his desire to publish in *Esprit* testify to his strong interest in a cross-fertilization between socialism and the social and political doctrine of the Christian nonconformists. Henri Moysset, Pétain's secretary of state, was a legitimate member of this cultural exchange between socialists and leftist Catholics, and it is not surprising that Tasca found in him a powerful point of reference.

As Marjorie Beale has pointed out, in his youth Moysset had been both a social Catholic and a socialist sympathizer. His interest in French socialists had led him to publish the collected works of Proudhon in collaboration with Marcel Déat. During the thirties, Moysset had developed an interest in the theory of elites, which had led him to his own formulation of the role of intellectuals in French society. According to this theory, the elites had lost part of their role in French society, and journalists and other publicists had supplanted them in shaping public opinion. This crisis of the French elites had left the masses at the mercy of the manipulative will of the economic enterprises behind the newspaper publishers. To restore a more balanced public opinion, he advocated a return to the figure of the militant intellectual, similar to the public intellectual of the Enlightenment. Thus, both because of his personal background and because of the nature of his reflections on the crisis of French society, Moysset exercised a powerful attraction on Tasca.

At the beginning of 1941, Moysset managed to enlist Tasca in his political projects, convincing him that he could provide a valuable service. In May of that year, Moysset asked Tasca to prepare a study on the creation of a youth movement for the regime. Through this study, which kept him engaged for the better part of 1941, Tasca defined his intellectual position inside the regime on the side of the Catholic antitotalitarians and tried to play an active political role, albeit from the position of ghostwriter for Moysset. Against those who wanted to create a single French youth movement, in order to establish a single orthodox ideology for the future generations of French citizens, Tasca's study aimed at giving young people an intellectual foundation different from fascism and Nazism.

Tasca's main adversaries were, in his words, "people coming from the Parti Populaire Français, who had been communists, and who wanted to create a single [youth] movement."[81] During the second half of 1940, Tasca continued, the opposition of the Catholics, who had insisted on the need to maintain multiple youth organizations, had defeated their projects. At the beginning of September 1940, the nomination of Georges Lamirand to the leadership of the Secretariat à la Jeunesse had temporarily settled the issue in favor of the Catholics. Pierre Dunoyer de Segonzac, a Catholic, had even managed to create and have recognized by the regime another important youth organization aimed at educating the regime's future leaders, the Uriage school.[82] However, in February 1941 the issue was reopened when the new leader of the Services de l'Information, Paul Marion, Tasca's old friend and former ideologue of the Parti Populaire, came out in favor of a single youth movement.

In Vichy, Marion and Tasca had resumed their friendship and Tasca had started to dine regularly at Marion's home.[83] Moysset, Tasca, and Marion had in common their past experience in the cultural milieu of the French nonconformists, but Marion, who was an ex-communist and not a Catholic, had no history in common with Moysset and had never been attracted by the Christian circles in which Tasca had pursued some of his political projects. Thus it is possible that Moysset chose Tasca as his advisor precisely to take advantage of Tasca's position as a link between his ideas and those of his powerful subordinate, with whom Tasca had been friends since the end of the twenties. Although we cannot know for sure if these were Moysset's intentions, Tasca's document on the youth movement carefully highlighted the strong cultural links that united Moysset, Tasca, and Marion. In fact, Tasca's reconstruction of the crisis of the Third Republic, which in his view had created the need for the National Revolution, was a long, albeit critical, tribute to the nonconformists.

In Tasca's analysis, France's moral, financial, and political crisis had been engendered by an overexpansion of the state's role. The ability to innovate and be creatively active had been denied to the younger generations after World War I by the pervasiveness of the state. Thus, the generation that had led France to victory during the war had been incapable of transmitting its own spirit to the new elites. The result of the state's intrusive presence had been the co-optation of the new elements into the old elites, rather than the replacement of the old elements. Consequently, the lack of a generational conflict had forestalled the rejuvenation of French society and made France "old." Both the extreme right and the extreme left had perceived this problem (Tasca named Pierre Drieu de la Rochelle and Paul Nizan as examples), but neither had been able to find a solution.

Only a few individuals had emerged with new ideas during the interwar period, Tasca thought: Bertrand de Jouvenel, who had reintroduced the idea of a directed economy; Paul Marion, who had coupled socialism and nation and provided the idea for the neosocialists; and Emmanuel Mounier, who had invented personalism.[84] They were united by the idea of overcoming ancient polarizations, and they had, directly or indirectly, inspired the political groups of the thirties. These groups were, Tasca wrote, the authors of the Plan du 9 Juillet; Dandieu, Aron, and their Ordre Nouveau; Galey, Izard, and the Troisième Force; Bergery and *La Flèche*; Mounier and *Esprit*; and Maulnier and *Combat*. All of them had clearly understood the need for a national revolution.[85] Nevertheless, they also had failed because, despite their attempts, they had not been able to start a revolution prior to the German invasion.

Tasca's insistence on the failure of his generation was a small tactical masterpiece on his part, and its main points deserve to be highlighted. What Tasca managed to create in a few pages was an internal critique of his opponents' support for a single youth movement. Under the guise of an overly generous tribute to the role of Marion in the nonconformist movement of the thirties, he was forcing Marion, the major supporter of compulsory participation in a state-sponsored youth movement, into a defensive position. He stressed that organizational unity was not a requirement for having common goals, as the plurality of nonconformist organizations proved. He also contested the right of the nonconformists who were then in power, including Marion, to claim that they had been complete outsiders in French politics, thus attacking their idea that everything that predated the National Revolution had to be changed. Finally, Tasca suggested that the idea of a movement sponsored by the state was a form of statism, one of the bêtes noires of the nonconformists.[86]

This critique of statism was Tasca's main support for his claim that a centralized and state-directed youth movement could be detrimental to France. If the crisis of French society had been caused by the lack of intellectual competition between generations, the solution to the crisis had to be found in the opposite direction: free competition of ideas among competing groups. A single youth movement sponsored by the state, on the other hand, was a recipe for the repetition of old errors. What the young French would learn from their participation in a state-sponsored youth movement was that their entire lives were managed by the state. They would also learn, Tasca insisted, to conform to the ideas of the old elites in the hope of being co-opted into them. Thus, Tasca suggested, everything that the nonconformists had despised in French society after World War I would be repeated and even worsened by the presence of a single youth movement. On the contrary, a plurality of movements able to develop their own ideas about the future of France but united by a common doctrine could ensure the success of the National Revolution.

As he had done in his analysis of the French situation right after the defeat, Tasca insisted on the importance of finding an original and national solution to France's problems. "There are those," Tasca wrote, "who turn toward Nazi Germany to wrest the secret of victory from her."[87] On the other side were those who, in Tasca's words, "wanted to question everything and critically examine their principles after putting them to the test."[88] His sympathy clearly was with the second group. Tasca affirmed that the German political experience had value only for Germany, and only for the specific time in which Nazism had seized power. Any plan for a French youth movement, therefore, had to start from the consideration that French youth had nothing in common with German or Italian youth at the time of the fascist revolutions. French youth had to face the harsh conditions of the German occupation, Tasca argued, and had to be trained in problem solving, not in quasi-religious experience and political mystique. The desire to import the German model into France was unrealistic and bound to condemn France to failure.

It is likely that Moysset was pleased by Tasca's three-hundred-page study on the youth movement. We do not know how he used it, but we do know that in 1942 Moysset was incorporating some of Tasca's political analysis in his speeches, starting with the concept of "l'appel du vide" that Tasca had developed in 1940.[89] Thus, it is probable that Moysset used Tasca's study in making his case against the single youth movement with Pétain, who on March 5, 1942, resolved the debate in Moysset's favor.[90] What is more surprising is that Tasca's active struggle against Marion's projects for a single youth movement, which kept him engaged throughout 1941, not only did not affect the personal relationship between Tasca and Marion but also created the conditions for an offer of employment that Marion made to Tasca in 1942. As soon as the question of the youth movement had been resolved by Pétain's intervention, Tasca started to work under Marion's direct control.

The key to understanding this seeming contradiction is to keep in mind that Tasca's ideological position, which remained substantially stable throughout his time in Vichy, was different from Marion's but not incompatible with it. The events of 1941, and in particular the beginning of the war between the Soviet Union and Germany, did not change Tasca's approach to the regime. Tasca's big political issue was the National Revolution and the possibility that France might join Italy, Germany, and the Soviet Union in the "new order" in an original French way, but he did not consider illegitimate the positions of those who wanted to copy Germany or Italy more closely. Only for the communist movement did he have real contempt, and that was because he considered the communists hypocritical agents of the Russian nationalist revolution.

Thus when Germany attacked the Soviet Union in June 1941 he had reached an ideological position that left him calm about those events. In fact, he looked at the situation from a utilitarian point of view. In a letter written to Liliane Chomette in July 1941, Tasca wrote that he had no regrets about what appeared to him as the fall of Stalin's regime, "whose crimes had been innumerable and, somehow, Asiatic"; he was simply afraid that Hitler's victory could worsen the conditions of France.[91] On the contrary, he wrote in his journal, he hoped for a Russian resistance to keep "the German war machine busy, so as to put the French government into a better position to negotiate with Germany."[92] Whatever the conclusion of the war, in fact, Tasca believed that the union between social and national revolution that he had identified as the key to the success of Hitler, Mussolini, and Stalin would have to be introduced in France.

Tasca thought that anyone who wanted to copy the totalitarian regimes was simply shortsighted. Those regimes, Tasca believed, had not yet completed their evolution, and their present status was simply dictated by the needs of the war. France, by contrast, "could skip a stage of the other evolved regimes and be their future and their history."[93] If France wanted to copy the Germans, it would become a colony, because "it will never be as

Nazi as the Nazis."[94] France's role, in his opinion, was to provide the universalism that the other national revolutions lacked, as it had done with the French Revolution. Thus Tasca had actively worked against the attempt to copy the German totalitarian model, not in the spirit of antifascist resistance but rather in the spirit of a nationalist distinction between France and the totalitarian states.

Such a perspective could easily be understood by Paul Marion, who had volunteered in the war against Germany and who had left the Parti Populaire when Doriot, its leader, had failed to denounce Italian claims on French territory. At the same time, however, Tasca's projects were also not incompatible with the anti-German activity that he and the leader of the Belgian underground in Vichy, Paul Cavyn, later claimed he engaged in. Since Tasca's goal was not victory by Germany but a form of French national socialism, he could desire the defeat of Germany while attempting to realize the transformation of France in concert with French fascists such as Paul Marion, who had similar anti-German feelings and a similar goal of combining socialism and nationalism.

Tasca, who, as we have seen, believed that the totalitarian states were still in evolution, worked from the assumption that the end of the war would bring about a new situation for which France needed to be ready. The National Revolution, he told the audience of the Cercle Jeune France de Vichy during a meeting presided over by Paul Estébe, "needs to be strong enough in the Free Zone to carry the weight of the rest of France when the other France will fall on the scale."[95] Such a position was able to attract the interest of much larger segments of the Vichy government than the small group of ex- socialists with whom Tasca had started his Vichy adventure. Thus Jean Rivain, a former member of L'Action Française who in Vichy edited *L'Unité Française* and who was close to Pétain, asked Tasca to prepare an article for his publication elaborating the three points that he had made during the conference: (1) the need for a variety of experiences among the leaders of a revolution, (2) the unfinished process of the European revolutions of the interwar period and the possibility that still existed for France to become the leading nation in the European revolution, and (3) the need for Vichy to complete its revolution before the return of the prisoners and the reunification with the rest of France.[96] As we have already mentioned, Tasca's position was also able to attract the interest of Paul Marion, who in the summer of 1942 offered him a job.

So from the second half of 1942 until his arrest in 1944, Tasca found a stable role in the Vichy regime as director of the research bureau (*bureau d'études*) under the secretary general for propaganda.[97] He was given, according to his testimony, 6,000 francs per month (approximately $1,500) and a secretary.[98] As director of this research bureau, Tasca went back to one of the activities he had been pursuing since his arrival in France in 1929: analysis of the political situation, both in France and on the international stage, based on the careful reading of an incredibly wide range of published material, including newspapers, magazines, journals, police reports, and other classified material. The central difference between his research before and after the invasion was that the focus of Tasca's analysis was no longer fascism and fascist countries but the ideological debate and the political moves of the French communists and of the USSR. After his experience at *L'Effort* and his study on youth organizations, Tasca's central activity in Vichy became the ideological and political struggle against the communist resistance and, as much as possible, against the Soviet Union.

Unlike the rest of his professional life, Tasca's activity during his time at the research bureau is poorly documented. Most of the material that survived in his archive can be classified under two headings: Tasca's papers on Marxism and on the communist parties, which he presented to the Ministry of Propaganda, and the books on the PCF, which we will discuss in the epilogue. It is easy to imagine, however, that Tasca's research bureau did more than prepare these occasional speeches and the research for books that were published only after the end of the war. For this reason, it is very important to pay attention to the only surviving document in Tasca's gigantic archive that offers us a glimpse of the routine activity of Tasca's office. This document, dated December 4, 1943, is entitled "The Goofy Maneuvers of the Algerian Committee" and was classified as "a daily report."[99]

In the first section of this document, Tasca emphasized the contrasts between the French Communist Party and the government led by Charles de Gaulle. According to what he had gathered from articles published by the international press and from police and secret service reports, the PCF wanted to retain control over which party members had a seat in the government, whereas de Gaulle wanted a free hand in the choice of the communist ministers.[100] This disagreement, in Tasca's account, was creating a major problem among the ranks of the Resistance, and the communists might be tempted to show their strength in metropolitan France to force de Gaulle to accept their point of view. In the second section of Tasca's report, he highlighted de Gaulle's failure to convince Great Britain to stop its "maneuvers" in the French colonial empire and grant him control over the administration of the colonies. According to Tasca, de Gaulle's was unquestionably responsible for failing to protect the integrity of the French colonies against British expansionism.[101]

The second section of the report was clearly nothing more than one of the traditional arguments raised by the regime: de Gaulle's alleged indifference to France's national interests. But the first section of Tasca's piece, where he analyzed the potential moves of the PCF, could provide information not only to the offices in charge of propaganda but also to the police and the secret service. Tasca's analysis, in fact, suggested that the French communists might increase their activities to demonstrate to the other parties associated with de Gaulle's government their capacity for action.[102] The police reports that Tasca put in the same file where he placed his document on the conflicts between de Gaulle and the communists suggest that he was right in predicting an increase in the communists' activities in France. A week after he wrote his report, the French police engaged in repressive measures in Paris to stop a series of small actions organized by the French communists. Tasca himself, in the way he organized his archive, left us a strong reason to believe that he had a part in orchestrating these repressive measures—his understanding of the internal dynamics of the Communist Party was put at the service of the repressive forces in occupied France.

This part of Tasca's activity, which must have produced an impressive amount of documents considering that his office produced a daily report, is not present in Tasca's archive because he must have considered it too compromising for his political persona. After the war, he rebuilt his credibility in part by presenting himself as a victim of communist persecution. As the communists were vocal in their accusations against Tasca for his role in Vichy, it was natural for him to seek to restore his reputation by discrediting his accusers. Tasca's role in providing the intelligence used against the PCF, on the other hand, explains why he believed that the communists wanted to kill him after the liberation of France.

By the same token, we can understand why Tasca, who technically had no political role in Vichy, could think that he might be arrested by de Gaulle's army for his activity in Vichy. Even assuming that Tasca was unconsciously exaggerating his importance, only his awareness that he was fighting against the Resistance can explain why he believed the new government might arrest him. As we will see in the epilogue, his hostility toward the people who fought against Vichy and its regime did not disappear even after the war, and he cited this "disgust" for the new leaders of liberated France as a reason to help Paul Marion with his legal problems.

When Vichy was finally liberated, Tasca's decision to stay in his job put him in the unpleasant position of being arrested, but also gave him the opportunity to claim that he had stayed to help the liberation. During the days that he spent in prison, Tasca was able to organize his defense against the legal and moral charges that the new France was preparing against him. However, the spectacle of people rallying around the new authorities after years of support for Pétain, he wrote in his diary, reminded him of what he had always wanted to avoid during his years in Vichy, and convinced him that he had been right: as he had always feared, the future of France had been decided by the Allies' victory in the war and not by a French revolution.[103] Tasca, who had not changed his routine after the Germans left, believed that, contrary to the conformism of the crowd, he had always been faithful to his ideas and to himself in pursuing his political projects. He still desired to see a revolution that combined the social and the national, but he knew that he had been defeated. Thus, the end of the occupation marked the end of Tasca's career as a revolutionary, whether socialist or national socialist.

In 1944, he was only fifty-two years old, potentially with many more years in front of him. Since 1938, though, he had wanted to retire from active politics, and at the end of the war, in prison and with an uncertain future ahead of him, Tasca found that his enthusiasm for politics was at its lowest level ever. He needed to come up with a defense for himself and, potentially, for some of his friends. The desire to justify his actions and to prove that they had been moral—when most of the people around him believed otherwise—forced Tasca to play a defensive game. From that moment onward, his activity as a historian was no longer directed toward influencing the future but only at explaining his own past. Tasca could no longer hope to change history, his lifelong dream; at most, all he could do was write his own interpretation of it.

As we will see in the epilogue, Tasca used all the means at his disposal to try to mitigate the infamy that his choice for Vichy had impressed upon his political persona. The twenty years that he had effectively spent fighting fascism, from the birth of Mussolini's movement to his radio broadcast in 1940, had been erased by his life in the 1940s. In the name of antifascism, he had accepted the loss of his communist identity in 1929, when his idea of a coalition of leftist parties to fight fascism prompted his comrades to say that he was not truly a communist. When his credibility as an antifascist was compromised and, thanks to the Resistance, the communists' credentials as antifascists were at their highest, very little was left of his former prestige and credibility. Only his anticommunism, as we will see, still gave him some authority in France and in the United States. Nevertheless, it was more an epilogue to his life than a true last chapter.

Epilogue

During the forty days he spent in prison in September 1944, Tasca still talked about socialism, but he dreamed of a trip to Italy with Liliane Chaumette. Surrounded by inmates who wanted to see a new German-Russian alliance that would embarrass the French communists, and by the military police who tortured some of the prisoners, he wished to go back to the Italy that he had left in 1926: Turin, Milan, Naples, and all the other places that carried memories for him.[1]

At that point, he still toyed with the idea of making an intellectual contribution to the reconstruction of Europe. Among his projects was still the idea of a book discussing the future political architecture of France. Increasingly, however, he wanted to distance himself from active politics. In the past, he had periodically entertained the idea of a more theoretical engagement, far from the exigencies of everyday politics, but this time he felt that he had the opportunity, and certainly the need, for a more traditional life. He was sure that he did not want to be a journalist any longer, and he desired more time for himself and his family. He also wanted to go back to Paris and live with one of his daughters, Valeria, and visit his eldest daughter, Elena, in Turin. He hoped that Liliane Chomette would agree to live with him and was distressed when in one of her letters she addressed him formally as *vous*.[2] He also knew that his desire to live with Chomette and go back to Paris meant that his youngest daughter, Catherine, would stay with her mother.[3]

After being released from prison, Tasca managed to realize almost all his dreams. He married Liliane Chomette and moved with her and his daughter Valeria into a new apartment in Paris.[4] In 1949 he visited Italy, where he saw his daughter Elena. He wrote for journals, including the conservative French publication *Le Figaro Littéraire* and the Italian *Il Mondo*, but never about everyday politics. He earned his income publishing books, which were well received. He stayed away from party politics and, despite an invitation from André Malraux to join the Rassemblement du Peuple Français, refused to lend his name to any specific party.[5] Most important, he never had to return to prison, and his incarceration in 1944 was his last. Thus at the end of his life, Tasca managed to reinvent a normal life for himself and his family, far from the revolutionary dreams that he had cultivated for almost forty years.

Tasca's longing for a normal life certainly was one reason he did not resume the activities that had characterized his life until the end of the war, but his personal wishes were not the only factor that kept him from playing a direct role in postwar France or Italy. Tasca's trajectory from revolutionary socialism to Vichy no longer allowed him to think positively about the future of France, Italy, or Europe more generally. It was his own role in the first half of the "age of extremes" that continued to be the center of interest for the people around him and, consequently, for his intellectual activity.[6] In this context, Tasca's vocation as a historian acquired a new importance, and his entire cultural production became oriented toward the project of justifying his own past. In the years immediately after the war, France's attempt to cope with the history of Vichy through the legal system further complicated Tasca's position, constantly producing an intellectual short circuit between moral, political, and legal responsibilities. On one hand, Tasca took advantage of the confusion created by the attempt to define moral and political problems in the language of criminal law. On the other hand, his need to create multiple truths—one legal, one moral, and one political—and the constant confusion between these different realms prevented him from facing his own past critically and from leaving behind the events of his earlier life.

The confusion started with his incarceration in 1944. Tasca, brought to prison unaware of the charges against him, naturally believed that the new Republican government had an interest in prosecuting him for his role in Vichy. But, as we have seen, the charges against him were absurd and had nothing to do with Vichy, and Tasca did not have too many problems in convincing the prosecutor that he had never been a Trotskyist, that his activity at *Monde* in the early thirties was not criminal, and that the idea of a fascist-Trotskyist-Spanish-Synarchist conspiracy to bring down de Gaulle's government in Algiers was ludicrous. During those days, however, he had also had the opportunity to create for himself an identity as a member of the Resistance. Since his role in Vichy was not at the center of the investigation, the people in charge of determining his fate had no special reason to pay too much attention to the proof Tasca presented for his Resistance claims.

As we have seen, Tasca's evidence for his role in the Resistance was at best dubious. He affirmed that his contact with the Resistance had been established through Jef Rens, who had been a close political associate of de Man and who had left Belgium after the German invasion to go into exile in London. But Rens specifically denied any association with Tasca after his decision to remain in Vichy and work for *L'Effort*. As Rens clearly stated in a letter to André Tixier, minister of social affairs in de Gaulle's government, he had indeed suggested contacting Tasca in order to obtain information about the Vichy regime, but that didn't mean he thought of him as anything less than fully committed to Vichy. In their conversations in 1940, Tasca had explicitly expressed his desire to play the role of the "socialist consciousness" of the authoritarian regime, and this had created a permanent political rift between Rens and Tasca. Rens refused to play along with Tasca's attempt to present "his continued presence in Vichy as a way to do him a favor and be useful."[7]

Paul Cavyn, on the other hand, fully confirmed his relationship with Tasca, and his testimony was the only positive proof that Tasca could offer about his role. In a letter to Georges Bidault, Cavyn, who introduced himself as a former unofficial underground representative of the Belgian government in France, confirmed that Tasca had given him information that prevented the arrest of four Belgian representatives in Nice. He had also learned from Tasca that other Belgian agents in Grenoble were under surveillance. Finally, Tasca had provided him with unspecified material on the French situation, material that Cavyn had transmitted to London. According to Cavyn, Tasca had been collaborating with him since 1941, but their association had been hidden from the other members of the Belgian underground organization for security reasons.[8]

We do not know what personal relationship Tasca and Cavyn had. Nor do we know Cavyn's political ideas and the exact role he played in Vichy France.[9] Furthermore, we do not know why Cavyn, in his first letter to Bidault, had spoken generically "of an interrupted service to the Belgian and French Resistance," or why he asserted that both Paul-Henri Spaak and Jef Rens were aware of Tasca's role, when Rens reacted as we have seen and Spaak never spoke out to defend Tasca.[10] What we do know is that it was thanks to Cavyn, and only to Cavyn, that Tasca was proposed as a recipient of a Belgian gold medal for his role in the Resistance. In October 1944 Cavyn petitioned his government to award Tasca either the Croix de Chevalier de l'Ordre de Léopold or the Rosette de l'Ordre de la Couronne; Tasca eventually received a decoration, but not a job from the Belgian government, as he had requested from Rens.[11] Thanks to his many connections and to the relatively low level that he had occupied in Vichy, Tasca was able to solicit the help he needed to end his imprisonment.

By the time he came out of prison, Tasca had managed to have his version of his role in Vichy on record for the new French military authorities, and officially certified by the Belgian authorities, who accepted Cavyn's version of events. The problem was that even if Tasca had truly helped Cavyn with the activities that earned him his gold medal, his version of the meaning of the events was certainly false. It was untrue that in 1944, at the moment of his arrest, he was engaged in an activity for the Resistance that could be jeopardized by his arrest, as he had stated. It was untrue that he had stayed in Vichy after the spring of 1941 in order to be able to assist the Belgian Resistance. It was also untrue that he had resumed his job at *L'Effort* in order to provide a cover for his role. Paul Cavyn never mentioned such requests, and Jef Rens explicitly denied that they had been made. Thus Tasca's official version of his role in Vichy was substantially false.[12]

Undoubtedly Tasca had made those declarations under the pressure of his imprisonment, when he believed that his ability to quickly regain his freedom depended on his role in Vichy.[13] After he had presented this version of the events to the prison authorities, to his friends, to the French ministers whom he was able to contact, and to the Belgian king, his credibility depended completely on the truthfulness of his statements. Tasca found himself in a position that constantly prevented him from either fully defending or completely rejecting the motives behind his collaboration with the Vichy government. Since officially he had deserted Vichy in the spring of 1941, he could not discuss explicitly the reasons he remained there and could never admit, to others or to himself, that he had made the wrong choice. In order not to appear as a liar, he needed to defend the version of the events that he had concocted while in prison.

In the years immediately after the liberation of France, Tasca was able to make use of the official version of his association with Vichy to help some of his friends who had made the same choice. The first to take advantage of Tasca's gold medal was Georges Monnet.[14] Monnet's decision to abstain in the vote that had assigned constitutional powers to Pétain had given rise to rumors about his unfaithfulness toward Léon Blum, and he was accused of personally betraying Blum.[15] Blum himself felt that Monnet's behavior had not been what he expected from a friend.[16] Thus in November 1944 Monnet had been excluded from the SFIO for misconduct. After the end of the war, Monnet appealed the decision, and the Jury of Honor of the Socialist Party, presided over by Charles Lussy, reviewed his case. On May 7, 1947, Tasca was called by Monnet to be a witness for his defense. Tasca testified as a decorated member of the Resistance, and Monnet was acquitted of all charges.[17] Tasca also wanted to help Paul Marion and Henri Moysset, with whom he had collaborated constantly since the spring of 1941. However, Moysset died on August 1, 1949, before the high court in charge of the purge could try his case and reach a verdict. Tasca never managed to present his defense of the ex-minister.[18]

In the case of Paul Marion, Tasca not only managed to submit an exculpatory brief on behalf of his old friend but also was paramount in the court's decision to shorten drastically the length of Marion's imprisonment.[19] Marion, who had been an expert on propaganda since his days in the Communist Party, was able to send letters to Tasca from his cell in 1947 and organize his own defense. In these letters, Marion told Tasca exactly what to say in order to help him in the trial.[20]

The version of their friendship that they invented for Marion's defense was based on small modifications of true events. Marion asked Tasca to say that they had first met in the circle of socialist activists that gravitated around *Monde*. When it came to Vichy, Marion suggested emphasizing the role of Henri Moysset in putting them in contact for the purpose of discussing theoretical matters, underlining that these had no direct practical consequences. After their renewed contacts through Moysset, it was Tasca's job that required constant meetings between them. Overall, Tasca had to say that he knew Marion very well, but only for professional reasons and only in Vichy: he was a very qualified witness but not Marion's friend.

Once he had established his credentials, Tasca was to present Marion as a politician who had been in favor of collaboration with the Germans, but at the government level only, always opposing the Parisian collaborators. In order to explain some of the most compromising facts of Marion's activity in Vichy, Tasca was to declare that Marion was studying techniques of resistance in occupied countries in order to plan France's revenge against the Germans. To testify to Marion's compassionate personality and personal decency, Tasca was to say that Marion had been in favor of a Red Cross government in occupied France, and that he had always led a modest life.[21] Marion, as he presented himself with the help of Tasca, was a French patriot who had done everything in the service of France and nothing for himself, always in good faith and never acting against other French citizens.

Tasca went further. In his letter to the court, he testified that Marion had helped Jews, communists, and Gaullists. Marion, according to Tasca's testimony, had personally intervened to free both famous communists, including Jacques Sadoul, and simple militants. Moreover, after achieving their release, he had also made certain that they would not be required to sign documents attesting to their support for Pétain, and he personally ensured that they would be allowed to find a job and support themselves.

Given such a favorable portrait, and especially since it was painted by a decorated hero such as Tasca, the high court was lenient with Marion. In the end, Marion, who had been a fascist and a collaborator, was sentenced to only ten years in prison.[22]

Tasca's testimony was crafted to omit the real history of his relationship with Marion. Their common past in Moscow and their common militancy in the Bukharinist faction of the International were hidden in order to avoid the impression of too close a parallel between their lives. Tasca's disagreement with Marion in 1933 over what he saw as a fascist turn in his friend's political ideology was kept secret because it would have damaged Marion rather than helping him. The debate between Marion, who in Vichy wanted the creation of a unified youth movement, and Moysset and Tasca, who opposed the totalitarian aspirations present in Marion's project, was transformed into the appearance of a perfect collaboration among Tasca, Moysset, and Marion.[23] To round out this gallery of lies there was Marion's request, carefully underlined in the letter, that Tasca declare he had worked at the Institut de Recherches Économiques et Sociales, not at the *bureau d'études*, probably in order to conceal the fact that Tasca was employed by Marion in Vichy. As a consequence, in front of the high court, the complex ideological turns that had characterized the lives of both men were erased in favor of a deceptive version that made them accomplices.

In helping Marion, Tasca was motivated by friendship, but also by his awareness that, despite their political differences and their different responsibilities in the regime, the charges against Marion also applied to him. In the context of the trials of all the protagonists of Vichy, the charges against Marion were charges against the regime itself, and as such, they symbolically encompassed all the people who had contributed to the functioning of the regime. As Tasca's declarations make clear, the defense strategy with which Marion and Tasca countered the prosecutors' intent to put the regime on trial consisted in claiming that, as an individual, Marion had not committed any crimes.[24] As an individual, Tasca declared, Marion had helped people, had not profited from his position, and had led a modest life. Thus Tasca was able to marshal the liberal-democratic principle of individual responsibility against the political nature of the trial. Rather than defending the regime, Tasca and Marion took advantage of the legal system to claim that Marion had not broken any laws.

The feeling that his political ideas were on trial created in Tasca a permanent resentment against the new republic. As he wrote to Marion, he had nothing but distaste for Marion's prosecutors.[25] This resentment was particularly strong against the communists, whom he saw as responsible for betraying France both at the national level and internationally. To Tasca, it seemed a moral and political injustice that the Communist Party had found in the resistance against Vichy and the Germans a source of legitimation in the political framework of the restored Republic. Consequently, he devoted his intellectual efforts to the fight against the communists.

The books he published from 1948 to 1954—*Physiologie du parti communiste français, Deux ans d'alliance germano-soviétique, Les communistes français pendant la drôle de guerre, Les cahiers du Bolchévisme pendant la campagne 1939–1940*, and *Le pacte germano-soviétique*—were all intent on proving a single proposition: that the communist movement had betrayed antifascism during the time of the Molotov-Ribbentrop Pact. The Italian communists, in their effort to keep Italy out of the war, "supported any defeatist and isolationist argument, and thus joined forces with Hitler's fifth column."[26] The British communists, on October 3, 1939, "demanded that negotiations for peace should begin immediately," and all the different communist movements had adopted similar positions.[27] It was in France, however, "that the communists made the most intensive and systematic efforts to spread defeatism," actively campaigning to "stir up an anti-war movement, making use of every possible means, legal and illegal."[28] The communist propaganda "undermined the morale of the French troops to an extent which helped the Wehrmacht when it delivered its onslaught."[29] Thus, in Tasca's reconstruction of the events of 1940, the communist movement had played a fundamental part in the French defeat: the pact between the Soviet Union and Germany had allowed Hitler to start the war against Great Britain and France, and the communist movement had campaigned against a military resistance against the Germans.

Tasca's anticommunism did not stop at the events of 1939–40 but encompassed the entire communist movement. Because of their absolute faithfulness to Moscow and to their party, Tasca presented the French communists as individuals fundamentally foreign to the French national community. "The point to grasp," he wrote, "is that this new kind of Frenchman [the communist] represents a sharp break with the social pattern hitherto dominant in France. The relevant specifications are taken from a blueprint imported from abroad."[30] Thus Tasca transformed the political identity of the French communists into an anthropological difference between the communists and the French.

In these passages, he employed the concept of a supposed French "national pattern" to mobilize against the Communist Party precisely the nationalist mythology that he had so strongly and coherently criticized during his life as a socialist.[31] The communists, Tasca believed, were doing exactly the same: "Today, Moscow excites and maneuvers the national sentiment in France . . . while it exalts all the national memories that can create anti-French feelings in Germany, and especially in East Germany."[32] All the Russian communist leaders, in fact, were simply Russian nationalists, whose goal, from Lenin to Trotsky, from Stalin to Malenkov, was simply the "territorial expansion of the USSR at the expense of all the other independent countries."[33]

Tasca's constant focus on the Molotov-Ribbentrop Pact certainly reveals the extent to which he had felt personally betrayed by the events of the summer of 1939. The chain of events that had led the French communists to accept the dictates of Stalin's policy, while Tasca and Blum, in their writings for *Le Populaire*, were desperately hoping for a different decision on the part of the French communist leadership, had left a permanent mark on Tasca's relationship with the communist movement.[34] As we have seen, the ruthlessness of Stalin's policy inspired Tasca to be as ruthless as his opponents in his political choices.[35] After the end of the war, Tasca did not abandon the spirit that he had cultivated in 1939.

Consequently, despite the accuracy of some of his historical reconstructions, Tasca's books on the communist parties were more propaganda than scientific history. The books themselves were initially conceived in the context of Tasca's job, which was in effect a branch of the Vichy propaganda secretariat. As Marion wrote to Tasca when the first of his books on the French Communist Party was published, it was Tasca's "abundant Vichyssoise research that was finally taking off," and Marion was "looking forward to the publication of his first volume."[36]

Even more important was that Tasca applied a double standard in judging the communists' behavior between 1939 and 1941 and his own. Indirectly, he blamed the communists for his own downfall and absolved himself of the same crimes that he blamed on the communists. He stressed the collaboration between the Germans and the Russians as proof of the communists' unworthiness, but, as we have seen, he himself had been in favor of collaboration with the Germans after the invasion of France.[37] He resented the communists' ability to present themselves as if they had always been at the forefront of antifascism when they had previously engaged in an alliance with fascism, hiding the fact that he himself had fully collaborated with openly fascist politicians such as Paul Marion. He wanted to discredit the communists' credentials as legitimate participants in the political life of France by debunking their history in the Resistance, but he was taking full advantage of his own ambiguous role in the Resistance to legitimize himself.

Without indulging in simplistic psychological analysis, we can affirm that Tasca blamed the communists for the fall of the Third Republic and the birth of Vichy and, in doing so, he blamed his entire Vichy past on them. Without the Molotov-Ribbentrop Pact, Tasca implied in all his books, Vichy would have not existed, and he would not have been in the position of having to choose collaboration and an authoritarian government over his democratic ideals. He ignored the observation made by Salvemini about his manuscript of *Le pacte germano-soviétique*—"Stalin . . . could not have predicted such a disastrous defeat of France. Hitler put him in the position of choosing between an agreement with him or a war against him with the consent of the West. What would you have done in that situation?"[38]—because this consideration would have put him in the difficult position of explaining that he had not been far from Stalin's political realism. The communists had betrayed France because they were not really French but anthropological specimens forged in Russia, whereas he had acted to defend France and the Enlightenment tradition from the assaults coming from the east. This psychological self-deception allowed Tasca to write his books as if he was the same antifascist intellectual that he had been in 1939. But he was no longer that person.

In the political climate of the Cold War, Tasca's past in Vichy was of no special concern to some of the intellectuals engaged in the ideological battle against communism. Tasca's books, financed by the Vichy government, became an international success. Yale University Press immediately translated *Physiologie du parti communiste français* as *A Communist Party in Action*, and the book appeared on the American market in 1949 and again in 1970. Two years later, Beacon Press published *Deux ans d'alliance germano-soviétique* as *The Russo-German Alliance*, which appeared the same year as the French edition. Other editions of *Physiologie du parti communiste français* appeared in Taiwan, in Brazil (where it was published with the title *A filosofia do comunismo*), in Italy, and in Norway (where *Deux ans d'alliance germano-soviétique* was also published in 1954), anointing Tasca as an internationally recognized Cold War warrior.[39]

This success as an anticommunist propagandist, however, did not erase the questions of some of Tasca's friends who, without themselves being communists, were not ready to accept Tasca's simplification of the policies of the communist parties and of his own past. Some of Tasca's former fellow travelers in the socialist movement or in the area of democratic antifascism, including Jef Rens, refused to resume their friendship with him. Léon Blum, for instance, declared: "What a pity. If Rossi [Tasca] had held out a few days longer, he would be playing a major role today in Italy."[40] Victor Serge, whom Tasca had helped both during and after his imprisonment in a Russian gulag, wrote in his memoir that Tasca's decision to stay in Vichy was a "moral failure," and hinted that he had done so to save his huge personal archive.[41] Even Charles-André Julien, who was so close to Tasca that he had raised his daughter during the war, suggested that Tasca had stayed in Vichy because he could not bear to start his life all over again.[42]

Tasca rejected with anger these judgments, and privately continued to claim the legitimacy of his choice in 1940. His comment on Blum's remark shows that Tasca always believed that his decision to work in Vichy was the opposite of a moral failure. "I 'held out' for four years and for quite different ambitions than to become a deputy or minister in the French or Italian Constituent Assembly,"[43] Tasca wrote in his diary. In his mind, Tasca continued to see his entire period in Vichy, the four years from 1940 to 1944, as an unbroken continuity. It was not his supposed role in the Resistance that legitimized his actual role in Vichy but the political ideas that he had developed in the early summer of 1940. Tasca rejected the accusations of opportunism and wanted to publicize the reasons behind his choice, convinced, as he was, that his choice had been rational and disinterested.

But even the idea of giving voice to his real motivations was an impossibility for Tasca. In order to fight the charges of moral indignity, he would have had to declare publicly that he still believed in the reasons behind his support for Vichy. This public declaration would have conflicted with Tasca's claim that he had worked against the Vichy regime in the ranks of the Resistance, and it would also have revealed his opportunistic use of his activities for Cavyn in order to help his Vichy friends. Even more important, the value of his anticommunist books would have been put in question, since they were authored by someone who had collaborated with Pétain's regime and, indirectly, with the Nazis. Therefore, if Tasca had wanted to fight the charges of "moral failure," he would have been forced to admit that after the war he had refused to face his responsibilities because of the contempt he felt for the new French Republic—presenting an impossible conundrum.

Tasca had no intention of losing his legitimacy as a *résistant.* In the spring of 1950, in *France Nouvelle,* the official journal of the French Communist Party, the communist journalist Roger Maria published an article that attacked Tasca for his past in Vichy. Maria did not mince words: he accused Tasca of being a collaborator and connected his activities in Vichy with Pierre Laval. Tasca's support for Pétain, the journal claimed, proved that he had always been a traitor and that the communists had been right in expelling him from their movement. Tasca immediately decided to sue

Maria and *France Nouvelle,* and a trial for defamation was scheduled first for October 6, 1950, and then postponed until January 12, 1951.[44]

At the trial, Tasca presented documents similar to those that he had used in 1944. In his written declaration to the court, Tasca declared:

> After a few weeks I had to abandon any hope of realizing the unity of the French people with the help of the Vichy government. Therefore, at the beginning of November 1940, I quit *L'Effort,* where I started to work again after many months, since I had agreed to work for the Resistance, work that justified my presence in Vichy. Needless to say, not a single line in my articles echoed the slogans of Vichy's propaganda.[45]

The statement repeats his usual mix of subjective truths (Tasca's concern for the unity of the French) and objective lies (his work for *L'Effort* as a consequence of his role in the Resistance). He included the declaration by Cavyn, which was crucial to his case, and an unsigned letter by Field Marshal Bernard Montgomery dated May 6, 1946, which said: "By this certificate of service I record my appreciation of the aid rendered by Tasca Jean Ange [*sic*] as a volunteer in the service of the United Nations for the great cause of freedom."[46] Tasca also listed, for the first time, the testimony of Jacques Fouques-Duparc, the French ambassador in Rome, who had left Vichy after Laval's return to power, and who declared that Tasca had saved many antifascists, including communists.[47] Needless to say, this was an entirely post facto fabrication, since neither Tasca nor Cavyn had mentioned the fact in 1944.

The trial against *France Nouvelle* mobilized in Tasca's favor unexpected sectors of the anticommunist movement. From the United States, David Dubinsky, the president of the International Ladies' Garment Worker's Union and vice president of the American Federation of Labor, offered by letter his and his organization's support for Tasca in the trial.[48] We do not know for sure why Dubinsky took an interest in Tasca's case, but it is not difficult to speculate that Jay Lovestone, who had long been an associate of Dubinsky, might have played a part in it. Lovestone, as we have seen, had been expelled from the American Communist Party at the same time as Tasca's expulsion and for the same reasons.[49] In 1930, Lovestone's journal, *Revolutionary Age,* had reported with great emphasis Tasca's expulsion from the PCI, and Lovestone and Tasca had known each other since the end of the twenties, when they were both in Moscow and, together with Marion, were prominent figures of the Bukharinist wing of the International. Thus, at the beginning of the fifties, when anticommunism became their new common ideological ground, Lovestone, leader of an

American anticommunist union, might have wanted to help his old comrade in his fight against communism.

In the trial against the communist journal, Tasca was also able to obtain the support of Gaetano Salvemini, with whom he had reestablished contact after the war.[50] Salvemini's help was ideologically, if not practically, important for Tasca. Most of the people who offered their assistance to Tasca for his trial either were motivated by their anticommunism or had entertained an ambiguous relation with Vichy.[51] Salvemini, by contrast, had real moral authority among the democratic antifascists.[52] Thus, despite the fact that Salvemini "did not know the facts under the court's scrutiny," his favorable opinion of Tasca became quickly very important for Tasca's defense, both in his case against *France Nouvelle* and against the attacks that continued to be directed against him.[53]

Tasca's victory in the trial created a legal truth that did nothing to convince Tasca's accusers of his innocence. In Italy in particular, where Tasca had been an important figure of the socialist movement, the publication of books by members of the Resistance who had lived in exile in France and in Belgium was increasingly reinforcing the idea that Tasca's past was not that of a *résistant*. In July 1951, the socialist Paolo Alatri wrote in his review of *La naissance du fascisme* that after the invasion of France, Tasca "ended up in Pétain's and Laval's circle, a strange development for which the word 'betrayal' [was] probably appropriate."[54] Six months later, Alberto Jacometti, a reformist socialist who had been arrested by the Gestapo in 1940 in Belgium and who had spent three years in confinement before joining the Resistance in 1943 after Mussolini's fall, wrote in his memoir that in 1940 "Tasca had already become a traitor."[55] Tasca asked Salvemini to reply to these charges, which had been directed against him by socialists whom Tasca accused of being lackeys of the communists. Salvemini accepted and partially protected Tasca with his moral authority. More important, Salvemini's voice helped to generate a debate around Tasca, who therefore had the opportunity to present his own account of his presence in Vichy.

At the beginning of 1952, Mario Pannunzio, the founder of the journal *Il Mondo*, one of the most prestigious publications in post–World War II Italy, which regularly featured articles by Salvemini, contacted Tasca to ask him to publish a series of articles on his experience in France during the war. Jacometti's reply to Salvemini's defense, in fact, was so detailed that only Tasca could provide an adequate answer.[56] The six articles that Tasca published in *Il Mondo* between July and August 1952 gave him the opportunity to present his last self-defense on the controversial subject of his support for Vichy.

In these articles, republished as a book a year later, Tasca tried to present the political reasons behind his support for Pétain and for the regime while seeking to counter Jacometti's charges. The legal side of his role in Vichy had been definitely closed at the end of April 1952, when a French appeals court had confirmed the judgment against *France Nouvelle,* but the moral and political charges against him had not received a full reply, and Tasca wanted to reaffirm the validity of his choice. Thus, as he did with his books on the French Communist Party, he used his historiographic work as a tool for self-justification. The result was an account of the events of the first year of Vichy from Tasca's point of view, in which he did not shy away from using the documents that he had produced for *L'Effort* at the end of the summer of 1940.

Tasca's rhetorical strategy consisted in presenting his subjective desires and the objective problems of the context in which he moved after the German invasion, while hiding the concrete solutions that he derived from his reading of the situation. He reminded his readers that a vast majority of the French parliament had voted to grant constitutional powers to Pétain and that he had not been alone in his belief that the Third Republic had to be replaced with a new political system after the defeat. He quoted the passages that he had written in 1940 to prove that his long-term goal was to organize, as we have seen, a new French state to preserve the possibility of a lasting revenge against the Germans.[57] But he failed to mention that from this analysis he also derived the idea that a form of collaboration with the Germans was necessary if an independent French state was ever to be created. He also did not mention that he believed that a single French party had to be created to give legitimacy to Pétain's regime and overcome the political divisions of the Third Republic. And he did not have to inform his readers that in 1940 his projects so neatly meshed with Laval's that Laval had financed the publication of *L'Effort.*[58]

Deploying the same rhetorical strategy, Tasca defended Pétain. To his Italian readers, he claimed that the marshal had been a "shield," presenting the thesis that the marshal's goal had been "to shield France with his person" and insisting on the good intentions of the regime.[59] Thus, in his apologetic reconstruction, Tasca inverted the logic that had inspired his actions in 1940. Tasca had consciously advocated the pursuit of policies that he knew were morally repugnant to a majority of the French, such as collaboration, citing the need for the political elite to make unpopular choices for the good of France. By 1952, however, Tasca was asking to be judged not from the point of view of the effects that these policies had had on France but from the point of view of his intentions. Tasca's book displayed the same logic that had inspired the legal defense of the leaders of the regime who, like Marion, had insisted on their lack of a criminal intent. In focusing on his intentions, Tasca remained silent on the real political crimes that he had committed.

Tasca's claim that "he never repeated the official propaganda of the regime," for instance, was made without mentioning one incontrovertible fact: he had directed the *bureau d'études*, whose task was to provide documentation to Paul Marion, then in charge of the regime's propaganda.[60] More important, Tasca never said a word about the publication on the first page of *L'Effort* of the *statut des juifs* while he was writing, in the same issue of the newspaper, an elegant analysis of the political situation in the Balkans.[61] He did not explain why he had agreed to publish an article with his signature in the same issue of *L'Effort* in which an editorial claimed that Jews and foreigners were to be blamed for France's defeat, and welcomed the racial laws as a means to prevent further damage. Presenting himself as an isolated figure who pursued an almost personal political project, Tasca sought to absolve himself of indirectly supporting the regime's acts through his political presence.

Despite his unwillingness to take responsibility for the crimes of the regime, Tasca still wanted to be exonerated in the context of a positive reconsideration of his project of a National Revolution and not for his role against Vichy. In Vichy he had been an attentive observer and, occasionally, a participant in the political struggle among the multiple components of the dictatorial regime. After the war, he could not accept being placed in the same political camp as Maurras and L'Action Française.[62] He had tried to influence the policy of the regime and had certainly been defeated in his projects, as we have seen. Therefore he considered it unfair to be judged along with an entire regime.

Tasca claimed that his position had been inspired by the idea that one "cannot and should not abandon a struggle at the first contradictions and when the fight becomes unpleasant and morally disturbing for some secondary aspects."[63] He used this idea, which he said he had learned in the communist movement, to imply that he should not be judged by the objective conditions in which he had conducted his struggle, but simply by his projects within those difficult conditions. Having been in the minority all his life, he now refused to be guilty by association.

Perhaps it was precisely Tasca's experience in the communist movement that played a substantial part in the absolution he chose to give himself. He always rejected the reason the communists gave for expelling him. He had always considered himself innocent of the crimes of Stalinism because he believed that his own "communism" had been different from Stalinism. The very fact that he himself had participated in the political activities of a movement that included Stalin convinced Tasca that not all the communists were clones of Stalin. He clearly believed that if had he been successful in his attempt to lead the communists in a policy of alliance with the socialist parties to defend the Italian and French institutions against the assault of fascism, the tragic end of democracy in these two countries would have been avoided. Under these circumstances, he felt that he did not bear responsibility for the actual direction taken by the communist movement. By the same token, he did not bear responsibility for the actual direction taken by Vichy.

After writing his articles on Vichy, Tasca also wrote a series of articles, published in *Il Mondo* in 1953, on the first ten years of the PCI that were, like his account of his experience in 1940, a combination of history and autobiography.[64] In these articles, Tasca's main thesis was similar to the one he had advanced in reconstructing his experience in Vichy. He had been a communist for good and honest reasons. His opposition to Stalin, Bordiga, and Togliatti proved that he could not be held responsible for the direction in which Stalin in Russia and Togliatti in Italy had taken the communist party. More convincingly than in his rationalizations about Vichy, Tasca showed how a political idea that had started as a project of liberation became responsible for the weakening of the workers' movement on the eve of the fascist seizure of power.[65] He also reconstructed the process of Stalinization undergone by the Italian Communist Party, showing how all the original aspirations of the key participants in the creation of the PCI had been perverted by the development of the situation in Russia. Thus Tasca was able to present himself in these articles as having remained for some time in a party whose politics he considered wrong because he wanted to change those politics, leaving only when he understood that Stalin had won.[66] His indirect claim was that he had behaved similarly in Vichy. He had tried to change the course of the regime but had switched to helping the Resistance as soon as he realized that the regime could not be changed.

Tasca's refusal to be guilty by association had some legitimacy in the legal system, but not in the moral or political realm. He never understood that he was not entitled to be the sole judge of what was "morally disturbing" in a specific regime and what was "a secondary aspect." Thus he was never able to regain the full confidence of the Italian or French left, to which he felt he belonged. Despite the help of Salvemini, who continued to defend him publicly and privately, Tasca's choice continued to be met with strong disapproval, even among the group of liberal socialists who published *Il Ponte* and *Il Mondo* and considered Salvemini a founding father.[67] Bruno Trentin, for instance, whose father, Silvio, had been one of the most famous Italian antifascists, continued to argue with Salvemini about Tasca. Trentin found Tasca's political ambiguities too disturbing to accept him as part of the European resistance against fascism. Even if Tasca's work had been useful, Trentin wrote to Salvemini, the political and moral damage caused by the presence in Vichy of a well-known socialist and antifascist such as Tasca had been much greater.[68]

The polemics surrounding Tasca's name came to a halt not because he was able to convince his detractors of the rightness of his decision but by the sudden deterioration of Tasca's health after 1955. In 1957 he still managed to publish his last work on the end of Stalinism, which he saw exposed in all its brutality by the Russian leadership itself.[69] But his memory and his intellect were quickly failing him. His daughter Valeria described his illness as a series of small brain hemorrhages that left him first physically and then mentally incapacitated.[70] In the last five years before his death, his capacity for work, which had been enormous throughout his life, was first seriously impaired and finally completely destroyed. In the very last years of his existence, he depended completely on his wife, who took care of him until the end. Angelo Tasca died in Paris on March 3, 1960.

The short obituary published by *Il Ponte* immediately after his death is a portrait of his forty years of political activity: "He had been a communist, but without feeling at ease in the communist movement. He had been a member of the Socialist Party, but without being consistent in his positions. After the French defeat in 1940, his desire to be a realist was responsible for the biggest mistake of his life. It is likely that he helped the Resistance; nobody claimed that he had been personally responsible of any crime. Nevertheless, his political life after the liberation was over."[71] What still lived on, *Il Ponte* wrote in 1960, was his book on the birth of fascism, which was then, and remains now, a milestone in the historiography on fascism.

Angelo Tasca's political activity spanned the most dramatic years of the twentieth century and, more than was the case for most of his contemporaries, his life was deeply marked by those years. His desire to change history, rather than just studying it, put him in the position of having to make a choice between political alternatives that he would rather have avoided. In the end, the political context in which he moved changed him much more than he was able to change the context itself, and he was left only with the conviction of the morality of his own political aspirations. This conviction was not enough for his contemporaries, and it is certainly still not enough for us. His attempt to use history to rehabilitate himself failed because the difficulties of the French context after the invasion did not prevent other people from making different choices. Nevertheless, the history of his multiple political failures can help us trace the history of the political catastrophes from which Europe learned the lesson of the moral value of democracy.

Notes

Introduction

1. The latest biography of Palmiro Togliatti (and the only new biography published since 1973) is Aldo Agosti, *Palmiro Togliatti: A Biography* (London: I. B. Tauris, 2008).

2. Tasca's multiple pseudonyms continue to constitute a challenge even for the most thorough scholars. Julian Jackson, for instance, did not realize, or at least did not tell his readers, that the "Angelo Tasca who worked in Vichy's propaganda services" is the A. Rossi who wrote *Les communistes français pendant la drôle de guerre*, a book he cites as a source on the communists in the Phony War (Jackson, *France: The Dark Years, 1940–1944* [Oxford: Oxford University Press, 2001], 639, 114). As another example, France's National Library identifies A. Rossi as Amilcare Rossi, a name that Tasca never used; Amilcare Rossi is in fact the name of another author, who continued to publish books in the 1970s, sixteen years after Tasca's death, including *Nell'occhio del ciclone come già nella cresta dell'onda*; Wikipedia, unfortunately, makes the same mistake.

3. Paolo Spriano, *Storia del Partito comunista italiano*, 2nd ed. (Turin: G. Einaudi, 1978); Alceo Riosa and Angelo Tasca, *Angelo Tasca socialista: Con una scelta dei suoi scritti (1912–1920)* (Venice: Marsilio, 1979); Sergio Soave, *Un eretico della sinistra: Angelo Tasca dalla militanza alla crisi della politica* (Milan: Franco Angeli, 1995).

4. Angelo Tasca, *La France de Vichy: Archives inédits d'Angelo Tasca* (Milan: Fondazione Giangiacomo Feltrinelli, 1996); Angelo Tasca and Denis Peschanski, *Vichy, 1940–1944: Quaderni e documenti inediti di Angelo Tasca: Archives de guerre d'Angelo Tasca* (Milan: Fondazione Giangiacomo Feltrinelli, 1986).

5. Ibid., 41.

6. Ibid., 46.

7. Peschanski titled his first essay on Tasca "Le régime de Vichy a existé" [The Vichy regime existed] to signify that the regime was not simply a puppet government controlled by the Germans and in which the French had no responsibility. Denis Peschanski, "Le régime de Vichy a existé," in Tasca and Peschanski, *Vichy, 1940–1944*, 3–51.

8. Jackson, *France: The Dark Years*, 92.

9. Alexander J. De Grand, *In Stalin's Shadow: Angelo Tasca and the Crisis of the Left in Italy and France, 1910–1945* (DeKalb: Northern Illinois University Press, 1986).

10. Philippe Burrin, "La France dans le champ magnétique des fascisms," *Le Débat* 32 (November 1984): 52–72.

11. I owe this second definition to Martin Jay's analysis of the concept as used by Theodor W. Adorno. See Martin Jay, *Force Fields: Between Intellectual History and Cultural Critique* (New York: Routledge, 1993), 2–3.

12. Jean-Paul Sartre and W. D. Redfern, *Les mains sales* (London: Methuen, 1985).

1. Into the Battlefield

1. See David King, *The Commissar Vanishes: The Falsification of Photographs and Art in Stalin's Russia* (New York: Metropolitan Books, 1997).

2. István Rév, *Retroactive Justice: Prehistory of Post-Communism* (Stanford, CA: Stanford University Press, 2005), 12.

3. The bibliography on Antonio Gramsci is simply too vast to be inserted in a note. However, it is worth mentioning here Carlos Nelson Coutinho, *Gramsci: Um estudo sobre seu pensamento político* (Rio de Janeiro: Editora Campus, 1989), which suggests that politics rather than culture was the central focus of Gramsci's reflection; thus Coutinho amplifies the distance between Tasca and Gramsci. The thesis is interesting and certainly well documented but reinforces a teleological reading of the Sardinian communist.

4. The Communist Party of Italy (PCd'I) officially changed its name to the Italian Communist Party (PCI) only in 1943, when the Third International was terminated. Here, however, I will use the acronym PCI throughout.

5. Leonardo Rapone's *Cinque anni che paiono secoli: Antonio Gramsci dal socialismo al comunismo* (Rome: Carocci, 2011) and Albertina Vittoria's *Storia del PCI: 1921–1991* (Rome: Carocci, 2006) are two perfect examples of how excellent historians can still unwittingly underestimate and obscure Angelo Tasca's role in the history of the Italian Communist Party. Rapone, by presenting Gramsci as a hero who creates a radically new approach to socialism, recognizes the role Tasca played in Gramsci's formation but describes their drifting apart as a consequence of Gramsci's development of "a new sensitivity, a new vision, an original vision," whereas Tasca's vision is described as based "on the methods of the past" (98; my translation). This judgment might be justified in light of the *Prison Notebooks*, but Rapone has no hesitation about presenting it without explaining to his readers why at that point Gramsci was the future and Tasca the past. Vittoria, by condensing seventy years into 164 pages, makes Tasca almost disappear from the narrative with the exception of the events around his

expulsion, thus involuntarily reinforcing the idea that Tasca was important only because of his expulsion, rather than for his presence.

6. Umberto Terracini, "Uscii di scuola e andai in Corso Siccardi," in *L'Unità*, January 22, 1967. Quoted in Francesco Trocchi, *Angelo Tasca e l'Ordine nuovo. La formazione del Partito comunista italiano* (Milan: Jaca, 1973), 29.

7. Antonio Gramsci, "Pietro Gavosto," in *Il Grido del Popolo*, January 22, 1916, reprinted in Antonio Gramsci, *Scritti giovanili, 1914–1918*, 4th ed. (Turin: Einaudi, 1975), 21.

8. Quoted in Alceo Riosa, *Angelo Tasca socialista: Con una scelta dei suoi scritti (1912–1920)* (Venice: Marsilio, 1979), 12.

9. Ibid.

10. For a biography of Palmiro Togliatti (besides the one by Aldo Agosti mentioned in the notes to the introduction), see Ernesto Ragionieri, *Palmiro Togliatti: Per una biografia politica e intellettuale* (Rome: Editori Riuniti, 1976).

11. Contrary to what some authors affirm, Tasca's testimony is clear on the fact that he lived in Moretta (Cuneo) only from 1892 to 1894.

12. Archivio Tasca (hereafter in notes "A.T."), "Cahiers AG, June-September 1944."

13. Angelo Tasca, *I primi dieci anni del PCI*, 2nd ed. (Bari: Laterza, 1973), 87.

14. Ibid.

15. See Riosa, *Angelo Tasca socialista*, 20.

16. Quoted in ibid., 20.

17. Tasca, *I primi dieci anni del PCI*, 84.

18. Ibid. Tasca's point is corroborated by Antonio Gramsci's famous article "Our Marx." Gramsci, providing an intellectual genealogy of Marx, wrote in 1919: "His work falls into just the period when the great battle was taking place between Thomas Carlyle and Herbert Spencer on the role of Man in history." Though this genealogy of Marx is surprising today, Gramsci's understanding of Marx's philosophy as part of the debate around positivism was common in Turin in the first decades of the twentieth century. Antonio Gramsci, Richard Bellamy, and Virginia Cox Balmaceda, *Antonio Gramsci: Pre-Prison Writings* (Cambridge: Cambridge University Press, 1994), 55.

19. On *La Voce*, see Diana Rüesch and Bruno Somalvico, *La voce e l'Europa: Il movimento fiorentino de* La voce*: Dall'identità culturale italiana all'identità culturale europea* (Rome: Presidenza del Consiglio dei ministri Dipartimento per l'informazione e l'editoria, 1989), and Walter L. Adamson, *Avant-Garde Florence: From Modernism to Fascism* (Cambridge, MA: Harvard University Press, 1993).

20. On Salvemini, see Charles L. Killinger, *Gaetano Salvemini: A Biography* (Westport, CT: Praeger, 2002). On Salvemini's *L'Unità*, see Gaetano Arfé, "Il meridionalismo di Gaetano Salvemini," *Ponte* 11, no. 12 (1955); Valerio Cantafio, "*L'Unità* di Gaetano Salvemini e la battaglia antiprotezionista," *Rassegna*

Storica Toscana 38, no. 2 (1992); Cesare Vasoli, "*L'Unità* di Salvemini," *Ponte* 14, no. 11 (1958).

21. For the intellectual biography of Amadeo Bordiga, see Andreina De Clementi, *Amadeo Bordiga* (Turin: G. Einaudi, 1971); Franco Livorsi, *Amadeo Bordiga: Il pensiero e l'azione politica, 1912–1970* (Rome: Editori Riuniti, 1976); Franco De Felice, *Serrati, Bordiga, Gramsci e il problema della rivoluzione in Italia. 1919–1920* (Bari: De Donato, 1971); Arturo Peregalli and Sandro Saggioro, *Amadeo Bordiga: La sconfitta e gli anni oscuri: 1926–1945* (Milan: Colibrì, 1998); Richard Drake, *Apostles and Agitators: Italy's Marxist Revolutionary Tradition* (Cambridge, MA: Harvard University Press, 2003), 138–65.

22. Amadeo Bordiga, in *L'Avanguardia*, June 1, 1913.

23. Quoted in Riosa, *Angelo Tasca socialista*, 23.

24. Angelo Tasca, "Note di un culturista," *L'Avanguardia*, December 22, 1912.

25. During the congress the motion written by Tasca received 2,465 votes, Bordiga's 2,730.

26. Tasca, "Note di un culturista."

27. Ibid.

28. Ibid.

29. On Turin and its working class, see Paolo Spriano, *Socialismo e classe operaia a Torino dal 1892 al 1913* (Turin: Einaudi, 1958).

30. Gramsci, in his *La questione meridionale* (Rome: Edizioni Rinascita, 1951), 14–16, offered a slightly different version of this story, but Salvemini confirmed Tasca's version. Gaetano Salvemini, "La mia autobiografia politica," in *Scritti sulla questione meridionale* (Milan: Feltrinelli, 1955), 5.

31. On Mussolini's role in the Socialist movement until his break in 1914, see Renzo De Felice, *Mussolini il rivoluzionario, 1883–1920*, 2nd ed. (Turin: G. Einaudi, 1965).

32. A.T., "Quaderno 28" (1934–35).

33."In Mussolini the young [socialists] saw the supreme leader." Amadeo Bordiga, *Storia della sinistra comunista* (Milan: Ediz. del Programma comunista, 1964), 68.

34. Bordiga wrote an article titled "Il socialismo a Napoli e nel Mezzogiorno," which was published in the same issue of *Utopia* in which Tasca's article was published. Benito Mussolini, *Utopia. Rivista quindicinale del socialismo rivoluzionario* (Milan: Feltrinelli, 1973), 361.

35. On Giuseppe Lombardo Radice and his pedagogy, which was influenced by Gentile's neoidealism and by Dewey's activism, see Giacomo Cives and Giuseppe Lombardo Radice, *Attivismo e antifascismo in Giuseppe Lombardo Radice: "Critica didattica" o "didattica critica"?* (Florence: La Nuova Italia, 1983). Lombardo Radice was later asked by Gentile to organize Italian elementary schools along the lines of Gentile's reform of the Italian school system, but, in

1925, Lombardo Radice interrupted his collaboration with Gentile and with the fascist regime .

36. Angelo Tasca, "I socialisti e la scuola," *Utopia*, February 15–28, 1914, reprinted in Mussolini, *Utopia*, 101–11.

37. See Tasca, *I primi dieci anni del PCI*, 92.

38. See Paolo Spriano, *Storia di Torino operaia e socialista. Da De Amicis a Gramsci* (Turin: G. Einaudi, 1972).

39. According to Tasca, Mussolini replied: "*Alea iacta est.* I need to address the crowd every day," adding that many Marxists, including Arturo Labriola, agreed with him. Tasca, *I primi dieci anni del PCI*, 93.

40. Benito Mussolini, "Dalla neutralità assoluta alla neutralità attiva ed operante," *L'Avanti*, October 18, 1914.

41. Angelo Tasca, "Il mito della guerra," *Il Grido del Popolo*, October 24, 1914.

42. Antonio Gramsci, "Neutralità attiva ed operante," *Il Grido del Popolo*, October 31, 1914; reprinted in Gramsci, *Scritti giovanili, 1914–1918*, 3–4.

43. Tasca, *I primi dieci anni del PCI*, 93.

44. Ibid. It is certainly true that Tasca never mentioned the episode in his later polemics with Gramsci. The event was well known, and during the congress that divided the socialists from the communists, many socialists claimed that Gramsci, who was physically impaired, had been a soldier in an elite regiment. Tasca, however, never took advantage of the situation.

45. Piero Gobetti wrote to Prezzolini that Tasca "hid himself in Turin and remained hidden for four years without even setting foot in a socialist circle" (quoted in Riosa, *Angelo Tasca socialista*, 53). Riosa's perfect reconstruction of Tasca's life in this period is also the source of the information gathered in this and the next paragraphs.

46. Quoted in Riosa, *Angelo Tasca socialista*, 53.

47. A.T., f. 111: "Processo contro Angelo Tasca." In 1940, after his break with Marxism, Tasca could see a parallel between his generation of historical materialists and Leopardi's generation of materialists, but we cannot be sure it was in his undergraduate thesis.

48. See Annamaria Russo, *De Sanctis e Croce: Dalla filosofia alla critica* (Naples: Edizoni del Delfino, 1993).

49. Antonio Gramsci, "Il nostro Marx," in *Il Grido del Popolo*, May 4, 1918, reprinted in Gramsci, *Scritti giovanili, 1914–1918*, 219–20.

50. Balbino Giuliano became, from 1929 to 1932, minister of education of the fascist regime. I have not been able to identify the title of the article or the journal where it was published.

51. Angelo Tasca, "Perché sono socialista," in *Energie Nuove*, March 15–31, 1919, reprinted in Riosa, *Angelo Tasca socialista*, 155. Gramsci had written:

"Karl Marx is for us an instructor of moral and spiritual life" (*Scritti giovanili, 1914–1918*, 220).

52. Riosa, *Angelo Tasca socialista*, 158.

53. Ibid., 156.

54. Tasca quoted the version published by Engels in 1886 as an appendix to his *Ludwig Feuerbach and the End of Classical German Philosophy.* The thesis, which Tasca quoted almost in its entirety (and which he mistakenly identified as thesis number five), is: "The materialist doctrine concerning the changing of circumstances and upbringing forgets that circumstances are changed by men and that it is essential to educate the educator himself. This doctrine must, therefore, divide society into two parts, one of which is superior to society. The coincidence of the changing of circumstances and of human activity or self-changing can be conceived and rationally understood only as revolutionary practice." Karl Marx and Friedrich Engels, *Selected Works* (Moscow: Progress Publishers, 1969), 1:13–15.

55. On Labriola's role in Italian Marxism, see Paul Piccone, *Italian Marxism* (Berkeley: University of California Press, 1983), 92–104.

56. Riosa, *Angelo Tasca socialista*, 156.

57. Giovanni Gentile had originally published "La filosofia della praxis" with Marx's "Theses on Feuerbach" in an appendix. It is therefore possible that Tasca had first read it in Gentile's work. "La filosofia della praxis" is reprinted in Gentile, *La filosofia di Marx. Studi critici* (Florence: Sansoni, 1962). On Gentile and Marxism, see Carmelo Vigna, *Le origini del marxismo teorico in Italia: Il dibattito tra Labriola, Croce, Gentile e Sorel sui rapporti tra marxismo e filosofia* (Rome: Città Nuova, 1977); Nicola Badaloni and Carlo Muscetta, *Labriola, Croce, Gentile* (Bari: Laterza, 1981); Eugenio Garin, "Croce e Gentile interpreti di Marx, in Croce e Gentile: fra tradizione nazionale e filosofia europea," in *Croce e Gentile: fra tradizione nazionale e filosofia europea*, ed. Michele Ciliberto (Rome: Editori Riuniti, 1993).

58. On Tasca and Mondolfo, see Riosa, *Angelo Tasca socialista*, 23–37.

59. Gramsci and Togliatti, the other two key founders of *L'Ordine Nuovo*, held similar views on how to interpret Marx. Years later, Gramsci, as is well known, still used "philosophy of praxis" as a code word for Marxism in his *Prison Notebooks.* Togliatti, in the first issue of the journal, referred to Gentile as the "most respected and influential philosopher of the Italian philosophical school." Empedocle [Palmiro Togliatti], *L'Ordine Nuovo* I (1919).

60. The sum is roughly equivalent to $7,000. The table I used to calculate the conversion is in ISTAT, *Il valore della lira dal 1961 al 2004* (Rome: ISTAT, 2004), Appendix 1.

61. Elena Tasca was born in May 1919.

62. Angelo Tasca, "Battute di preludio," *L'Ordine Nuovo* 1, no. 1 (1919).

63. On Western Marxism, see Perry Anderson, *Considerations on Western Marxism* (London: Verso, 1979), and Martin Jay, *Marxism and Totality: The Adventures of a Concept from Lukács to Habermas* (University of California Press, 1986).

64. Angelo Tasca, "La casa," *L'Ordine Nuovo*, 1919.

65. Riosa, *Angelo Tasca socialista*, 20.

66. Tasca, *I primi dieci anni del PCI*, 86.

67. On the subject, from an author who gives a positive interpretation of Bordiga's policy, see Maria Luongo, "Amadeo Bordiga e il movimento operaio napoletano (1910–1920)," *Cahiers Internationaux d'Histoire Economique et Sociale* 17 (1985).

68. Angelo Tasca, "Fare ognuno il proprio dovere," *L'Ordine Nuovo* 1 (1919).

69. Ibid.

70. Angelo Tasca, "Relazione al congresso camerale di Torino," *L'Ordine Nuovo* 2, no. 3 (1920).

71. Antonio Gramsci, "La relazione Tasca e il congresso camerale di Torino," *L'Ordine Nuovo* 2, no. 4 (1920).

72. Ibid.

73."Cronache dell'Ordine Nuovo," *L'Ordine Nuovo* 2, no. 5 (1920).

74. Antonio Gramsci, "Editorial," *L'Ordine Nuovo* 2 no. 6 (1920).

75. Paolo Spriano, *Storia del Partito comunista italiano*, 2nd ed. (Turin: G. Einaudi, 1978), 163.

76. Riosa, *Angelo Tasca socialista*, 98.

77. For Palmiro Togliatti's account of some of the events narrated in this chapter, see Togliatti, *La formazione del gruppo dirigente del Partito comunista italiano nel 1923–1924*, 2nd ed. (Rome: Editoria Riuniti, 1969).

78. V. I. Lenin, *"Left-Wing" Communism, an Infantile Disorder* (Moscow: Foreign Language Publishing House, 1952), 83n.

79. On the Comintern in those years, see Fernando Claudín, Aldo Agosti, and Fondazione Luigi Einaudi, *Problemi di storia dell'Internazionale comunista (1919–1939): Relazioni tenute al Seminario di studi organizzato dalla Fondazione Luigi Einaudi (Torino, aprile 1972)* (Turin: La Fondazione, 1974), and Aldo Agosti, *La Terza internazionale: Storia documentaria* (Rome: Editori Riuniti, 1974).

80. Tasca, *I primi dieci anni del PCI*, 122.

81. Amadeo Bordiga, "Theses of the Abstentionist Communist Faction of the Italian Socialist Party," *Communist Program* 5 (1979).

82. Spriano, *Storia del Partito comunista italiano*, 163.

83. Ibid.

84. Ibid., 189.

85. Tasca, *I primi dieci anni del PCI*, 132.

86. Ibid.

87. Ibid., 139.

88. Serra (Tasca) to the *Comitato Esecutivo del PCI*, February 8, 1923, in Archivio Storico del PCI, Partito Comunista d'Italia, ff. 99.

89. See Tasca, *I primi dieci anni del PCI*, 180–81.

90. On February 2, 1923, Piero Gobetti, a liberal democrat, was arrested. On August 23, Father Giovanni Minzoni, who refused to merge his group of Boy Scouts with the organization of the young fascists, was killed by the fascists for "small political differences," as stated by the police report. At the end of the year, Giovanni Amendola, another liberal democratic leader, was assaulted by the fascists; he never recovered and died soon after.

91. Spriano, *Storia del Partito comunista italiano*, 279.

92. Tasca, *I primi dieci anni del PCI*, 115.

93. Ibid., 107.

94. Ibid., 137.

95. Tasca, *I primi dieci anni del PCI*, 137.

96. *L'Unità* was also the name of Salvemini's journal, read with passion by the young socialists who created *L'Ordine Nuovo*.

97. Antonio Gramsci, "Intervento alla conferenza organizzativa," *Lo Stato Operaio*, 1924.

98. Ibid.

99. In his reply to Gramsci, Bordiga insisted that the PCI would have conquered the entire working class if Gramsci had not changed its policy toward the Socialist Party. See Amadeo Bordiga, "Intervento alla conferenza organizzativa," *Lo Stato Operaio*, 1924.

100. Spriano, *Storia del Partito comunista italiano*, 249.

101. Ibid.

102. Ibid., 251.

103. See Alexander J. De Grand, *In Stalin's Shadow: Angelo Tasca and the Crisis of the Left in Italy and France, 1910–1945* (DeKalb: Northern Illinois University Press, 1986), 42–43.

104. Amadeo Bordiga, "Tesi per il terzo congresso," in *Il terzo congresso del Partito Comunista d'Italia (Sezione dell'Internazionale Comunista)*, ed. Partito Comunista d'Italia (Rome: Società An. Poligrafica Italiana, 1926).

2. Learning Russian

1. On Tasca's youth, see also Alceo Riosa, *Angelo Tasca socialista: Con una scelta dei suoi scritti (1912–1920)* (Venice: Marsilio, 1979), 10–88; Alexander J. De Grand, *In Stalin's Shadow: Angelo Tasca and the Crisis of the Left in Italy and France, 1910–1945* (DeKalb: Northern Illinois University Press, 1986), 11–33; Francesco Trocchi, *Angelo Tasca e l'Ordine nuovo. La formazione del Partito comunista italiano* (Milan: Jaca, 1973).

2. Angelo Tasca, *I primi dieci anni del PCI*, 2nd ed. (Bari: Laterza, 1973), 152–53.

3. *Annali Istituto Feltrinelli*, ed. Giuseppe Berti (Milan: Feltrinelli, 1966), 516.

4. For the documents and the bylaws approved by the Sixth Congress, see Communist International, *The Program of the Communist International: Together with the Statutes of the Communist International* (London: Modern Books, 1932).

5. On the subject of Stalin's invention of the rules of obedience for the different communist parties, see Erik van Ree, "Stalin's Organic Theory of the Party," *Russian Review* 52, no. 1 (April 1993): 43–57.

6. See Isaac Deutscher, *The Prophet Unarmed: Trotsky, 1921–1929* (New York: Verso, 2003); Pierre Broué, *Trotsky* (Paris: Fayard, 1988); Paolo Spriano, *Storia del Partito comunista italiano*, 2nd ed. (Turin: Einaudi, 1978); Tasca, *I primi dieci anni del PCI*, 125–39.

7. *Annali Istituto Feltrinelli*, 493–95.

8. Spriano, *Storia del Partito comunista italiano*, 3–17.

9. On Palmiro Togliatti, see Aldo Agosti, *Palmiro Togliatti: A Biography* (London: I. B. Tauris, 2008), and Ernesto Ragionieri, *Palmiro Togliatti: Per una biografia politica e intellettuale* (Rome: Editori Riuniti, 1976). See also Giorgio Bocca, *Palmiro Togliatti* (Rome: Laterza, 1973).

10. Cf. Spriano, *Storia del Partito comunista italiano*, 174–75.

11. Ibid.

12. *Annali Istituto Feltrinelli*, 505.

13. The Russians also refused to publish this part of Togliatti's speech in the proceedings of the meeting. See ibid., 494.

14. Spriano uses a euphemism and says that Togliatti had an "awareness that became vigilant of dangers coming from above, namely the Comintern." Spriano, *Storia del Partito comunista italiano*: 184.

15. *Annali Istituto Feltrinelli*, 516.

16. See Hermann Weber and Bernhard Bayerlein, *Der Thälmann-Skandal: Geheime Korrespondenzen mit Stalin* (Berlin: Aufbau-Verlag, 2003); *Annali Istituto Feltrinelli*, 512–13; Ruth Fischer, *Stalin and German Communism: A Study in the Origins of the State Party* (London: G. Cumberlege, 1948).

17. Jules Humbert-Droz had been one of the three secretaries of the Executive Committee of the International and was very close to the Italian Communist Party and its events. See Jules Humbert-Droz, *Il contrasto tra l'Internazionale e il C. I.* (Milan: Feltrinelli, 1969).

18. See *Annali Istituto Feltrinelli*, 512–13, and Robert Jackson Alexander, *The Right Opposition: The Lovestoneites and the International Communist Opposition of the 1930s* (Westport, CT: Greenwood Press, 1981), 157–62.

19. Joseph Stalin, *Works*, Russian ed. (Moscow: Foreign Languages Publishing House, 1954), 11:103–20.

20. Angelo Tasca et al., *A Cécile* (Turin: N. Aragno, 2001), 50–52.

21. See Renzo De Felice, *Mussolini il fascista*, vol. 2: *L'organizzazione dello Stato fascista* (Turin: Einaudi, 1995).

22. Tasca, *I primi dieci anni del PCI*, 147–48; Giovanni Germanetto, *Le Memorie di un barbiere* (Paris: Edizioni di Coltura Sociale, 1931), 355–57.

23. Tasca, *I primi dieci anni del PCI*, 152–53.

24. Ibid.

25. François Furet, *The Passing of an Illusion: The Idea of Communism in the Twentieth Century* (Chicago: University of Chicago Press, 1999), 179–80.

26. Ibid.

27. See A.T., "Quaderno 2," 1928, note dated November 26, 1928.

28. *Annali Istituto Feltrinelli*, 244. This situationism had, to my knowledge, no relation whatsoever to the artistic/political movement that became famous under this name at the end of the fifties and had in Guy Debord one of its most famous exponents.

29. Ibid. The Italian word *tempo* suggests both the idea of time and the idea of a rhythm, a pace, as in the musical term.

30. Ibid., 244–46.

31. Ibid., 284–85.

32. Ibid., 286.

33. Ibid.

34. Ibid., 287.

35. Ibid.

36. The representative was Hungarian Communist Julius Sachs, also known as Giulay Sas and Giulio Aquila.

37. *Annali Istituto Feltrinelli*, 277–79.

38. Antonio Gramsci, Palmiro Togliatti, and Chiara Daniele, *Gramsci a Roma, Togliatti a Mosca: Il carteggio del 1926* (Turin: Einaudi, 1999), 184.

39. *Annali Istituto Feltrinelli*, 279.

40. See Giuseppe Vacca, *Gramsci Togliatti* (Rome: Editori Riuniti, 1991).

41. *Annali Istituto Feltrinelli*, 365.

42. He opposed the expulsion of Boris Souvarine from the PCF and was against the exclusion of Trotsky from the Executive Committee of the Russian Party. See Gramsci, Togliatti, and Daniele, *Gramsci a Roma*, 224.

43. On Luigi Longo's critique of Palmiro Togliatti from the left, see Elio Franzin, *Longo contro Togliatti nel 1927* (Rome: SBL Agenzia 70, 1970).

44. *Annali Istituto Feltrinelli*, 515.

45. Ibid., 520.

46. Stalin, *Works*, 11:307–24.

47. *Annali Istituto Feltrinelli*, 592.

48. Ibid., 533.

49. Ibid.

50. Ibid., 583.

51. Stalin, *Works,* 11:316.

52. Ibid.

53. Ibid., 11:320.

54. Stalin, *Works,* 11:308. For Humbert-Droz's account of the events, see Jules Humbert-Droz, *De Lénine à Staline: Dix ans au service de l'Internationale communiste, 1921–1931* (Neuchatel: Éditions de la Baconnière, 1971).

55. On the so-called right opposition, see Alexander, *The Right Opposition.*

56. For a short but very precise biography of Paul Marion, see Jean Maitron and Claude Pennetier, *Dictionnaire biographique du mouvement ouvrier français,* vol. 35, part 4: *1914–1939: De la première à la seconde guerre mondiale* (Paris: Editions Ouvrières, 1990).

57. *Annali Istituto Feltrinelli,* 596.

58. Ibid.

59. This representative, known by the code name "Pellicano," was the Ukrainian Dmitrij Manuil'skij.

60. *Annali Istituto Feltrinelli,* 607–8.

61. Ibid., 628. The use of *dear* without a name is uncommon in Italian and lends an ironic overtone to the letter.

62. Ibid., 654.

63. Ibid., 626.

64. Ibid., 979. *Misadventure* is the word that Tasca uses ironically to refer to his expulsion.

65. Ibid., 180.

66. On September 14, 1929, Boris Souvarine sent him a letter in which he invited Tasca to keep quiet (*se taire*) to avoid being expelled. Souvarine, who had been expelled for being a Trotskyist, knew firsthand the problems that Tasca could face if he were expelled. See A.T., "Corrispondenza" (1929), Boris Souvarine to Tasca, September 14, 1929.

67. *Annali Istituto Feltrinelli,* 806–7. This expression is as uncommon in Italian as it is in English.

68. Ibid.

69. Ibid., 941.

70. On the issue of the invention of Stalin as a major Marxist theoretician, see Robert C. Tucker, "The Rise of Stalin's Personality Cult," *American Historical Review* 84, no. 2 (1979).

71. *Vie Prolétarienne* 25 (1929).

72. Ibid.

73. Ibid.

74. Ibid.

75. Ibid.

76. Tasca, *I primi dieci anni del PCI.*

77. On October 1, 1929, Tasca wrote to Jezierska that "the bad illness [politics], which my wife says is worse than syphilis and tuberculosis because it's incurable, is back." *Annali Istituto Feltrinelli,* 977.

78."A uno a uno. Tasca espulso dal P.C.," *L'Avanti,* October 13, 1929.

79. *Annali Istituto Feltrinelli,* 977.

80. *Revolutionary Age* 7 (1930).

81."Comunicato del CE," *Prometeo* 26 (1930).

82. A.T., "Quaderno 9" (1929–1930).

83. ISTAT, *Il Valore della Lira dal 1961 al 2004* (Rome: ISTAT, 2004).

84. On *Monde,* see Guessler Normand, "Henri Barbusse and His *Monde* (1928–35): Progeny of the Clarté Movement and the Review Clarté," *Journal of Contemporary History* 11, nos. 2/3 (1976): 173–197.

85. See Chapter 1.

86. A.T., "Quaderno 9," 109.

87. Ibid.

88. Ibid.

89. Ibid.

90. Ibid.

91. On the so-called nonconformists, the French intellectuals of the thirties who refused the hegemony of the interwar period's leading political currents, see Jean-Louis Loubet del Bayle, *Les non-conformistes des années 30: Une tentative de renouvellement de la pensée politique française,* rev. ed. (Paris: Seuil, 2001). See also Julian Jackson, *France: The Dark Years, 1940–1944* (Oxford: Oxford University Press, 2001), 37–44.

3. In Limbo

1. See David Caute, *The Fellow-Travellers: Intellectual Friends of Communism,* rev. ed. (New Haven: Yale University Press, 1988).

2. On the complex relation between French intellectuals and communism in the years of the Stalinization of communist parties, see David Caute, *Communism and the French Intellectuals, 1914–1960* (New York: Macmillan, 1964), 93–111.

3. See Guessler Normand, "Henri Barbusse and His *Monde* (1928–35): Progeny of the Clarté Movement and the Review *Clarté,*" *Journal of Contemporary History* 11, nos. 2/3 (1976). On the general problem of the function absolved by intellectuals close to the communist movement, see also Caute, *Communism and the French Intellectuals,* 35.

4. Union Internationale des Écrivains Révolutionnaires, "La littérature de la revolution mondiale, numéro special," paper presented at the Deuxiéme Conférence Internationale des Ecrivains Révolutionnaires, Moscow, June 1931, 180.

5. Ibid., 15.

6. See Normand, "Henri Barbusse," 184.

7. On Barbusse's understanding of the role of the intellectuals in the communist movements, see David James Fisher, "The Rolland-Barbusse Debate," *Survey* 20, nos. 2–3 (1974).

8. Henri Barbusse, "Editorial," *Monde* 3, no. 124 (1930).

9. The inquiry titled "La crise doctrinale du socialisme" was announced in the pages of *Monde* on July 20, 1929. Contributions in later issues of *Monde* included those by Henri de Man in no. 76 (1929); by Émile Vandervelde in no. 77 (1929); by Jean Zyromski in no. 78 (1929); by Karl Renner in no. 80 (1929); by Henriette Roland-Holst in no. 83 (1930); and by Marcel Déat in no. 87 (1930).

10. A. Rossi, "La crise doctrinale du socialisme," *Monde* 3, no. 122 (1930).

11. Ibid.

12. Ibid.

13. Ibid.

14. Ibid.

15. Ibid.

16. See Renzo De Felice, *Il fascismo: Le interpretazioni dei contemporanei e degli storici*, new ed. (Rome: Laterza, 1998), 4–6.

17. On the subject of American responses to the rise of fascism, see John P. Diggins, *Mussolini and Fascism: The View from America* (Princeton, NJ: Princeton University Press, 1972), 22–72; on the subject of the German and Italian responses and also on the subject of the first socialist and communist reactions, see De Felice, *Il fascismo*, 3–22; on the French conservative press and its reaction to fascism, see Robert Soucy, *French Fascism: The First Wave, 1924–1933* (New Haven: Yale University Press, 1986), 23; and on Paul Hazard's *L'Italie vivante*, the first book published by a French liberal author on the rise of fascism, see Giuseppe Recuperati, "Paul Hazard," *Belfagor* 23 (1968): 580–83.

18. A. Rossi, "Sur le fascisme en Europe," *Monde* 3, no. 100 (1930).

19. A.T., "Quaderno 16" (1931–32).

20. Ibid.

21. Union Internationale des Écrivains Révolutionnaires, "La littérature," 23.

22. A.T., "Quaderno 16."

23. Ibid.

24. Ibid.

25. Angelo Tasca to Henri Barbusse, March 6, 1932, in A.T., "Quaderno 22" (1932).

26. H. Neveu to Angelo Tasca, January 20, 1932, in A.T., "Corrispondenza: 'Monde.'"

27. Normand, "Henri Barbusse," 186–87.

28. Henri Barbusse to Angelo Tasca, July 21, 1933 in A.T., "Corrispondenza: 'Monde.'"

29. See Stephan Vallot to *Monde,* October 2, 1933, in A.T., "Corrispondenza: 'Monde.'" Tasca received 7,500 francs in reparations for unfair labor practice.

30. See Sergio Soave's introduction to Angelo Tasca et al., *A Cécile* (Turin: N. Aragno, 2001).

31. A.T., "Quaderno 16."

32. Ibid.

33. Valeria Tasca, Angelo's daughter, gave me this information during a meeting we had in Paris, where she lives, in November 2002.

34. Angelo Tasca to M. Zimmer, secretary of the *préfet de police,* February 23, 1933, in A.T., "Quaderno 24" (1933–34).

35. Tasca to the Italian consul general, February 23, 1933, in A.T., "Quaderno 24" (1933–34).

36. Ibid.

37. See Sergio Soave's introduction in Tasca et al., *A Cécile,* 16.

38. *L'Humanité,* September 20, 1933.

39. See Philippe Burrin, *La dérive fasciste: Doriot, Déat, Bergery, 1933–1945* (Paris: Seuil, 2003). On Déat, see also Jean-Paul Cointet, *Marcel Déat: Du socialisme au national-socialisme* (Paris: Perrin, 1998).

40. See Roger Griffin and Matthew Feldman, *A Fascist Century* (Basingstoke: Palgrave Macmillan, 2008), 132–80. See also Michael Arthur Ledeen, *Universal Fascism: The Theory and Practice of the Fascist International, 1928–1936* (New York: H. Fertig, 1972).

41. See Zeev Sternhell, *Neither Right nor Left: Fascist Ideology in France* (Princeton, NJ: Princeton University Press, 1996), 90–118. See also Soucy, *French Fascism: The First Wave.*

42. A. Rossi, "Le technicien au carrefour," *Monde* 4, no. 164 (1931).

43. On Edmondo Rossoni and his relation to the workers' movement, see Edward R. Tannenbaum, "The Goals of Italian Fascism," *American Historical Review* 74, no. 4 (1969). See also Emanuel Rota, "La tentazione corporativa: Corporativismo e propaganda fascista nelle file del socialismo europeo," in *Progetti corporativi tra le due guerre mondiali,* ed. Matteo Pasetti (Roma: Carocci Editore, 2006). On Emilio Caldara, see Guido Alpa's introduction in Camilio Cavagnari and Emilio Caldara, *Avvocati e Procuratori* (Bologna: Il Mulino, 2005), 3–27.

44. Giuseppe Faravelli to Pallante Rugginenti, in Stefano Merli, *La rinascita del socialismo italiano e la lotta contro il fascismo, 1934–1939: Documenti inediti dell'Archivio Angelo Tasca* (Milan: Feltrinelli, 1963), 91–96.

45. The regime refused to accept Caldara's request to authorize the publication of a socialist newspaper in Italy, and this refusal ended the experiment. The socialists around Caldara, however, had agreed to publish a "manifesto" in which they would have declared that they had embraced a form of socialism that was

"anti-democrat and anti-Marxist" along the lines of the French neosocialists. See Rota, "La tentazione corporativa."

46. Henri de Man to Angelo Tasca, November 4, 1933, in A.T., "Corrispondenza 'De Man'" (1929–50). On Tasca's difficult relationship with Carlo Rosselli and his movement, Giustizia e Libertà, see Stanislao G. Pugliese, *Carlo Rosselli: Socialist Heretic and Antifascist Exile* (Cambridge, MA: Harvard University Press, 1999), 155. Tasca was convinced that Giustizia e Libertà was looking for the political spotlight at the cost of sacrificing the unity of the antifascist front.

47. On Henri de Man, see Dick Pels, *The Intellectual as Stranger: Studies in Spokespersonship* (London: Routledge, 2000), 110–30. See also Sternhell, *Neither Right nor Left*, 119–41.

48."Le congrès de SFIO," *L'Humanité*, July 13, 1933.

49. On the creation of neosocialism, see Burrin, *La dérive fasciste*, 139–75. Richard Griffiths is right when he writes that Déat was "respectable" ("Fascism and the Planned Economy: 'Neo-Socialism' and 'Planisme' in France and Belgium in the 1930s," *Science and Society* 69, no. 4 [2005]: 583), but Tasca's testimony and the quoted passage suggest that the fascist component was no mystery at the time for careful observers.

50. Marcel Déat was quickly becoming the most prominent figure of *planisme* in France. See Comité du Plan Paris and Marcel Déat, *Le plan français: Doctrine et plan d'action* (Paris: Fasquelle, 1935).

51. See "Paul Marion," in Jean Maitron and Claude Pennetier, *Dictionnaire biographique du mouvement ouvrier français*, vol. 35, part 4: *1914–1939: De la première à la seconde guerre mondiale* (Paris: Editions Ouvrières, 1990).

52. Even before they were both expelled, the newspaper of the Italian communists in France had presented them together as the perfect examples of social fascism. "Malavita Politica," *Vie Prolétarienne*, 1929.

53. Conversation with Valeria Tasca, November 2002.

54. Paul Marion to Angelo Tasca, August 18, 1933, in A.T., "Quaderno 24."

55. Angelo Tasca, *De la démocratie au socialisme: Marxisme 33* (La Chaux-de-Fonds: Coopératives Réunies, 1934), 3.

56. Ibid., 24.

57. Ibid., 19–20.

58. Ibid., 31–36.

59. Angelo Tasca to Charles-André Julien, in A.T., "Quaderno 24."

60. Angelo Tasca to Giuseppe Faravelli, in Merli, *La rinascita del socialismo italiano*, 125.

61. See Jean Louis Loubet del Bayle, *Les non-conformistes des années 30: Une tentative de renouvellement de la pensée politique française*, rev. ed. (Paris: Seuil, 2001).

62. See François Chaubet, *Paul Desjardins et les Décades de Pontigny* (Villeneuve-d'Ascq: Presses Universitaires du Septentrion, 2000), 29.

63. These meetings lasted ten days, hence the name.

64. In the *Agir* group, both Angelo Tasca and Pierre Viènot (who in Pontigny had met his wife, Andrée, an important political figure on her own and a former vice minister in two Popular Front governments) were assiduous participants in the Décades.

65. Chaubet, *Paul Desjardins*, 41–42.

66. Paul Desjardins to Angelo Tasca, September 23, 1934, in A.T., "Corrispondenza 'De Man.'"

67. See Angelo Tasca to Paul Desjardins, August 15, 1934, in A.T., "Corrispondenza 'De Man.'"

68. See Tasca, *Marxisme 33*, 6.

69. A.T., "Quaderno 24."

70. Tasca had the opportunity to repeat these points in front of the entire leadership of the Belgian Socialist Party during a second meeting held in Pontigny in 1934. At this second meeting, Tasca was praised by Paul-Henri Spaak, who affirmed that Tasca's critique of de Man was his as well. See A.T., "Quaderno 25."

71. On *planisme*, see Griffiths, "Fascism and the Planned Economy."

72. A.T., "Quaderno 24."

73."My fatherland," he wrote in his diary, "is my conception of life, is my relation with the others." Ibid.

74. Angelo Tasca, "Una sconfitta e una lezione," *Nuovo Avanti*, January 19, 1935, and "La lezione della Sarre," *Nuovo Avanti*, January 26, 1929.

75. Angelo Tasca, "Una sconfitta e una lezione."

76. In 1935, for instance, commenting on Jaurès's idea of the persistence of specific national identities after the construction of socialism, he had called the French socialist "a sophist," despite his admiration for other elements of his work. If the abolition of capitalist tyranny meant anything, he wrote, it meant the integral liberation of the working class, including the division of labor of capitalist economies at the international level. *Annali Istituto Feltrinelli*, ed. Giuseppe Berti (Milan: Feltrinelli, 1966), 365–66.

77. If Marion's *Socialisme et nation*, with its call for "a rejuvenation of the state through a popular mystique," had already provoked a break between Tasca and his friend, Marion's career in the formation led by Jacques Doriot temporarily ended their relationship. On the Parti Populaire Français, see Robert Soucy, *French Fascism: The Second Wave, 1933–1939* (New Haven: Yale University Press, 1995). See also Bernard Henry Lejeune, *Historisme de Jacques Doriot et du Parti populaire français* (Amiens: Nouveaux Cahiers du CERPES, 1977). For a biography of Doriot, who, contrary to Tasca, seems to have been always on the side that

he thought was going to win, see Jean-Paul Brunet, *Jacques Doriot, du communisme au fascisme* (Paris: Balland, 1986).

78. See A.T., "Quaderno 32."

79. A.T., "Quaderno 24."

80. Tasca became a French citizen on August 7, 1936. See A.T., "Processo a Angelo Tasca," the document signed by Henri Moysset on Tasca's behalf to support the latter's new application for the French citizenship in 1941.

81. As Tony Judt remarked in his study on the reconstruction of the Socialist Party in the 1920s, some of the socialist federations had a tradition of chauvinism to the point of localism. See Tony Judt, *La reconstruction du parti socialiste: 1921–1926* (Paris: Presses de la Fondation nationale des sciences politiques, 1976), 59.

82. See A.T., "Quaderno 32."

83. Ibid.

84. Ibid.

85. In fact, according to Tasca, Stalin was pursuing goals similar to those of the prerevolutionary czars. See *Annali Istituto Feltrinelli*, 615–16.

86. See A.T., "Quaderno 32."

87. Ibid.

88. Ibid.

89. Angelo Tasca, "Economia mondiale ed economie nazionali," *Nuovo Avanti*, February 16, 1935.

90. Angelo Tasca, "Editorial," *Nuovo Avanti*, November 28, 1936.

91. *Annali Istituto Feltrinelli*, 605.

92. André Leroux [Angelo Tasca], "La situation," *Le Populaire*, January 12, 1937.

4. The Road to Vichy

1. Angelo Tasca, *La naissance du fascisme: L'Italie de 1918 à 1922* (Paris: Gallimard, 1938).

2. Sergio Soave, "Prefazione," in *Angelo Tasca, Nascita e avvento del fascismo l'Italia dal 1918 al 1922* (Florence: La Nuova Italia, 1950), xv.

3. Pierre Assouline, *Gaston Gallimard: A Half-Century of French Publishing* (San Diego: Harcourt Brace Jovanovich, 1988), 192.

4. See Pierre Assouline, *Gaston Gallimard: Un demi-siècle d'édition française* (Paris: Balland, 1984), 199–207.

5. A.T., "Quaderno 34," March 14, 1938.

6. Tasca, *La naissance du fascisme*, 34.

7. Ibid., 9.

8. Ibid., 74.

9. Ibid., 35.

10. Ibid., 142.

11. Ibid., 124.
12. Ibid., 268.
13. Ibid., 267.
14. Ibid., 268.
15. Ibid., 269–70.
16. Ibid., 283.
17. Léon Blum, *L'œuvre 1937–1940*, vol. 4, part 2 (Paris: A. Michel, 1965), 160.
18. Ibid.
19. Émile Vandervelde, "Pour s'initier au socialism," *Peuple*, June 5, 1938.
20."Pour le premier mai. Une tactique antifasciste," *Combat*, 1938.
21. Ibid.
22. Mounier to Angelo Tasca, in A.T., "Corrispondenza," f. 270, February12, 1938.
23. Mounier to Angelo Tasca, in A.T., "Corrispondenza," f. 270, February12, 1938, January 20, 1933.
24. On Luigi Sturzo, see Gabriella Fanello Marcucci, *Luigi Sturzo: Vita e battaglie per la liberta' del fondatore del Partito popolare italiano* (Milan: Mondadori, 2004).
25. Jacques Madaule, "A. Rossi: La naissance du fascism," *Esprit* 6, no. 72 (1938): 777.
26. On the subject of the position of the *Esprit* group and of Mounier in particular toward Catholicism and politics, see Michel Winock, *Histoire politique de la revue Esprit, 1930–1950* (Paris: Seuil, 1975), and Michel Winock, *Esprit: Des intellectuels dans la cité* (Paris: Editions du Seuil, 1996), 30–42.
27. A.T., "Quaderno 34."
28. Ibid., 152–53.
29. Ibid.
30. See Tony Judt, *La reconstruction du parti socialiste: 1921–1926* (Paris: Presses de la Fondation Nationale des Sciences Politiques, 1976), 59.
31. Ibid.
32. *Gringoire*, March 28, 1940.
33. A.T., "Quaderno 34," August 7, 1938.
34. Ibid.
35. Tasca was financially helping Andrea Caffi and Mario Levi, two Italian antifascists close to Rosselli's Giustizia e Libertà.
36. A.T., "Quaderno 34."
37. Boris Souvarine was an ex-leader of the French Communist Party. Classified as a Trotskyist in the Stalinist hunt for traitors, he had been expelled from the Communist Party during the first wave of Stalinist persecutions and had been in constant contact with Tasca. At the time of his expulsion, the Italian delegation, composed of Tasca and Togliatti, was the only section of the

Comintern that voted against the motion to exclude him. This event had strengthened the friendship between Tasca and the French intellectual. At the time of Tasca's expulsion, it had been Souvarine's turn to provide the Italian with the necessary information to survive the experience. Despite their political differences, Souvarine offered Tasca a job in his journal, *Critique Sociale,* when the latter had to find a way to support himself and a new role to continue his political engagement. Their friendship lasted through time, and when Souvarine finally left France in 1941, he sent letters to Tasca to describe his journey and his new life in the United States. See Souvarine to Tasca in A.T., "Corrispondenza Souvarine," September 19, 1929, and Souvarine to Tasca in A.T., "Corrispondenza Souvarine," December 3, 1941.

38. Laurat had also been a victim of Stalinism and, like Tasca, had ended up in France after being purged. His real name was Otto Maschl; he was Austrian and had been a member of the Austrian Communist Party. A friend of Souvarine since the early 1920s, he went to Moscow in 1923 to work with his French friend as an interpreter. In the Soviet Union, he became professor of Economics at the Communist University of Western Minorities (KUNMZ) and worked there until 1927. His anti-Stalinism prompted him to organize meetings of the "right opposition" in his room at the famous Hotel Luxe. Among those who went to the meetings there was Angelo Tasca, who worked with him at *Monde.* Unlike the Italian, Laurat actively contributed to Souvarine's *Critique Sociale,* and was more active in the CGT (Confédération Générale du Travail)—close to the positions of René Belin—than in the SFIO. This ended in 1939, when he became more interested in the life of the SFIO, close to Paul Faure's positions, just in time to work as Tasca's Faurist counterpart in the organization of a meeting for the renewal of French socialism at Pontigny Abbey. See Jean Maitron and Claude Pennetier, *Dictionnaire biographique du mouvement ouvrier français,* vol. 35, part 4: *1914–1939: De la première à la seconde guerre mondiale* (Paris: Editions Ouvrières, 1990), 337–38.

39. Daniel Villey, "Les Nouveaux Cahiers," *Esprit* 6, no. 65 (1938): 540–45.

40. Ramon Fernandez (1894–1944), son of a Mexican diplomat, was affiliated in 1923 with the *Nouvelle Revue Française.* He was the author of many books of literary criticism, and is a novelist. Founder with Emmanuel Berl of the journal *Marianne* and one of the key organizers of the Décades at Pontigny, Ramon Fernandez was one of the many French intellectuals who went from left to right in the interwar period. He was first a socialist, then a communist sympathizer, then a member of Doriot's *Parti Populaire,* and finally a member of the collaborationist NRF. At the beginning of October 1941, he was one of the seven French writers—Marcel Jouhandeau, Jacques Chardonne, Robert Brasillach, Pierre Drieu la Rochelle, Abel Bonnard, and André Fraigneau were the others—who went to visit Nazi Germany at the invitation of Goebbels.

41. See A.T., "Quaderno 34" (1938), 221.

42. See Eric Bussière, *La France, la Belgique et l'organisation économique de l'Europe: 1918–1935* (Paris: Comité pour l'Histoire Économique et Financière de la France, 1992).

43. See A.T., "Cahier AA, April 1941."

44. Emmanuel Mounier, "Prefascisme français: Les deux sources du prefascisme," *Esprit* 7, no. 75 (1938): 325–26.

45. Simone Weil, "Ne recommençons pas la Guerre de Troie," *Les Nouveaux Cahiers*, 1937.

46."Manifesto," *Les Nouveaux Cahiers*, special issue, 1938.

47. Auguste Detoeuf, "Pour la France et la liberté," *Les Nouveaux Cahiers*, special issue, 1938.

48. Quoted in Olivier Dard, *Les années trente: Le choix impossible* (Paris: Librairie Générale Française, 1999), 197.

49. Léon Blum, "Editorial," *Le Populaire*, October 1, 1938.

50. On the subject of the reactions of the French political parties to Munich, see Julian Jackson, *France: The Dark Years, 1940–1944* (Oxford: Oxford University Press, 2001), 92–101; Jean-Baptiste Duroselle, *La décadence, 1932–1939* (Paris: Imprimerie Nationale, 1979).

51. Only one socialist voted with the communists. See Bruce Desmond Graham, *Choice and Democratic Order: The French Socialist Party, 1937–1950* (Cambridge: Cambridge University Press, 1994), 225.

52. See chapter 3.

53. Graham, *Choice and Democratic Order*, 183.

54. A.T., "Quaderno 34," October 1938, 252–55.

55. Pierre-Étienne Flandin, prime minister of France from November 8, 1934, to May 31, 1935, argued in 1938 that France ought to accommodate itself to Germany's dominance of the continent. He refused to join a proposed all-party government at the time of the Anschluss, applauded the Munich Pact, and urged Daladier to abandon Poland.

56. A.T., "Quaderno 34." October 1938, 252–55.

57. Ibid.

58. Ibid.

59. Ibid.

60. André Leroux [Angelo Tasca], "Les sauvages de l'air du general Franco," *Le Populaire*, October 10, 1938.

61. After the beginning of October, Tasca completely ceased his work for Blum's newspaper and Pierre Brossolette took his place.

62. In 1939 Viénot voluntarily enlisted in the army, and after the defeat he embarked on the *Massilia* to go to North Africa with other French deputies.

There he was arrested together with Pierre Mendès-France, Jean Zay, and Alex Wiltzer. Tried for desertion, he was condemned to eight years in prison. See Maitron and Pennetier, *Dictionnaire*, 209–11.

63. Thanks to a famous article he wrote for *L'Oeuvre* on May 4, 1939, where he announced that he did not want to die for Danzig, Déat became an emblem of the opposition to war. Even before that article, though, Déat's pacifist positions were well known. See Marcel Déat and Laurent Theis, *Mémoires politiques* (Paris: Denoël, 1989), 442.

64."Pourquoi nous publions *Agir*," *Agir* 1 (1939).

65. André Leroux [Angelo Tasca], "La leçon d'une vie," *Agir* 1 (1939).

66. André Leroux [Angelo Tasca], "Pacifisme bourgeois, impérialisme fasciste," *Agir* 3 (1939).

67. André Leroux [Angelo Tasca], "Assez de verbalisme et de course aux mandats! Luttons dans la réalité," *Agir* 7 (1939).

68. See Gaston Bergery, "Pour un 'coup d'arrêt' aux états fascistes," *La Flèche* 4, no. 83 (1937).

69. Gaston Bergery, "Tchecoslovaquie," *La Flèche* 6, no. 112 (1938).

70. Ibid.

71. Bernard Serampuy, "La Flèche, le frontisme, Esprit," *Esprit* 6, no. 72 (1937): 735–46.

72. Georges Izard, "Pour fonder le démocratie véritable il faut un Richelieu," *La Flèche* 4, no. 79 (1937).

73. See Gaston Bergery, "La faiblesse de l'état est une menace pour les libertés du peuple. Elle mène droit au fascisme," *La Flèche* 6, no. 100 (1938).

74. Georges Monnet, "Un an de gouvernement Daladier. La démocratie en péril," *Agir* 6 (1939).

75. See Graham, *Choice and Democratic Order*, 236.

76. André Leroux [Angelo Tasca], "Le parti et les clans," *Agir* 10 (1939).

77. In the pages of *L'Ordre*, between June 1938 and August 1940, Benda published seventy-seven articles on the theme of antifascism. For an analysis of Benda's positions in the late 1930s, see Sandra Teroni, *La passione della democrazia: Julien Benda* (Rome: Bulzoni, 1993). See also David L. Schalk, *The Spectrum of Political Engagement: Mounier, Benda, Nizan, Brasillach, Sartre* (Princeton, NJ: Princeton University Press, 1979), 26–48.

78. André Stibio, "Les Anciens et les Modernes," *Ordre*, 1939.

79. Jean Lebas, "La révision des statuts," *Le Populaire*, August 1, 1939.

80. Adrien Brill, "Des vicissitudes du Pouvoir au calme de l'abbaye de Pontigny," *La Flèche* 7 (1939).

81. See François Chaubet, *Paul Desjardins et les Décades de Pontigny* (Villeneuve-d'Ascq: Presses universitaires du Septentrion, 2000), 29.

82. See Angelo Tasca and Denis Peschanski, *Vichy, 1940–1944: Quaderni e documenti inediti di Angelo Tasca; archives de guerre d'Angelo Tasca* (Milan: Fondazione Giangiacomo Feltrinelli, 1986), 224.

83. André Philip was a professor of law at the University of Lyon. In the SFIO he had distinguished himself for his interest in Henri de Man's ideas on planning. In particular, he had taken from de Man's the idea of the foundation of socialism in the Christian humanist tradition. After the war he became minister of economy in several governments. See Graham, *Choice and Democratic Order,* 39.

84. Tasca and Peschanski, *Vichy,* 222–23.

85. Despite all the divisions, for instance, nobody could contest Spinasse's authority on the economy, which he had managed as a minister of finance in the Blum governments. The same was true for Faure and the organization of the SFIO, which the secretary of the party controlled with undisputed authority, and for all the other speakers.

86. On Georges Lefranc, see Graham, *Choice and Democratic Order,* 175.

87. Spinasse was one of the editors of *Pays Socialiste,* the Faurist journal at the forefront of the antiwar polemics in the SFIO. See Maitron and Pennetier, *Dictionnaire,* 407.

88. The German parliament during the Nazi era, which Hitler used to announce to the world his war plans for Czechoslovakia and then Poland.

89. See Maitron and Pennetier, *Dictionnaire,* 370–71.

90. See, for instance, Graham, who in his intelligent reconstruction *Choice and Democratic Order,* 241–43, does not pay any attention to the delicate months between the beginning of the war and the invasion of France. Graham, *Choice and Democratic Order: the French Socialist Party, 1937–1950.*

91. André Leroux [Angelo Tasca], "La situation," *Le Populaire,* September 16, 1939.

92. Léon Blum, "Le mystère stalinienne," *Le Populaire,* September 17, 1939.

93. Ibid.

94. *Le Populaire,* September 18, 1939.

95. Léon Blum, "L'atroce évènement," *Le Populaire,* September 18, 1939.

96. André Leroux [Angelo Tasca], *Le Populaire,* September 18, 1939.

97. Léon Blum, "Silence accablant," *Le Populaire,* September 19, 1939.

98. André Leroux [Angelo Tasca], "La situation," *Le Populaire,* September 20, 1939.

99. André Leroux [Angelo Tasca], "La situation," *Le Populaire,* September 24, 1939.

100. André Leroux [Angelo Tasca], "La situation," *Le Populaire,* September 26, 1939.

101. Léon Blum, *Le Populaire,* September 27, 1939.

102. A.T., "Quaderno 37," November 29, 1939.

103. Ibid., January 10, 1940.

104. Ibid.

105. On this point Tasca's words in January 1940 were the same that Rives would use a few months later in Vichy. It is also important to note that, even before the political logic of Vichy further encouraged the phenomenon of secret societies and paranoia about their omnipotence, institutions such as Pontigny, with their goal of personal connections between members of an elite, fostered a mentality similar if not equivalent to the technocratic conception of politics dominant in Vichy.

106. See Philippe Burrin, *La dérive fasciste: Doriot, Déat, Bergery, 1933–1945* (Paris: Seuil, 2003), 139–75.

107. A.T., "Quaderno 37." January 10, 1940.

108. Ibid.

109. Angelo Tasca, "Il comitato direttivo della sezione Socialista italiana di Parigi," in A.T., "PCI-PSI," (1939).

110. See chapter 5.

111. Tasca and Peschanski, *Vichy*, 224.

112. Émile Buré, "La position de l'Italie," *Ordre*, 1940.

113. XX [Angelo Tasca], "La situation," *Le Populaire*, April 3, 1940.

114. Giorgio Sansa, "Il Mediterraneo e i rapporti Italo-francesi," *La Stampa*, April 4, 1940.

115. Georges Th. Girard, "Oui, vive la nation," *Le Populaire*, July 19, 1939.

5. A Socialist in Vichy

1. A.T., "Cahiers AI, September-October 1944."

2. Ibid.

3. Ibid.

4. Ibid.

5. A.T., "Cahiers AE, August 1943–January 1944," 521.

6. Ibid.

7. A.T., "Cahiers AG, June-September 1944."

8. Tasca identified his accuser a few years later. See Angelo Tasca, *In Francia nella bufera* (Parma: Guanda, 1953). 233. The Centre d'Écoutes was the office in charge of translating foreign transmissions in France under the Vichy regime.

9. A.T., "Cahiers AG, June-September 1944."

10. Ibid., 646.

11. See the epilogue.

12. The first one obtained, thanks to Tasca's testimony, a light sentence: only ten years in prison for the only minister in the Vichy government openly recognized as a fascist. The second one obtained readmittance to the SFIO, from

which he had been expelled for allegedly abandoning Léon Blum. In A.T., "Processo a Angelo Tasca."

13. Angelo Tasca and Denis Peschanski, *Vichy, 1940–1944: Quaderni e documenti inediti di Angelo Tasca; archives de guerre d'Angelo Tasca* (Milan: Fondazione Giangiacomo Feltrinelli, 1986), 230.

14. Ibid., 231.

15. Ibid.

16. See chapter 4.

17. Tasca, *In Francia nella bufera*, 22.

18. Ibid.

19. Ibid.

20. Ibid., 27.

21. Quoted in Alceo Riosa, "Dalla 'drôle de Guerre' all' 'autre Résistance,'" in Tasca and Peschanski, *Vichy*, 204. François Chasseigne had been a communist, then a socialist close to Paul Faure. He became minister of agriculture in 1944.

22. It was true that since the beginning of the Russian-German alliance he had increasingly become anticommunist, and therefore a fundamental disagreement with the right of the socialist party, which had opposed the war against Germany, no longer existed, but this was also true for Léon Blum, who had supported the outlawing of the Communist Party, and it could hardly be considered a sufficient reason to eliminate all the suspicions against him.

23. Tasca joined the number of intellectuals who became unlikely collaborators because they were convinced that a new constitution could save France. Gertrude Stein is another interesting example but, contrary to Stein, who seems to have welcomed the defeat as a way to restore "a spirit of sacrifice," Tasca was never taken by the cultural despair that seems to characterize modernist writers such as Stein and, in a different context, José Ortega y Gasset. On Stein, see Barbara Will, *Unlikely Collaboration: Gertrude Stein, Bernard Faÿ, and the Vichy Dilemma* (New York: Columbia University Press, 2011). On Ortega y Gasset, see María Isabel Ferreiro Lavedán, *La teoría social de Ortega y Gasset: los usos*, 2nd ed. (Madrid: Biblioteca Nueva: Fundación José Ortega y Gasset, 2005).

24. On *L'Effort*, see Yves Bongarçon, "Un vichysme de gauche? Les débuts de l'effort, quotidien socialiste lyonnais," *Cahiers d'Histoire* 32, no. 2 (1987): 123–46. This article provides very basic information on the newspaper but ignores any information on the publication that could not be gleaned from reading the publication itself.

25. On July 3, 1940, the Royal Navy arrived at Mers-el-Kébir, on the coast of Algeria, and ordered the French forces to surrender or be attacked. After hours of unsuccessful negotiations, the British fleet opened fire on the French navy. One battleship was sunk and two were seriously damaged. A total of 1,147 sailors were killed in the attack. See David Brown, *The Road to Oran: Anglo-French*

Naval Relations, September 1939–July 1940 (New York: Frank Cass, 2004), 182–205. See also Tasca and Peschanski, *Vichy*, 233.

26. Tasca and Peschanski, *Vichy* 234.

27. Ibid.

28. Ibid., 236.

29. Ibid., 239.

30. Ibid., 240.

31. Ibid.

32. Ibid. Tasca believed that communism was not part of this tradition and that French socialism, from Louis Blanc to Jean Jaurès, had nothing in common with the Marxist version of socialism that characterized the communist movement.

33. Tasca and Peschanski, *Vichy*, 238.

34. Ibid., 241.

35. As documented by the recent historiography on Vichy, Tasca's position was common among the supporters of the regime. Julian Jackson notes that the Germans, who could damage the French economy, "also provided the only prospect of its recovery. Negotiations were therefore unavoidable." Julian Jackson, *France: The Dark Years, 1940–1944* (Oxford: Oxford University Press, 2001), 187. Robert Gildea, who studies the issue of collaboration at the local level, argues that collaboration was interpreted as a way of "maintaining good relations between French and Germans, whether at the public or private levels, in order to benefit all concerned." Robert Gildea, *Marianne in Chains* (London: Macmillan, 2002), 242.

36. Tasca and Peschanski, *Vichy*, 241.

37. Angelo Tasca, "Nationalisme ou socialisme, " *Monde*, no. 259 (1933).

38. See chapter 4.

39. Peter Gay, *Weimar Culture: The Outsider as Insider* (New York: Harper and Row, 1968), 23.

40. Angelo Tasca, *La France de Vichy: Archives inédits d'Angelo Tasca* (Milan: Fondazione Giangiacomo Feltrinelli, 1996), 238.

41. On collaborationism in Paris, see Philippe Burrin, *France Under the Germans: Collaboration and Compromise* (New York: New Press, 1996), 372–85.

42. A.T., "Quaderno 34," *fine d'anno*, 1938.

43. Ibid.

44. Ibid.

45. Ibid.

46. See the epilogue.

47. See Jackson, *France: The Dark Years*, 129–32. On Laval, see Jean-Paul Cointet, *Pierre Laval* (Paris: Fayard, 1993).

48. See Bongarçon, "Un vichysme de gauche?" 128.

49. Angelo Tasca, "L'accord franco-japonais," *L'Effort*, September 25, 1940.

50. XX [Angelo Tasca], "La bataille d'Angleterre," *L'Effort*, August 20, 1940.

51. Tasca was right on the issue of the German opposition to the creation of such a party. As Philippe Burrin has shown in his study on the collaborationists, Abetz had received orders directly from Hitler to prevent the formation of a united French front. Citing German sources, the French historian shows that Hitler feared that the construction of a single party could result in a rallying point for the French nationalists and in a stronghold of resistance against German influence. See Philippe Burrin, "Le collaborationisme," in *La France des années noires*, ed. Jean-Pierre Azéma and François Bédarida (Paris: Seuil, 1993), 363–83.

52. During his trips to Bellerives to see Rives, Tasca met Alice Naturel, who worked in the city hall of the village, and with whom, at the end of 1941, Tasca had a daughter, Catherine.

53. Paul Rives, "Bilan d'une expérience," *L'Effort*, August 11, 1940.

54. Henri De Man, "Le mouvement ouvrier belge prend position," *L'Effort*, September 3, 1940.

55. See, for instance, Marcel Déat, "Rassemblement pour la Révolution Nationale," *L'Effort*, August 30, 1940.

56. See, for instance, Gaston Bergery, "Du libéralisme expirant à la révolution nationale," *L'Effort*, August 9, 1940.

57. Ibid.

58."Statut des Juifs," *L'Effort*, October 18, 1940.

59. See the epilogue.

60. In 1939, writing a small column on the future of the SFIO on *Le Populaire*, Girard had quoted extensively from Tasca's analysis of the need for a revolutionary class to represent the general interest. According to Girard, the general interest that needed to be represented was that of France. Georges Th. Girard, "Oui, vive la nation," *Le Populaire*, July 19, 1939.

61. See chapter 4.

62. The so-called *Massilia* affair refers to the twenty-six parliamentarians who, on June 20, 1940, embarked on the *Massilia* for Casablanca. When the boat reached the African city, three parliamentarians who were serving in the French army, Jean Zay, Pierre Mendès-France, and Pierre Viénot, were arrested for desertion. The affaire is narrated, and slightly fictionalized, in Christiane Rimbaud, *L'affaire du Massilia, été 1940* (Paris: Seuil, 1984). See also Jackson, *France: The Dark Years*, 127–32.

63. A.T., "Processo a Angelo Tasca."

64. There are no good reasons to doubt Tasca's reconstruction of the events. It is possible that before February 1941 his application received some help not only from Charles Vallin and Henri Moysset but also from the entourage of Laval.

However, it is clear that in 1941, after Darlan had been appointed to the vice presidency, Moysset, who had always had important connections in the French navy and who was one of Darlan's main collaborators, was in the best position to help him.

65. On Darlan, see Henri Michel, *François Darlan: Amiral de la flotte* (Paris: Hachette, 1993).

66. A.T., "Cahier L," 209–10. On Marion's role in Vichy, see Jackson, *France: The Dark Years*, 158–61, 254–58.

67. A.T., "Cahier L," 173.

68. Ibid., 160.

69. Ibid., 182.

70. Ibid., 174.

71. Ibid.

72. Ibid., 166.

73. Ibid., 168.

74. Ibid., 169.

75. Ibid., 170.

76. The *charte du travail* was later approved on October 4, 1941. Tasca refers here to the debate in the first Laval government, with Laval's opposition to the projects of Belin, that led to the showdown of December 13. Contrary to Belin's expectations, during the meeting Pétain dismissed Laval and not him. See ibid., 173.

77. Robert O. Paxton, *Vichy France: Old Guard and New Order, 1940–1944* (New York: Columbia University Press, 2001), xv.

78. A.T., "Cahier L," 255.

79. Ibid.

80. On Henri Moysset, see Jackson, *France: The Dark Years*, 252.

81. A.T., "Journal de guerre," in Tasca, *La France de Vichy*, 256.

82. On the Uriage school, see John Hellman, *The Knight-Monks of Vichy France: Uriage, 1940–1945* (Montreal: McGill-Queen's University Press, 1993).

83. Tasca kept regular notes of these meetings in his journal. See A.T., "Cahier L."

84. A.T., "Cahier X, 1 April 1941–6 May 1941."

85. Ibid.

86. As Loubet del Bayle has shown in his study of the nonconformists, the critique of statism and centralization was one of the central themes of all the new political groups of the thirties. *L'Ordre Nouveau* had written that "the state is against man." Paul Marion himself wrote in *Socialisme et Nation*, a twenty-three-page pamphlet that Tasca strategically overemphasized in his presentation, that socialism was doomed if it did not escape from a "statism falsely presented as proletarian." Jean-Louis Loubet del Bayle, *Les non-conformistes des années 30:*

Une tentative de renouvellement de la pensée politique française, rev. ed. (Paris: Seuil, 2001), 190–91.

87. A.T., "Cahier L," 267.

88. Ibid.

89. See Henri Moysset, "L'appel du vide," in Tasca and Peschanski, *Vichy*, 263–64.

90. Moysset himself declared in December 1941 that Tasca's work "was destined for the marshal and to the marshal only" (ibid., 322). Pétain declared: "The creation of a single youth movement is out of the question" (quoted in ibid., 264).

91. A.T., "Cahier L," 276.

92. Ibid., 293.

93. Ibid.

94. Ibid.

95. Tasca, *La France de Vichy*, 312. Paul Estèbe was adjunct director of Pétain's *Gabinet civil.* See Assemblée nationale, "Biographies des députés de la IVe République," www.assemblee-nationale.fr/histoire/biographies/IVRepublique/estebe-paul-jean-marie-raymond-02081904.asp.

96. Jean Rivain to Angelo Tasca, in Tasca, *La France de Vichy*, 312.

97. See Alexander J. De Grand, *In Stalin's Shadow: Angelo Tasca and the Crisis of the Left in Italy and France, 1910–1945* (DeKalb: Northern Illinois University Press, 1986), 159–62.

98. A.T., "Cahiers AG, June-September 1944," 662. Conversion based on "Pouvoir d'achat de l'euro et du franc," available at www.insee.fr/fr/indicateur/achatfranc.htm.

99. Ibid.

100. Ibid.

101. Ibid.

102. Ibid.

103. Ibid., 660.

Epilogue

1. A.T., "Cahiers AG, June-September 1944," September 18, 1944.

2. A.T., "Cahiers AI, September-October 1944," October 3, 1944.

3. Tasca moved back to Paris at the beginning of November 1944. He married Liliane Chomette in 1946. See Alexander J. De Grand, *In Stalin's Shadow: Angelo Tasca and the Crisis of the Left in Italy and France, 1910–1945* (DeKalb: Northern Illinois University Press, 1986).

4. Tasca's new address was 7, Rue César-Frank, in the Fifteenth Arrondissement.

5. Letter of Angelo Tasca to Lucien Laurat, A.T., "Correspondence ff. Laurat," November 6, 1948. The Rassemblement du Peuple Français was the

political party launched by General de Gaulle on April 14, 1947. De Gaulle wanted it to be a movement that gathered people of different political orientations but excluded communists.

6. According to the definition given by Hobsbawm; see E. J. Hobsbawm, *The Age of Extremes: A History of the World, 1914–1991* (New York: Vintage Books, 1996).

7. See Jef Rens to André Tixier, in Angelo Tasca and Denis Peschanski, *Vichy, 1940–1944: Quaderni e documenti inediti di Angelo Tasca; archives de guerre d'Angelo Tasca* (Milano: Fondazione Giangiacomo Feltrinelli, 1986). 639.

8. Paul Cavyn to Georges Bidault, in A.T., "Correspondence ff. Cavyn," October 14, 1944.

9. For instance, it is difficult to understand the meaning of a letter sent by Alice Naturel to Tasca on September 25, 1944, where she says: "Patrick's father received this morning the answer from your friend of Mayet de Montagne. He will take care of the problem in question and hopes for a quick solution." Patrick's father is Paul Cavyn. Mayet de Montagne is the school for state functionaries founded by Paul Marion in 1941 on the model of the communist school in Bobigny. Why were Naturel and Tasca using a code to hide the identities of the people to whom they referred in the letter? Was Cavyn trying to help Paul Marion as Tasca did after his release? Or were they trying to help Henri Moysset, who also taught at Mayet de Montagne? If this is the case, why did Cavyn want to help them, since they certainly did not play any role in the Resistance? Alice Naturel's letter is reported in A.T., "Cahiers AG, June-September 1944," September 27, 1944.

10. Angelo Tasca to Paul Cavyn, in Tasca and Peschanski, *Vichy*, 652.

11. Paul Cavyn to Angelo Tasca, in A.T., "Correspondence ff. Cavyn." October 31, 1944.

12. See chapter 5. Tasca clearly lied many times during the interrogations. For instance, when the military police asked him if he knew "Moisset known as Moyse," he replied that he was unaware of "the existence of such a person," but it is very unlikely that Tasca did not recognize the name of Moysset under the misspellings. See A.T., "Cahiers AG, June-September 1944," September 11, 1944.

13. See A.T., "Cahiers AG, June-September 1944," September 27, 1944, September 11, 1944.

14. For Georges Monnet's relation to Tasca, see chapter 4.

15. See "Georges Monnet," in Jean Maitron and Claude Pennetier, *Dictionnaire biographique du mouvement ouvrier français*, vol. 34, part 4: *1914–1939: De la première à la seconde guerre mondiale* (Paris: Editions Ouvrières, 1990).

16. See Léon Blum, *L'oeuvre de Léon Blum: 1940–1945. Mémoires, La prison et le procès, A l'échelle humaine*, (Paris: A. Michel, 1965), 324–26.

17. Monnet left the SFIO and France and, from 1959 to 1961, served as minister of agriculture of Côte d'Ivoire and as personal advisor to President

Félix Houphouët-Boigny. See "Georges Monnet," in Maitron and Pennetier, *Dictionnaire.*

18. The impossibility of helping Moysset saddened Tasca, who gathered in a dossier a series of articles about his friend and planned to write a "Note sur l'affaire Henry Moysset [sic] devant la haute cour," which was never completed.

19. See "Paul Marion" in Maitron and Pennetier, *Dictionnaire.*

20. See Jean-Paul Cointet, *Expier Vichy: L'épuration en France (1943–1958)* (Paris: Perrin, 2008).

21. Paul Marion to Angelo Tasca, no date, in A.T., "Correspondence ff. Marion."

22. See "Paul Marion" in Maitron and Pennetier, *Dictionnaire.*

23. See chapter 5.

24. As Jean-Paul Cointet underlines, the trials against the regime, covered under article 75 of the Penal Code, could not count on a coherent jurisprudence. See Cointet, *Expier Vichy,* 253–57.

25. Angelo Tasca to Paul Marion, January 23, 1949, in A.T., "Correspondence ff. Marion."

26. Angelo Tasca, *The Russo-German Alliance, August 1939–June 1941* (Boston: Beacon Press, 1951), 107.

27. Ibid.

28. Ibid.

29. Ibid.

30. Angelo Tasca and Willmoore Kendall, *A Communist Party in Action: An Account of the Organization and Operations in France* (New Haven: Yale University Press, 1949), 216.

31. See chapter 3.

32. Angelo Tasca, *Le pacte germano-soviétique: l'histoire et le mythe* (Paris: Cahiers des Amis de la Liberté, 1954), 94.

33. Ibid., 95.

34. See chapter 4.

35. See chapter 5.

36. Paul Marion to Angelo Tasca, October 22, 1947, A.T., "Correspondence ff. Marion."

37. See chapter 5.

38. Gaetano Salvemini to Angelo Tasca, in Gaetano Salvemini, Angelo Tasca, and Elisa Signori, *Il dovere di testimoniare: Carteggio* (Naples: Bibliopolis, 1996), 183–84. Salvemini also noted that the series in which the book was scheduled to be published included a book with a preface by Daniel Halévy, who was an ex-socialist who had become pro-Nazi and a collaborationist under Pétain and Laval. He commented: "I suspect that the series' goal is not only to present history books, but also political material in the service of anti-communist, anti-socialist, anti-democratic, reactionary projects." Ibid., 182.

39. The international fame that his book on fascism and his anticommunism gave him allowed Tasca to present himself as a respected scholar. In 1953, Tasca was invited to give a lecture on Western Europe at Johns Hopkins University, in the context of a conference on international studies in Washington. Tasca accepted the invitation and left Paris on August 6, 1953, for his first and only trip to the United States. Ironically, Tasca had problems obtaining a visa because his name figured in a list of communist activists held by the Department of State. See Angelo Tasca to Gaetano Salvemini, in ibid., 175.

40. Quoted in De Grand, *In Stalin's Shadow*, 172.

41. Victor Serge, Jean Rière, and Jil Silberstein, *Mémoires d'un révolutionnaire et autres écrits politiques, 1908–1947* (Paris: Laffont, 2001).

42. Quoted in Alceo Riosa, "Dalla 'drôle de guerre' all' 'autre Résistance,'" in Tasca and Peschanski, *Vichy*, 199.

43. A.T., "Cahiers XX, September-October 1944," Feltrinelli Foundation, Milan.

44. Angelo Tasca to Gaetano Salvemini, in Salvemini, Tasca, and Signori, *Il dovere di testimoniare*, 175.

45. A.T., "Processo a Angelo Tasca."

46. Ibid.

47. Salvemini, Tasca, and Signori, *Il dovere di testimoniare*, 175.

48. A.T., "Processo a Angelo Tasca."

49. See chapter 3.

50. See Salvemini, Tasca, and Signori, *Il dovere di testimoniare*, 152.

51. For instance, this was the case of Albert Buchalet, who reminded Tasca that he himself had come under suspicion for his role in Vichy after de Gaulle had abandoned active politics in 1947. Buchalet, who later became the head of the bureau that developed the French nuclear bomb, wrote to Tasca that he knew nothing of Tasca's activities because they had had only a short contact in 1943. Therefore, he could say nothing of Tasca's role in the years before 1943. See A.T., "Processo a Angelo Tasca." For a biography of Buchalet, see *Who's Who in France*, s.v. "Buchalet, Albert, Louis, George."

52. For a biography of Gaetano Salvemini, see Charles L. Killinger, *Gaetano Salvemini: A Biography* (Westport, CT: Praeger, 2002).

53. Salvemini wrote that it was absurd to think that Tasca could fight against his old comrades using or being used by the police, Salvemini, Tasca, and Signori, *Il dovere di testimoniare*, 178.

54. Paolo Alatri, "La Nascita del Fascismo," *Belfagor*, 1951, 479–84.

55. Alberto Jacometti, *Quando la storia macina* (Novara: La Foresta Rossa, 1952), 108.

56. Jacometti did his best to document the charges present in his book, sending a letter to *Il Mondo* in which he reconstructed, with only a few mistakes, Tasca's experience in Vichy. He claimed that Tasca had not left France because

he could not find a ride to go to Great Britain, which was not true. He also misspelled the name of *L'Effort* and claimed that Tasca had worked for Laval after 1942, both minor mistakes. Jacometti's letter is reported by Tasca in a letter sent by Angelo Tasca to Gaetano Salvemini on June 9, 1952, in Salvemini, Tasca, and Signori, *Il dovere di testimoniare*, 240.

57. See chapter 5.

58. See chapter 5.

59. Angelo Tasca, *In Francia nella bufera* (Parma: Guanda, 1953), 84.

60. Ibid., 73.

61. *L'Effort*, October 18, 1940.

62. Tasca, *In Francia nella bufera*, 81.

63. Ibid., 75.

64. Angelo Tasca, *I primi dieci anni del PCI*, 2nd ed. (Bari: Laterza, 1973).

65. Ibid., 109–24.

66. Ibid., 155–72.

67. Salvemini, Tasca, and Signori, *Il dovere di testimoniare*, 273; Elena Ragonesi, "La tradizione intellettuale de 'Il Mondo': Tra Croce e Salvemini," *Il Cristallo* 2 (1996): 23–32.

68. Salvemini, Tasca, and Signori, *Il dovere di testimoniare*, 85–86.

69. Angelo Tasca and Nikita Sergeevich Khrushchev, *Autopsie du stalinisme* (Paris: P. Horay, 1957).

70. Valeria Tasca gave me this information during our meeting in November 2002.

71."Angelo Tasca," *Il Ponte*, 1960, 18–19.

Bibliography

Adamson, Walter L. *Avant-Garde Florence: From Modernism to Fascism.* Cambridge, MA: Harvard University Press, 1993.

Agosti, Aldo. *La Terza Internazionale: Storia Documentaria.* Rome: Editori Riuniti, 1974.

———. *Palmiro Togliatti: A Biography.* London: I. B. Tauris, 2008.

Alatri, Paolo. "La nascita del fascismo." *Belfagor,* July 1951.

Alexander, Robert Jackson. *The Right Opposition: The Lovestoneites and the International Communist Opposition of the 1930s.* Westport, CT: Greenwood Press, 1981.

Anderson, Perry. *Considerations on Western Marxism.* London: Verso, 1979.

Arfé, Gaetano. "Il meridionalismo di Gaetano Salvemini." *Ponte* 11, no. 12 (1955).

Assouline, Pierre. *Gaston Gallimard: A Half-Century of French Publishing.* San Diego: Harcourt, Brace, Jovanovich, 1988.

———. *Gaston Gallimard: Un demi-siècle d'édition française.* Paris: Balland, 1984.

Barbusse, Henri. "Editorial." *Monde* 124 (October 18, 1930): 3.

Bergery, Gaston. "Du libéralisme expirant à la révolution nationale." *L'Effort,* August 9, 1940.

———. "La faiblesse de l'état est une menace pour les libertés du peuple. Elle mène droit au fascisme." *La Flèche* 6, no. 100 (August 1, 1938).

———. "Pour un 'coup d'arrêt' aux états fascistes." *La Flèche* 4, no. 83 (September 11, 1937).

———. "Tchecoslovaquie." *La Flèche* 6, no. 112 (April 1, 1938).

Berti, Giuseppe, ed. *Annali Istituto Feltrinelli.* Milan: Feltrinelli, 1966.

Blum, Léon. "Editorial." *Le Populaire,* October 1, 1938.

———. "L'atroce évènement." *Le Populaire,* September 18, 1939.

———. "Le mystère stalinienne." *Le Populaire,* September 17, 1939.

———. *L'œuvre 1937–1940.* Paris: A. Michel, 1965.

———. "Silence accablant." *Le Populaire,* September 19, 1939.

Bocca, Giorgio. *Palmiro Togliatti.* Rome: Laterza, 1973.

Bongarçon, Yves. "Un vichysme de gauche? Les débuts de l'effort, quotidien socialiste lyonnais." *Cahiers d'Histoire* 32, no. 2 (1987): 123–46.

Bordiga, Amadeo. "Intervento alla conferenza organizzativa." *Lo Stato Operaio*, May 29, 1924.

———. *Storia della sinistra comunista*. Milan: Ediz. del Programma Comunista, 1964.

———. "Tesi per il terzo congresso." In *Il Terzo congresso del partito comunista d' Italia (Sezione dell'internazionale comunista)*. Edited by Partito Comunista d' Italia. Rome: Società An. Poligrafica Italiana, 1926.

———. "Theses of the Abstentionist Communist Faction of the Italian Socialist Party." *Communist Program* 5 (June 1979).

Brill, Adrien. "Des vicissitudes du pouvoir au calme de l'abbaye de Pontigny." *La Flèche* 7 (June 28, 1939).

Broué, Pierre. *Trotsky*. Paris: Fayard, 1988.

Brown, David. *The Road to Oran: Anglo-French Naval Relations, September 1939–July 1940*. New York: Frank Cass, 2004.

Brunet, Jean-Paul. *Jacques Doriot, du communisme au fascisme*. Paris: Balland, 1986.

Buré, Émile. "La position de l'Italie." *Ordre*, April 2, 1940.

Burrin, Philippe. "Le collaborationisme." In *La France des années noires*, edited by Jean-Pierre Azéma and François Bédarida. Paris: Seuil, 1993.

———. *La dérive fasciste: Doriot, Déat, Bergery, 1933–1945*. Paris: Seuil, 2003.

———. "La France dans le champ magnétique des fascisms." *Le Débat* 32 (November 1984): 52–72.

———. *France Under the Germans: Collaboration and Compromise*. New York: New Press, 1996.

Bussière, Eric. *La France, la Belgique et l'organisation économique de l'Europe: 1918–1935*. Paris: Comité pour l'Histoire Economique et Financiere de la France, 1992.

Cantafio, Valerio. "*L'Unità* di Gaetano Salvemini e la battaglia antiprotezionista." *Rassegna Storica Toscana* 38, no. 2 (1992): 193.

Caute, David. *Communism and the French Intellectuals, 1914–1960*. New York: Macmillan, 1964.

———. *The Fellow-Travellers: Intellectual Friends of Communism*. Rev. ed. New Haven: Yale University Press, 1988.

Cavagnari, Camilio, and Emilio Caldara. *Avvocati e procuratori*. Edited by Guido Alpa. Bologna: Il Mulino, 2005.

Chaubet, François. *Paul Desjardins et les Décades de Pontigny*. Villeneuve-d'Ascq: Presses Universitaires du Septentrion, 2000.

Cives, Giacomo, and Giuseppe Lombardo Radice. *Attivismo e antifascismo in Giuseppe Lombardo Radice: "Critica didattica" o "didattica critica"?* Florence: La Nuova Italia, 1983.

Claudín, Fernando, Aldo Agosti, and Fondazione Luigi Einaudi. *Problemi di storia dell'internazionale comunista (1919–1939): Relazioni tenute al seminario di studi organizzato dalla Fondazione Luigi Einaudi (Torino, Aprile 1972).* Turin: La Fondazione, 1974.

Cointet, Jean-Paul. *Expier Vichy: L'épuration en France (1943–1958).* Paris: Perrin, 2008.

———. *Marcel Déat: Du socialisme au national-socialisme.* Paris: Perrin, 1998.

———. *Pierre Laval.* Paris: Fayard, 1993.

Comité du plan and Marcel Déat. *Le plan français: Doctrine et plan d'action.* Paris: Fasquelle, 1935.

Communist International. *The Program of the Communist International: Together with the Statutes of the Communist International.* London: Modern Books, 1932.

"Comunicato del ce." *Prometeo* 26 (January 1, 1930).

"Le Congrès de SFIO." *L'Humanité,* 13 July 1933.

Coutinho, Carlos Nelson. *Gramsci: Um estudo sobre seu pensamento político.* Rio de Janeiro: Editora Campus, 1989.

"Cronache dell'*Ordine Nuovo.*" *L'Ordine Nuovo* 2, no. 5 (June 12 ,1920).

Dard, Olivier. *Les années trente: Le choix impossible.* Paris: Librairie Générale Française, 1999.

De Clementi, Andreina. *Amadeo Bordiga.* Turin: G. Einaudi, 1971.

De Felice, Franco. *Serrati, Bordiga, Gramsci e il problema della rivoluzione in Italia 1919–1920.* Bari: De Donato, 1971.

De Felice, Renzo. *Il fascismo: Le interpretazioni dei contemporanei e degli storici.* Rev. ed. Rome: Laterza, 1998.

———. *Mussolini il fascista,* vol. 2: *L'organizzazione dello stato fascista.* Turin: Einaudi, 1995.

———. *Mussolini il rivoluzionario, 1883–1920.* 2nd ed. Turin: G. Einaudi, 1965.

De Grand, Alexander J. *In Stalin's Shadow: Angelo Tasca and the Crisis of the Left in Italy and France, 1910–1945.* DeKalb: Northern Illinois University Press, 1986.

Déat, Marcel. "La crise doctrinale du socialisme." *Monde* 3, no. 87 (February 1, 1930).

———. "Rassemblement pour la révolution nationale." *L'Effort,* August 30, 1940.

Déat, Marcel, and Laurent Theis. *Mémoires politiques.* Paris: Denoël, 1989.

Detoeuf, Auguste. "Pour la France et la liberté." *Les Nouveaux Cahiers,* special issue, September 15, 1938.

Deutscher, Isaac. *The Prophet Unarmed: Trotsky, 1921–1929.* New York, NY: Verso, 2003.

Diggins, John P. *Mussolini and Fascism: The View from America.* Princeton, NJ: Princeton University Press, 1972.

Drake, Richard. *Apostles and Agitators: Italy's Marxist Revolutionary Tradition.* Cambridge, MA: Harvard University Press, 2003.

Duroselle, Jean-Baptiste. *La décadence, 1932–1939*. Paris: Imprimerie Nationale, 1979.

Empedocle [Palmiro Togliatti]. *L'Ordine Nuovo*, no. 1 (May 1st 1919).

Engels, Friedrich, and Karl Marx. *Selected Works*. Vol. 1. Moscow: Progress Publishers, 1969.

Fanello Marcucci, Gabriella. *Luigi Sturzo: Vita e battaglie per la liberta' del fondatore del Partito Popolare italiano*. Milan: Mondadori, 2004.

Ferreiro Lavedán, María Isabel. *La teoría social de Ortega y Gasset: Los usos*. 2nd ed. Madrid: Biblioteca Nueva/Fundación José Ortega y Gasset, 2005.

Fischer, Ruth. *Stalin and German Communism: A Study in the Origins of the State Party*. London: G. Cumberlege, 1948.

Fisher, David James. "The Rolland-Barbusse Debate." *Survey* 20, nos. 2–3 (Spring-Summer 1974): 121–59.

Franzin, Elio. *Longo contro Togliatti nel 1927*. Rome: SBL Agenzia 70, 1970.

Furet, François. *The Passing of an Illusion: The Idea of Communism in the Twentieth Century*. Chicago: University of Chicago Press, 1999.

Garin, Eugenio. "Croce E Gentile interpreti di Marx." In *Croce E Gentile: Fra tradizione nazionale e filosofia europea*, edited by Michele Ciliberto. Rome: Editori Riuniti, 1993.

Gay, Peter. *Weimar Culture: The Outsider as Insider*. New York: Harper and Row, 1968.

Gentile, Giovanni. *La filosofia di Marx. Studi critici*. Florence: Sansoni, 1962.

Germanetto, Giovanni. *Le memorie di un barbiere*. Paris: Edizioni di Coltura Sociale, 1931.

Gildea, Robert. *Marianne in Chains*. London: Macmillan, 2002.

Girard, Georges Th. "Oui, vive la nation." *Le Populaire*, July 19, 1939.

Graham, Bruce Desmond. *Choice and Democratic Order: The French Socialist Party, 1937–1950*. Cambridge: Cambridge University Press, 1994.

Gramsci, Antonio. "Editorial." *L'Ordine Nuovo* 2 (October 9, 1920).

———. "Intervento alla conferenza organizzativa." *Lo Stato Operaio*, May 29, 1924.

———. *La questione meridionale*. Rome: Edizioni Rinascita, 1951.

———. "La relazione Tasca e il congresso camerale di Torino." *L'Ordine Nuovo* 2, no. 4 (June 5, 1920).

———. *Scritti giovanili, 1914–1918*. 4th ed. Turin: Einaudi, 1975.

Gramsci, Antonio, Richard Bellamy, and Virginia Cox Balmaceda. *Antonio Gramsci: Pre-Prison Writings*. Cambridge: Cambridge University Press, 1994.

Gramsci, Antonio, Palmiro Togliatti, and Chiara Daniele. *Gramsci a Roma, Togliatti a Mosca: Il carteggio del 1926*. Turin: Einaudi, 1999.

Griffin, Roger, and Matthew Feldman. *A Fascist Century*. Basingstoke: Palgrave Macmillan, 2008.

Griffiths, Richard. "Fascism and the Planned Economy: 'Neo-Socialism' and 'Planisme' in France and Belgium in the 1930s." *Science and Society* 69, no. 4 (October 2005): 580–93.

Hellman, John. *The Knight-Monks of Vichy France: Uriage, 1940–1945*. Montreal: McGill-Queen's University Press, 1993.

Hobsbawm, E. J. *The Age of Extremes: A History of the World, 1914–1991*. New York: Vintage Books, 1996.

Humbert-Droz, Jules. *De Lénine à Staline: Dix ans au service de l'internationale communiste, 1921–1931*. Neuchatel: Éditions de la Baconnière, 1971.

———. *Il contrasto tra l'internazionale e il P.C.I., 1922–1928*. -Milan: Feltrinelli, 1969.

Izard, Georges. "Pour fonder le démocratie véritable il faut un Richelieu." *La Flèche* 4, no. 79 (August 14, 1937).

Jackson, Julian. *France: The Dark Years, 1940–1944*. Oxford: Oxford University Press, 2001.

Jacometti, Alberto. *Quando la storia macina*. Novara: La Foresta Rossa, 1952.

Jay, Martin. *Force Fields: Between Intellectual History and Cultural Critique*. New York: Routledge, 1993.

———. *Marxism and Totality: The Adventures of a Concept from Lucács to Habermas*. Cambridge: Polity, 1984.

Judt, Tony. *La reconstruction du Parti Socialiste: 1921–1926*. Paris: Presses de la Fondation Nationale des Sciences Politiques, 1976.

Killinger, Charles L. *Gaetano Salvemini: A Biography*. Westport, CT: Praeger, 2002.

King, David. *The Commissar Vanishes: The Falsification of Photographs and Art in Stalin's Russia*. New York: Metropolitan Books, 1997.

Lebas, Jean. "La révision des statuts." *Le Populaire*, August 1, 1939.

Ledeen, Michael Arthur. *Universal Fascism: The Theory and Practice of the Fascist International, 1928–1936*. New York: H. Fertig, 1972.

Lejeune, Bernard Henry. *Historisme de Jacques Doriot et du Parti Populaire Français*. Amiens: Nouveaux Cahiers du CERPES, 1977.

Lenin, V. I. *"Left-Wing" Communism, an Infantile Disorder*. Moscow: Foreign Language Publishing House, 1952.

Leroux, André [Angelo Tasca]. "Assez de verbalisme et de course aux mandats! Luttons dans la réalité." *Agir* 7 (May 1, 1939).

———. "La leçon d'une vie." *Agir* 1 (February 1, 1939).

———. "Pacifisme bourgeois, impérialisme fasciste." *Agir*, no. 3 (March 1, 1939).

———. "Le parti et les clans." *Agir* 10 (June 15, 1939).

———. "Les sauvages de l'air du General Franco." *Le Populaire*, October 10, 1938.

———. "La situation." *Le Populaire*, January 12, 1937.

———. "La situation." *Le Populaire*, September 16, 1939.

Livorsi, Franco. *Amadeo Bordiga: Il pensiero e l'azione politica, 1912–1970*. Rome: Editori Riuniti, 1976.

Loubet del Bayle, Jean Louis. *Les non-conformistes des années 30: Une tentative de renouvellement de la pensée politique française*. Rev. ed. Paris: Seuil, 2001.

Luongo, Maria. "Amadeo Bordiga e il movimento operaio napoletano (1910–1920)." *Cahiers Internationaux d'Histoire Economique et Sociale* 17 (1985): 155–203.

Madaule, Jacques. "A. Rossi: La naissance du fascism." *Esprit* 6, no. 72 (1938).

Maitron, Jean, and Claude Pennetier. *Dictionnaire biographique du mouvement ouvrier français*, vol. 35, part 4: *1914–1939: De la première à la seconde guerre mondiale*. Paris: Editions Ouvrières, 1990.

"Malavita Politica." *Vie Prolétarienne*, January 22, 1929.

Man, Henri de. "La crise doctrinale du socialisme." *Monde* 76 (November 16, 1929).

———. "Le mouvement ouvrier belge prend position." *L'Effort*, September 3, 1940.

"Manifesto." *Les Nouveaux Cahiers*, special issue, September 15, 1938.

Merli, Stefano. *La rinascita del socialismo italiano e la lotta contro il fascismo, 1934–1939; documenti inediti dell'archivio Angelo Tasca*. Milan: Feltrinelli, 1963.

Michel, Henri. *François Darlan: amiral de la flotte*. Paris: Hachette, 1993.

Monnet, Georges. "Un an de gouvernement Daladier. La démocratie en péril." *Agir* 6, April 15, 1939.

Mounier, Emmanuel. "Prefascisme français: Les deux sources du prefascisme." *Esprit* 7, no. 75 (December 1, 1938).

Muscetta, Carlo, and Nicola Badaloni. *Labriola, Croce, Gentile*. Bari: Laterza, 1981.

Mussolini, Benito. "Dalla neutralità assoluta alla neutralità attiva ed operante." *L'Avanti*, 18 October 1914.

———. *Utopia. Rivista quindicinale del socialismo rivoluzionario*. Reprint. Milan: Feltrinelli, 1973.

Normand, Guessler. "Henri Barbusse and His *Monde* (1928–35): Progeny of the Clarté Movement and the Review *Clarté*." *Journal of Contemporary History* 11, nos. 2/3 (July 1976): 173–97.

Paxton, Robert O. *Vichy France: Old Guard and New Order, 1940–1944*. New York: Columbia University Press, 2001.

Pels, Dick. *The Intellectual as Stranger: Studies in Spokespersonship*. London ; New York: Routledge, 2000.

Peregalli, Arturo, and Sandro Saggioro. *Amadeo Bordiga: La sconfitta e gli anni oscuri: 1926–1945*. Milan: Colibrì, 1998.

Piccone, Paul. *Italian Marxism*. Berkeley: University of California Press, 1983.

"Pour le premier mai. Une tactique antifasciste." *Combat*, April 30, 1938.

"Pourquoi Nous Publions *Agir*." *Agir* 1 (February 1, 1939).

Pugliese, Stanislao G. *Carlo Rosselli: Socialist Heretic and Antifascist Exile*. Cambridge, MA: Harvard University Press, 1999.

Ragionieri, Ernesto. *Palmiro Togliatti: Per una biografia politica e intellettuale.* Rome: Editori Riuniti, 1976.

Ragonesi, Elena. "La tradizione intellettuale de 'Il Mondo': Tra Croce e Salvemini,." *Il Cristallo* 2 (1996).

Rapone, Leonardo. *Cinque anni che paiono secoli: Antonio Gramsci dal socialismo al comunismo, 1914–1919.* Rome: Carocci, 2011.

Recuperati, Giuseppe. "Paul Hazard." *Belfagor* 23 (1968).

Ree, Erik van. "Stalin's Organic Theory of the Party." *Russian Review* 52, no. 1 (April 1993): 43–57.

Renner, Karl. "La crise doctrinale du socialisme." *Monde* 2, no. 80 (1929).

Rév, István. *Retroactive Justice: Prehistory of Post-Communism.* Stanford, CA: Stanford University Press, 2005.

Rimbaud, Christiane. *L'affaire du* Massilia, *été 1940.* Paris: Seuil, 1984.

Riosa, Alceo, and Angelo Tasca. *Angelo Tasca socialista: Con una scelta dei suoi scritti (1912–1920).* Venezia: Marsilio, 1979.

Rives, Paul. "Bilan d'une expérience." *L'Effort,* August 11, 1940.

Roland-Holst, Henriette. "La crise doctrinale du socialisme." *Monde* 3, no. 83 (January 4, 1930).

Rossi, A. [Angelo Tasca]. "La crise doctrinale du socialisme." *Monde* 3, no. 122 (October 3, 1930).

———. "Le technicien au carrefour." *Monde* 4, no. 164 (1931): 11.

———. "Sur le fascisme en Europe." *Monde* 3, no. 100 (May 3, 1930).

Rota, Emanuel. "La tentazione corporativa: Corporativismo e propaganda fascista nelle file del socialismo europeo." In *Progetti corporativi tra le due guerre mondiali,* edited by Matteo Pasetti. Rome: Carocci Editore, 2006.

Rüesch, Diana, and Bruno Somalvico. *La voce e l'Europa: Il movimento fiorentino de la voce: Dall'identità culturale italiana all'identità culturale europea.* Rome: Presidenza del Consiglio dei Ministri Dipartimento per l'Informazione e l'Editoria, 1989.

Russo, Annamaria. *De Sanctis e Croce: Dalla filosofia alla critica.* Napoli: Edizoni del Delfino, 1993.

Salvemini, Gaetano. *Scritti sulla questione meridionale.* Milan: Feltrinelli, 1955.

Salvemini, Gaetano, Angelo Tasca, and Elisa Signori. *Il dovere di testimoniare: Carteggio.* Naples: Bibliopolis, 1996.

Sansa, Giorgio. "Il Mediterraneo e i rapporti italo-francesi." *La Stampa,* April 4, 1940.

Sartre, Jean-Paul, and W. D. Redfern. *Les mains sales.* London: Methuen, 1985.

Schalk, David L. *The Spectrum of Political Engagement: Mounier, Benda, Nizan, Brasillach, Sartre.* Princeton, NJ: Princeton University Press, 1979.

Serampuy, Bernard. "*La Flèche,* le frontisme, esprit." *Esprit* 6, no. 72 (1937): 735–46.

Serge, Victor, Jean Rière, and Jil Silberstein. *Mémoires d'un révolutionnaire et autres écrits politiques, 1908–1947.* Paris: Laffont, 2001.

Soave, Sergio. *Un eretico della sinistra: Angelo Tasca dalla militanza alla crisi della politica.* Milan: FrancoAngeli, 1995.

———. "Prefazione." In *Angelo Tasca, nascita e avvento del fascismo l'Italia dal 1918 al 1922.* Florence: La Nuova Italia, 1950.

Soucy, Robert. *French Fascism: The First Wave, 1924–1933.* New Haven: Yale University Press, 1986.

———. *French Fascism: The Second Wave, 1933–1939.* New Haven: Yale University Press, 1995.

Spriano, Paolo. *Socialismo e classe operaia a Torino dal 1892 al 1913.* Turin: Einaudi, 1958.

———. *Storia del Partito Comunista Italiano.* 2nd ed. Turin: G. Einaudi, 1978.

———. *Storia di Torino operaia e socialista. Da De Amicis a Gramsci.* Turin: G. Einaudi, 1972.

Stalin, Joseph. *Works.* [Russian ed.] Moscow: Foreign Languages Publishing House, 1954.

"Statut des juifs." *L'Effort,* October 18, 1940.

Sternhell, Zeev. *Neither Right nor Left: Fascist Ideology in France.* Princeton, NJ: Princeton University Press, 1996.

Stibio, André. "Les anciens et les modernes." *Ordre,* June 7, 1939.

Tannenbaum, Edward R. "The Goals of Italian Fascism." *American Historical Review* 74, no. 4 (April 1969): 1183.

Tasca, Angelo. "Battute di preludio." *L'Ordine Nuovo* 1, no. 1 (May 1, 1919).

———. "La Casa." *L'Ordine Nuovo,* June 14, 1919.

———. *De la démocratie au socialisme: Marxisme 33.* La Chaux-de-Fonds: Coopératives Réunies, 1934.

———. "Economia mondiale ed economie nazionali." *Nuovo Avanti,* February 16, 1935.

———. "Fare ognuno il proprio dovere." *L'Ordine Nuovo,* August 16, 1919.

———. *I primi dieci anni del PCI.* 2nd ed. Bari: Laterza, 1973.

———. "Il mito della guerra." *Il Grido del Popolo,* October 24, 1914.

———. *In Francia nella bufera.* Parma: Guanda, 1953.

———. *La France de Vichy: Archives inédits d'Angelo Tasca.* Milan: Fondazione Giangiacomo Feltrinelli, 1996.

———. *La naissance du fascisme; L'Italie de 1918 à 1922.* Paris: Gallimard, 1938.

———. "Nationalisme ou socialisme." *Monde* 259 (May 20, 1933).

———. "Note di un culturista." *L'Avanguardia,* December 22, 1912.

———. *Le pacte germano-soviétique: L'histoire et le mythe.* Paris: Cahiers des Amis de la Liberté, 1954.

———. "Relazione al congresso camerale di Torino." *L'Ordine Nuovo* 2, no. 3 (May 24, 1920).

———. *The Russo-German Alliance, August 1939–June 1941*. Boston: Beacon Press, 1951.

Tasca, Angelo, Sergio Anelli, Sergio Soave, and Cécile Beitzmann. *A Cécile*. Turin: N. Aragno, 2001.

Tasca, Angelo, and Willmoore Kendall. *A Communist Party in Action: An Account of the Organization and Operations in France*. New Haven: Yale University Press, 1949.

Tasca, Angelo, and Nikita Sergeevich Khrushchev. *Autopsie du stalinisme*. Paris: P. Horay, 1957.

Tasca, Angelo, and Denis Peschanski. *Vichy, 1940–1944: Quaderni e documenti inediti di Angelo Tasca; Archives de guerre d'Angelo Tasca*. Milan: Fondazione Giangiacomo Feltrinelli, 1986.

Teroni, Sandra. *La passione della democrazia: Julien Benda*. Rome: Bulzoni, 1993.

Togliatti, Palmiro. *La formazione del gruppo dirigente del Partito Comunista Italiano nel 1923–1924*. 2nd ed. Rome: Editoria Riuniti, 1969.

Trocchi, Francesco. *Angelo Tasca e l'*Ordine Nuovo. *La formazione del Partito Comunista Italiano*. Milan: Jaca, 1973.

Tucker, Robert C. "The Rise of Stalin's Personality Cult." *American Historical Review* 84, no. 2 (April 1979): 347–66.

Union Internationale des Écrivains Révolutionnaires. "La littérature de la révolution mondiale, numéro special." Paper presented at the Deuxiéme Conférence Internationale des Écrivains Révolutionnaires, Moscow, June 1931.

"A uno a uno. Tasca espulso dal P.C." *L'Avanti*, October 13, 1929.

Vacca, Giuseppe. *Gramsci Togliatti*. Rome: Editori Riuniti, 1991.

Vandervelde, Émile. "La crise doctrinale du socialisme." *Monde* 2, no. 77 (1929).

———. "Pour s'initier au socialism." *Peuple*, June 5, 1938.

Vasoli, Cesare. "*L'Unità* di Salvemini." *Ponte* 14, no. 11 (1958): 1382.

Vigna, Carmelo. *Le origini del marxismo teorico in Italia: Il dibattito tra Labriola, Croce, Gentile e Sorel sui rapporti tra marxismo e filosofia*. Rome: Città Nuova, 1977.

Villey, Daniel. "*Les Nouveaux Cahiers*." *Esprit* 6, no. 65 (February 1, 1938).

Vittoria, Albertina. *Storia del PCI: 1921–1991*. Rome: Carocci, 2006.

Weber, Hermann, and Bernhard Bayerlein. *Der Thälmann-Skandal: Geheime Korrespondenzen mit Stalin*. Berlin: Aufbau-Verlag, 2003.

Weil, Simone. "Ne recommençons pas la guerre de Troie." *Les Nouveaux Cahiers*, April 1, 1937.

Will, Barbara. *Unlikely Collaboration: Gertrude Stein, Bernard Faÿ, and the Vichy Dilemma*. New York: Columbia University Press, 2011.

Winock, Michel. Esprit*, des intellectuels dans la cité.* Paris: Editions du Seuil, 1996.

———. *Histoire politique de la revue* Esprit*, 1930–1950.* Paris: Seuil, 1975.

XX [Angelo Tasca]. "La bataille d'Angleterre." *L'Effort,* August 20, 1940.

———. "La situation." *Le Populaire,* April 3, 1940.

Zyromski, Jean. "La crise doctrinale du socialisme." *Monde* 2, no. 78 (November 30, 1929).

Index

Agir, 99–112
Alatri, Paolo, 165
alliance, antifascist, 106–7, 112–14, 117–18
Amadesi, Gino, 54
Amendola, Giovanni, 178n90
antifascism: communist movement and, 160; *Monde* and, 66; Tasca charged with, 57; WWII foreign policy and, 118–19
antifascist fascism, 98–99
antipositivism, 13–14
anti-Semitism, 138–39, 167
armistice, between France and Germany, 126
arrest(s): of fascists in Italy, 46; of Tasca, 121–23, 152. *See also* imprisonment
autarky, 93, 106

Badoglio, Pietro, 1
Balabanoff, Angelica, 58
Barbusse, Henri, 59, 64, 66–68
Belin, René, 143
Benda, Julien, 109
Bergery, Gaston, 104, 106, 107, 138
Berti, Giuseppe, 50, 56
biennio rosso, 25, 29
Blum, Léon: *La naissance du fascisme* and, 93–94; on Munich conference, 100; Socialist Party and, 102–3; Tasca's relationship with, 83, 96, 162; WWII foreign policy and, 113
books, on PCF, 161–62
Bordiga, Amadeo, 14–16, 25–26, 30, 32–33, 36–39
Boris, Georges, 111
Bouhey-Allex, Georges, 104
Brandler, Heinrich, 54
Brill, Adrien, 109–10
Brossolette, Pierre, 104, 112
Brunet, René, 111
Buchalet, Albert, 201n51
budget, of Tasca, 59
Bukharin, Nikolai, 42–43, 45, 54
Buré, Émile, 118
bureau d'études, 149–52, 159, 167
Burrin, Philippe, 8, 71, 196n51

Caldara, Emilio, 72–73, 184–85n45
capitalism: fascism and, 57–58; in Marx and Engels's socialism, 60; unification under, 84, 86
Catholics and Catholic Church, 95, 98, 144–45
Cavyn, Paul, 123, 156–57, 199n9
Chasseigne, François, 126–27, 194n21
Chomette-Fernandez, Liliane, 98, 148, 154
Christianity, 25, 144–45
citizenship, French, 82–83, 95–96, 139–41
class and class consciousness, 15, 24, 65, 80–81
Cold War, 162
collaboration, 131, 134, 139, 158, 161, 195nn35,51
collaborations, of Tasca, 94–99
communist movement: alliance in, 106–7; manipulation of, 10, 51; *Monde* and, 70–71; National Revolution and, 134–35; struggle in, 42–44; Tasca and, 159–62, 167–68, 195n32
Communist Party in Action, A (Tasca), 162
Communist Party of Italy (PCI). *See* Italian Communist Party (PCI)
congress of socialist trade unions, 27–29
conscience, 134
consigli, 27–29
Croce, Benedetto, 22
culturalism, 15
culture: notion of, 14–15; Tasca on, 23–24
Czechoslovakia, 99–100

Daladier, Edouard, 99–100, 107–8
Damilano, Angela, 12
de Gaulle, Charles, 150–51
De Grand, Alexander, 6, 7
de Jouvenel, Bertrand, 146
de Man, Henri, 64–65, 73, 78–80, 94, 98
Déat, Marcel, 64, 74–75, 94, 138
Décades, 78–79
democracy: in construction of socialism, 65; fascism and, 66, 75–77; parliamentary, 33
Desjardins, Paul, 78–79, 110
determinism, economic, 21–22
Detoeuf, Auguste, 99

Deux ans d'alliance germano-soviétique (Tasca), 162
dialectics, 60, 85
Drieu de La Rochelle, Pierre, 94
Dubinsky, David, 164

economic determinism, 21–22
L'Effort, 128, 135–40, 167
Engels, Friedrich, 41, 60
Enlightenment, 21, 79
Esprit, 94–95, 99, 107
Europe Libre: Revue Socialiste et Syndicaliste, 117–18
Ewert, Arthur, 54
exile, of Tasca, 55–61

factories, occupation of northern, 29, 31
fascism: analysis of, 65–66; democracy in fight against, 66; *La naissance du fascisme* and, 89–94; Nazism and, 69–70; resistance to, 71–82, 98–99; Tasca's experience with, 5; Tasca's views on, 1–2, 48, 57–58; Togliatti's plan to overcome, 1
Faure, Paul, 96, 102, 109
Fernandez, Ramon, 189n40
Fifth Congress of the International, 38–39
"filosofia della prassi, La," 22
finances, of Tasca, 59
Finland, Soviet invasion of, 115
Flandin, Pierre-Étienne, 190n55
La Flèche, 107
force field metaphor, 8
Fortini, Franco, 1
Fouques-Duparc, Jacques, 164
Fourth Congress of the International, 46
France Nouvelle, 163–66
French citizenship, 82–83, 95–96, 139–41
French Communist Party, 67, 84, 114–15, 128, 150–51, 161–62
French Section of the Workers' International (SFIO): Monnet and, 100–101; neosocialism and, 74; nonconformist ideas in, 108–9; Pétain regime and, 128; Pontigny initiative and, 109–11; Tasca's role in, 82–83, 95–98, 101–2

Gallimard, Gaston, 89
Gentile, Giovanni, 22
German Communist Party, 44–45, 52–54
Gildea, Robert, 195n35
Girard, Georges Th., 119, 140, 196n60
Giuliano, Balbino, 21
Giustizia e Libertà, 185n46
Gobetti, Piero, 178n90
"Goofy Maneuvers of the Algerian Committee, The," 150–51
Graham, Bruce, 100
Gramsci, Antonio: attacks Tasca, 48–50; Communist Party of Italy and, 36–38; conflict with Tasca, 27–29; defends Mussolini, 19–20; influence of, on Tasca, 21, 172n5; *L'Ordine Nuovo* and, 23; on Marx, 173n18, 176n59; on Socialist Party and revolution, 30; struggle in communist movement and, 43; Tasca and, 3, 10, 11
Graziadei, Antonio, 33
Grieco, Ruggero, 56

Hitler, Adolf: invades Czechoslovakia, 99–100; opposition to, 88–89; Stalin and, 112–13, 114, 116–17
homes and households, Tasca on, 24
humanism, 60–61
Humbert-Droz, Jules, 45, 53–54

identities, of Tasca, 2–3, 171n2
Il Mondo, 165
Il Ponte, 169
imprisonment: Tasca's activities during, 152; Tasca's life after, 154–55, 157–59. *See also* arrest(s)
institutions, in construction of socialism, 65
Italian Communist Party (PCI): creation of, 29–40; Stalinization of, 168; Tasca's expulsion from, 41–42, 54–61; Tasca's role in, 3, 10–11, 47–48, 50–51, 172–73n5; third congress of, 49
Italian Socialist Party (PSI), 17–20, 25, 30–31, 77, 92
Izard, Georges, 104, 107, 109

Jackson, Julian, 4, 195n35
Jacometti, Alberto, 165, 201–2n56
Jaurès, Jean, 186n76
Jouvenel, Bertrand de, 146
Judt, Tony, 95–96
Julien, Charles-André, 123, 163

Kun, Bela, 45

"La filosofia della prassi," 22
La Flèche, 107
La naissance du fascisme (Tasca), 88, 89–95
La Voce, 13–14
Labriola, Antonio, 22, 60
Lagrange, Léo, 104
Laurat, Lucien, 97, 109–11, 189n38
Laval, Pierre, 135–36, 141, 142–43
Le pacte germano-soviétique (Tasca), 162
Le Populaire, 83, 95–96, 103, 112–14
Lebas, Jean, 109
L'Effort, 128, 135–40, 167
Left-Wing Communism: An Infantile Disorder (Lenin), 32
leggi fascistissime, 46
Légion Française des Anciens Combattants, 142

Lenin, Vladimir, 32
Leonetti, Alfonso, 36
Leopardi, Giacomo, 20–21
Leroux, André (pseudonym), 2, 3, 83, 90
Les mains sales (Sartre), 9
Les Nouveaux Cahiers, 97–98, 99
liberal democracy, 76
L'Ordine Nuovo, 21–29, 36, 37
Loubet del Bayle, Jean-Louis, 197n86
Lovestone, Jay, 54, 164–65
Lyon congress, 39–40, 49

Madaule, Jacques, 95
mains sales, Les (Sartre), 9
Manuil'skij, Dmitrij, 45
Marcia su Roma (1922), 32
Maria, Roger, 163–64
Marion, Paul: Moysset and, 145; neosocialism and, 74–75; Stalin attacks, 54; on statism, 197n86; Tasca testifies for, 157–59; on Tasca's books, 161; Tasca's relationship with, 186n77
marriage, of Tasca, 20, 68–69
Martoretti, Carlo, 23
Martoretti, Lina, 20, 68–69
Marx, Karl: antifascism and, 79; Gramsci and Togliatti on, 176n59; Gramsci on, 173n18; influence of, on Tasca, 21–23, 24; Tasca's abandonment of, 84–86; Tasca's study on, 60–61
Marxism: fascism and, 48, 58; influence of, on Tasca, 21–23, 24; Tasca on, 75–76; Tasca's abandonment of, 84–86, 116; Tasca's study on, 60–61
Marxisme 33 (Tasca), 75–76
Massilia affair, 196n62
Maurìn, Joaquin, 54
Maurras, Charles, 94
Mayer, Daniel, 104
metalworkers, insurrection of, 29, 31
military service, 20
Minzoni, Giovanni, 178n90
Molotov-Ribbentrop Pact, 112, 160, 161, 162
Monde, 59–60, 61, 63–71, 100
Mondo, Il, 165
Mondolfo, Rodolfo, 22
Monnet, Georges, 77, 100–102, 107–8, 126–27, 157
Montagnon, Barthélemy, 74
Montgomery, Bernard, 164
Montrouge congress, 102–3
Moscow, Tasca's time in, 45–52
Mounier, Emmanuel, 94–95, 98–99, 146
Moysset, Henri, 141, 144–45, 147–48, 158, 159
Munich agreements, 99–102, 106
Mussolini, Benito: antifascism and, 73; declares war against France, 125; nationalism and, 80; Tasca and, 17–20, 92

La naissance du fascisme (Tasca), 88, 89–95
national parties, 130–31, 137, 142
National Revolution: Tasca on, 134–35, 149; Tasca's plan for, 131–34
national unity, 129–31, 135–36
nationalism, 21–22, 80–81, 84, 116–17, 119, 138
naturalism, 14
naturalization, 82–83, 139–41
Naturel, Alice, 199n9
Nazism: fascism and, 69–70; National Revolution and, 134–35
neosocialism/Néos, 74–75
normal life, Tasca's desire for, 154–55
Norway, 137
Nouveaux Cahiers, Les, 97–98, 99

L'Ordine Nuovo, 21–29, 36, 37

pacifism, 105
Pannunzio, Mario, 165
parliamentary democracy, 33
Parti Populaire Français, 145
Pascal, Pierre, 47
Pastore, Ottavio, 17
Paxton, Robert, 143
Pays Socialiste, 103
"Perché sono socialista," 21–22
Peschanski, Denis, 3–4
Pétain, Philippe, 123–24, 126–29, 131–33, 166
Philip, André, 192n83
Physiologie du parti communiste français (Tasca), 162
"Plan du 9 Juillet," 132
Poland, USSR invasion of, 112–14
politics, Tasca's separation from, 154–55
Ponte, Il, 169
Pontigny Abbey, 78–79, 97, 109–12
Populaire, Le, 83, 95–96, 103, 112–14
Popular Front, 82–83, 86–87, 107
positivism, 13–14
proletariat: faith in, 117; in Marxism, 84–86
Prouvost, Jean, 100
pseudonyms, of Tasca, 2–3, 171n2
PSI (Italian Socialist Party), 77, 92
public speaking, Tasca and, 12–13

Radice, Lombardo, 174–75n35
Rapone, Leonardo, 172n5
Rassemblement National Populaire, 142
"rational republicans," 132
reformism, 26–27
religion, 25
Renner, Karl, 64
Rens, Jef, 127–28, 156
research bureau, 149–52, 159, 167
Resistance, Tasca as agent for, 122–25, 135, 155–58, 163–64
Rév, István, 10

revolution: Bordiga and Tasca on, 25–27; and conflict between Gramsci and Tasca, 27–29; failure of Italian, 29–40; Tasca's contributions to, 124
Rivain, Jean, 149
Rives, Paul, 137
Roland-Holst, Henriette, 64–65
Romain, Jules, 132
Roman, Jules, 104
Rosselli, Carlo, 73
Rossi, A. (pseudonym), 2, 3, 89–94, 109, 171n2
Rossi, Amilcare, 171n2
Rossoni, Edmondo, 72–73
Rougemont, Denis de, 97
Russo-German Alliance, The (Tasca), 162

Salvemini, Gaetano, 13–14, 17, 162, 165, 168–69, 200n38
Sartre, Jean-Paul, 9
Second International Congress of Revolutionary Writers, 63, 66–67
Seniorenkonvent, 44
Serampuy, Bernard, 106–7
Serge, Victor, 162–63
Serra (pseudonym), 2, 3
Serrati, Giacinto, 30
SFIO (French Section of the Workers' International). *See* French Section of the Workers' International (SFIO)
situationism, 48
Sixth Congress of the Communist International, 42–44
Smeral, Bohumir, 54
socialism: antifascism and, 72–80; Christianity and, 144; construction of, 86; debate on crisis of, 64–65; nationalism and, 132, 138; Tasca's early years in, 10–17
Sorel, Georges, 17
Souvarine, Boris, 58, 97, 181n66, 188–89n37
Soviet Union: alliance with, 106–7, 112–14; invades Finland, 115
Spaak, Paul-Henri, 156
Spanish Civil War, 86–87
Spinasse, Charles, 110, 111, 137–38
Spriano, Paolo, 44
Stalin, Josef: attacks Tasca, 52–55; Hitler and, 112–13, 114, 116–17; manipulation of, 10, 42–43; Tasca's abandonment of, 85–86; Tasca's expulsion from PCI and, 56
Stalinism, 167–68
Stalinization of communist parties: impact of, 41–42, 52–55; Italian Communist Party and, 168; *Monde* and, 63–64; and scandal in German Communist Party, 44–45; Sixth Congress of the Communist International and, 42–44; Tasca's expulsion from PCI and, 55–61; Tasca's stay in Moscow and, 46–47
statism, 147, 197n86
Stein, Gertrude, 194n23
Stibio, André, 109
Sudentenland, 99–100
suffrage, universal, 76

Tasca, Angela Damilano, 12
Tasca, Angelo: early years of, 12–13; final years of, 169; marital problems of, 68–69; marriage and military service of, 20
Tasca, Carlo, 12, 16
Terracini, Umberto: Communist Party of Italy and, 36; on Italian revolution, 32; *L'Ordine Nuovo* and, 23; Tasca's influence on, 11–12
Thalheimer, August, 54
Thälmann, Ernst, 44–45, 52
Third International: Communist Party of Italy and, 32, 34, 37–39; Italian revolution and, 30, 33; Socialist Party and, 25; Stalin and, 42–43; Tasca as delegate of, 46
Third Republic: breakdown of, 125–27, 129; political divisions in, 129; reformation of, 132
Tixier-Vignancour, Jean-Louis, 140–41
Togliatti, Palmiro: on alliance of Italian Communist Party, 1; attacks Tasca, 48–52; Communist Party of Italy and, 35, 36–37, 39, 42; *L'Ordine Nuovo* and, 23; on Marx, 176n59; on Serrati and Turati, 30; Stalinization of communist parties and, 46–47; struggle in communist movement and, 43–44; Tasca and, 3; Tasca's expulsion from PCI and, 54, 56
totalitarianism, 116, 133, 148–49
Touchard, Pierre-Aimé, 98
trade unions, 26–29, 31
Trentin, Bruno, 169
Trotsky, Leon, 33, 42
Turati, Filippo, 30

unity, national, 129–31, 135–36
universal suffrage, 76
USSR: alliance with, 106–7, 112–14; invades Finland, 115

Valois, Georges, 72
Vandervelde, Émile, 64, 94, 105
Vernunftrepublikaner, 132
Versailles Treaty, 105–6
Viénot, Pierre, 104, 111, 126, 140–41, 190–91n62
Viglongo, Andrea, 12–13
Vittoria, Albertina, 172–73n5
Voce, La, 13–14

war, as outcome of fascism, 93. *See also* World War I; World War II
Wittorf, John, 44–45
workers' movement, 55–56
World War I, 18–20

World War II: call for national unity in, 129–31; foreign policy during, 112–19; foreign policy preceding, 99–112; French defeat in, 125–26; National Revolution and, 131–34; Pétain regime and, 126–29; Tasca's contributions to, 119–20

XX (pseudonym), 2–4, 112–13, 136

youth movement, 145–48

Zinoviev, Grigory, 30, 42
Zyromski, Jean, 64

WORLD WAR II: THE GLOBAL, HUMAN, AND ETHICAL DIMENSION

G. Kurt Piehler, series editor

Lawrence Cane, David E. Cane, Judy Barrett Litoff, and David C. Smith, eds., *Fighting Fascism in Europe: The World War II Letters of an American Veteran of the Spanish Civil War*

Angelo M. Spinelli and Lewis H. Carlson, *Life Behind Barbed Wire: The Secret World War II Photographs of Prisoner of War Angelo M. Spinelli*

Don Whitehead and John B. Romeiser, *"Beachhead Don": Reporting the War from the European Theater, 1942–1945*

Scott H. Bennett, ed., *Army GI, Pacifist CO: The World War II Letters of Frank and Albert Dietrich*

Alexander Jefferson with Lewis H. Carlson, *Red Tail Captured, Red Tail Free: Memoirs of a Tuskegee Airman and POW*

Jonathan G. Utley, *Going to War with Japan, 1937–1941*

Grant K. Goodman, *America's Japan: The First Year, 1945–1946*

Patricia Kollander with John O'Sullivan, *"I Must Be a Part of This War": One Man's Fight Against Hitler and Nazism*

Judy Barrett Litoff, *An American Heroine in the French Resistance: The Diary and Memoir of Virginia d'Albert-Lake*

Thomas R. Christofferson and Michael S. Christofferson, *France During World War II: From Defeat to Liberation*

Don Whitehead, *Combat Reporter: Don Whitehead's World War II Diary and Memoirs*, edited by John B. Romeiser

James M. Gavin, *The General and His Daughter: The Wartime Letters of General James M. Gavin to His Daughter Barbara*, edited by Barbara Gavin Fauntleroy et al.

Carol Adele Kelly, ed., *Voices of My Comrades: America's Reserve Officers Remember World War II,* foreword by Senators Ted Stevens and Daniel K. Inouye

John J. Toffey IV, *Jack Toffey's War: A Son's Memoir*

Lt. General James V. Edmundson, *Letters to Lee: From Pearl Harbor to the War's Final Mission,* edited by Dr. Celia Edmundson

John K. Stutterheim, *The Diary of Prisoner 17326: A Boy's Life in a Japanese Labor Camp,* foreword by Mark Parillo

G. Kurt Piehler and Sidney Pash, eds., *The United States and the Second World War: New Perspectives on Diplomacy, War, and the Home Front*

Susan E. Wiant, *Between the Bylines: A Father's Legacy,* foreword by Walter Cronkite

Deborah S. Cornelius, *Hungary in World War II: Caught in the Cauldron*

Gilya Schmidt, *Süssen Is Now Free of Jews: World War II, the Holocaust, and Rural Judaism*

Emanuel Rota, *A Pact with Vichy: Angelo Tasca from Italian Socialism to French Collaboration*